Architecture as Material Culture

The work of Francis-Jones Morehen Thorp

Architecture as Material Culture
The work of Francis-Jones Morehen Thorp

Introduction by
Kenneth Frampton

**Francis-Jones Morehen Thorp
is an Australian architectural
practice dedicated to design
excellence and the enhancement
of the public domain.**

fjmt originated in the Canberra-
based practice of Mitchell/Giurgola
& Thorp (mgt) founded in 1980 by
Romaldo Giurgola and Richard Thorp
on their winning of the international
design competition for the Australian
Parliament in Canberra. In 1990,
Richard Francis-Jones began work
as a designer for the mgt Sydney
studio where he met his key
collaborator Jeff Morehen. In 2002
Francis-Jones, together with Morehen
and Thorp, established the practice
Francis-Jones Morehen Thorp (fjmt).
Richard Thorp retired from the
partnership in 2009.

Façade detail, Surry Hills Library & Community Centre

Atrium detail, Tyree Energy Technologies Building, University of New South Wales

Foreword

Jennifer Taylor

The material of the architecture and the culture which it seeks to serve or contribute to—at its most basic, perhaps, as the relationship between artefacts and social relations. That is, the twin focus of the work: the embodiment of social aspirations and values, together with the enhancement of the public domain (which necessitates an associated resistance to the reducing effects of consumption); and the material of construction itself together with the expressive precision of assembly as the means to achieve this embodiment.

— Richard Francis-Jones

Since its establishment in 2002, Francis-Jones Morehen Thorp has focused on the design and making of buildings and places for the western Pacific with an architecture that stands outside, and distinct from, the historical mainstreams of the region. Rather, it is concerned with its own mission arising from, and encompassing, a vision of what architecture might be. This vision is three-fold and embraces the philosophical, the conceptual and the material.

The book is both broad and penetrating in its communication of the narrative of fjmt and in its unveiling of the wide range of inspiration drawn from nature with its landscape, the tenets of architectural theory, and the inheritance of the past. Across its pages the path is traced, and the logic of the evolution of the architecture from critique to response is made known through the comprehensive coverage of the illustrations and text of its dual structure. *Architecture as Material Culture* first introduces the spectrum of this portfolio of Australian and New Zealand architecture onto an international stage.

The content of the work is introduced by Kenneth Frampton, with an essay that explores the major consistent themes of the oeuvre of the practice, and offers specific critiques of selected significant projects, relating them in context and locating them in the past and present.

The presentation of the projects is prefaced by the five brief treatises of "Architecture as the mediation of the universal and the specific," that offer the distillation of Francis-Jones's thinking over the past twenty years with its current evolution—words to be reflected on in concert with the design studies they precede.

Façade detail, Sydney Law School, University of Sydney

For fjmt, "The measure of the achievement is the building," and the total compendium of layered and interwoven graphic, pictorial and written material speaks of an architecture of confidence and conviction—revealing of itself. Forces, local and global, concerning climate and consumption, guide the advent of a responsive and responsible architecture, creating aesthetics from necessities. A bold, freely drawn sketch, starkly depicting an abstraction of the formal generative structure, heralds each of the twenty-six projects that are presented under "City, Community and Campus," to create a comprehensive album testifying to the performance of fjmt. This is a sincere, and in many ways, straightforward architecture, but one connecting with existence through an ever-present concern for habitation, neighbourhood, and well-being.

Seminal to the designs is the belief that "the poetic depth of the tectonic is the true expressive media of architecture," and the building is given immediate presence through the explicit readability of the materials—glass is brittle, and earth materials ponderous and heavy. These qualities are visually captured in the impressive imagery of the large photographic plates, notably those of details, which add to both the pleasure and knowledge to be gained from the pages of this book. The building and its place enact a complementary environmental and technical performance. There is no hesitation, but a conceptual clarity made evident through the disclosure of the tectonic assembly, the explicit singular materiality of the fabric, and the spatial order and established relationships existing within the building and extending without, connecting with the urban landscape. Primary importance is accorded this public domain with buildings that reject the notion of architecture as an independent entity, but rather, respect the reciprocal relationship between building and setting. Such an engagement also embraces heritage buildings and endows them with a renewed critical life, enhancing both the historical and the contemporary.

While the depiction of the buildings comprises the major part of the book, the essays that follow offer insights into the beliefs, reasoning and deductions that gave them form. The essays, primarily selected from previous publications, testify to Francis-Jones's "continuing interest in the theory of architecture and its manifestation in built projects," and throw light on the rationale guiding the constant pursuit of clearly defined goals.

While Francis-Jones has sought architectural excellence across many fields, the primary legacy lies in the experience of the exceptional buildings of Francis-Jones Morehen Thorp.

Concept sketch, Sydney Law School, University of Sydney

Contents

Stair and ceiling detail, Surry Hills Library & Community Centre

1 The Red Centre

Architecture as Material Culture

Kenneth Frampton

The ideology of our time, with its emphasis on efficiency, change, speed and the free market, in many ways establishes the antithesis of the necessary conditions for making architecture. Architecture is not efficiency; in fact it is often the way in which efficiency is subordinated to other values that distinguishes architecture.

— Richard Francis-Jones

The studio of Francis-Jones Morehen Thorp is a multi-disciplinary architectural practice: it is a co-operative endeavour involving a considerable number of talented architects, designers and specialists who together work closely to pursue the line of the office under design director Richard Francis-Jones's and managing director Jeff Morehen's leadership and guidance.

Prior to the formation of fjmt, Richard Francis-Jones collaborated closely with Romaldo Giurgola on the design of many projects as co-partners of Mitchell/Giurgola & Thorp. One of the most significant of these collaborations was the Red Centre. Francis-Jones led the design of this ambitious project, which explored many ideas of urban form, sustainability and tectonic expression that would become common to the work of fjmt. Won in competition in 1992, it was built for the University of New South Wales over the next four years. This long five-storey block faced in red terracotta was an addition to an existing structure and incorporated

specially designed facilities for the Faculty of the Built Environment and the School of Mathematics. Apart from its dynamic linear form, this building pioneered a range of innovative environmental systems, including ingenious sun-shading devices and balanced systems for the conditioning and re-circulation of air.

The Red Centre is a sustainable tour de force that challenged the environmental standards for Australian campus architecture. Four features determine the character of this work: one—the formal continuity of the linear mass-form, which is emphasized by long, shallow windows; two—a partially opened, reinforced concrete structural frame with cantilevers carrying the body of the building throughout its length; three—the expression of the building's services through clusters of metal intake and exhaust tubes on the roof; finally, four—marked emphasis on an existing pedestrian route running alongside and branching off to access pre-existing academic buildings lying behind its frontage.

Parti Pris

Francis-Jones declared his parti pris as an architect at the moment that fjmt was founded, via an essay entitled "The [Im]Possibility of Slowness: A Note on Globalisation, Ideology and Speed in Contemporary Architecture" which appeared in *10x10: 100 Architects 10 Critics*, published by Phaidon in 2000. This critical text concludes with six points, which while they were not numbered, nonetheless read as a manifesto:

The ideology of our time, with its emphasis on efficiency, change, speed and the free market, in many ways establishes the antithesis of the necessary conditions for making architecture. Architecture is not efficiency; in fact it is often the way in which efficiency is subordinated to other values that distinguishes architecture.

Architecture is not mere change: architecture is more about transformation and permanence; it is most often about uncovering what is in humanity that does not change.

Architecture cannot be the servant of the free market. Architecture should not be reduced to a market-dependent consumerable, as at this point it becomes merely decorated building within the flux of fashion.

Architecture does not move at speed, as any of us know who have tried to make architecture.

Architecture is slow.

Finally, an authentic contemporary architecture should not only attempt to somehow begin to reconcile humanity's place in the world but also be directed towards rejuvenating, repoliticising our desiccated public realm. We should pursue an architecture appropriate to citizens rather than consumers.[1]

Three years earlier Francis-Jones had already taken a stand against a semiotic interpretation of architecture in an essay entitled "Architecture Not Language—A Note on Representation,"[2] which appeared in the magazine *UME* in 1997. Herein he compellingly argues that architecture rather than being sign system, as per Robert Venturi's "decorated shed," is first and foremost a structural assembly and a craftwork of socio-cultural significance that arises not from some detached aesthetic commentary but rather from the way it frames and formulates both site and program from a socio-ethical standpoint.

Scientia

Francis-Jones first demonstrated this ethos in the John Niland Scientia Building completed on the campus of the University of New South Wales at Kensington, Sydney in 2000. Although mgt was still the architect of record, it is clear, from the make-up of the design team, that this was a transitional work that would definitively establish the tectonic syntax and the general, critically creative approach of the new practice. Iconographically, Scientia is focused about a four-column, tree-like canopy crowning the main pedestrian axis of the campus, which runs east-west across a rather non-descript domain. The glazed and louvred structure of this monumental canopy accommodates the axis of this long walkway while negotiating a dramatic change in level between the western and the eastern parts of the campus.

The overall honorific character of Scientia stems from four spaces which were of great social and symbolic import to the university; the two-storey Leighton Hall to the north of the axis, the Tyree Room, sitting on top of a two-storey recital hall (which was later realized as a "black box" experimental space), together with a small cinema beneath. Within this dense sectional arrangement, a glazed bridge running beneath the canopy unites the honorific spaces while two of the symbolic volumes were accessed independently, either from the lower level beneath the walkway or from the roof of the recital hall. These volumes were faced with sandstone which enabled them to read as podia on either side of the axis. Honorific roof-forms are employed twice in this work, first in the folded ceiling of Leighton Hall, supported on tapered, pin-jointed timber columns, and second in the aforementioned crowning canopy, which also carried on four tapered timber columns that give rise to timber brackets supporting the inner and outer metal purlins supporting the canopy itself. This is already the fjmt tectonic signature in that it combines a basic structural form with precisely wrought metal and glass elements, conceived and executed to the precise standards of the international hi-tech architecture. No one recognized more promptly the significance of this diminutive "city crown" than John Gosling when he compared Scientia to Francis-Jones's earlier Red Centre to the effect that:

The treed columns supporting a massive layered glass roof form are a highly successful and dramatic device to terminate the Mall axis. Yet at the same time the dialectic of both a ceremonial space and the secondary role as a device to link the once disparate parts of the campus is clear, even from a distance.

Using this form as a central device for both urban and architectural resolution proposes a clear simplicity in the planning composition. This is also expressed in the eastern and western walls of simple sandstone, where the horizontal is emphasized in a poetic manner, utilizing precast concrete string-course work. These linear elements are also used to veil the glass faced vertical stair not unlike the Red Centre…. The success of these two buildings lies in the subversion of an autonomous artefact in the urban landscape to the notion that the creation of architecture and urbanism is intrinsically interrelated and inseparable.[3]

Joondalup

An equally axial and much more monumental "city crown" is evident in the Chancellery and Business School complex realized in 2003 for the Joondalup Campus of the Edith Cowan University, Perth, on the west coast of Australia. Among its many other attributes this work is, above all else, an overwhelming tectonic exercise in timber construction, iconographically reminiscent of Renzo Piano's Kanak Centre in Noumea, New Caledonia (1998) by which it was surely influenced. What is key here are three stepped-building forms, two of them making up the twin halves of the bisected chancellery building, each half being a stepped formation

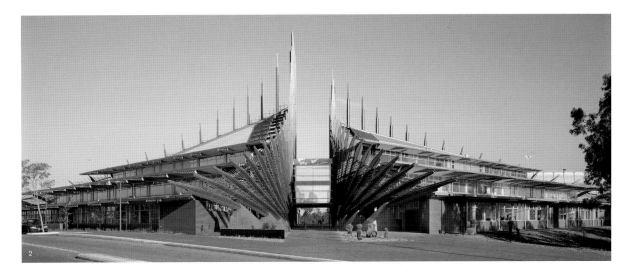

1 The tree-like structure is emblematic of Scientia.
2 The Chancellery at Edith Cowan University.

7

1

over a triangular plan, together with the enclosing form of the business school which is treated as a terrace structure overlooking a rectangular greensward separating it from of the chancellery. Of the two, the Chancellery is the more rhetorical by virtue of being lined on its inner face by brise soleil made up of laminated Jarrah spars held in place by a steel frame. These large timber spars assume the form of a fan-like progression as they pass from being virtually horizontal at the outer limits of the complex to becoming increasingly vertical in front of this bisected building. Irrespective of whether they are vertical or horizontal, the warp of these spars support the woof of a horizontal sun screen, echoing the tectonic form of Piano's so-called cases in Noumea. These vertical spars also make up a kind of a colonnade in front of the curtain wall to either side of a pedestrian axis as it passes from the entry plaza through the Chancellery to emerge on the other side and wend its way down towards the lake. The architect's description testifies to the "civic" character of this arrangement:

The new buildings are sited on a gentle rise, set amongst bushland and eucalyptus. On one side are the broad lanes of the Grand Drive leading into the new City of Joondalup and on the other a central pathway that leads down to a modest lake and peaceful green lawns… The Jarrah screen provides shelter and shade and structural support to the assembly… Within the interstitial space between the timber screen and the main enclosure the circulation is concentrated. Stairways and lifts occur in this shaded zone… Positioned on either side of the central space, within the sheltering screen are located the Council Chamber and the executive offices of the Vice Chancellor, held in visible democratic balance either side of the vista and connecting bridge… The organic forms of the architecture have been developed to appear to rise almost 'naturally' out of the landscape itself….[4]

Australian academic Gevork Hartoonian remarks that Joondalup already demonstrates two key aspects of the work of fjmt: topographic placemaking and a sustainable approach to local climatic conditions.[5]

Camperdown

The fjmt emphasis on the roofwork surely derives to considerable extent from the so-called woolshed tradition stemming from the Sydney based practices of Richard Leplastrier, Glenn Murcutt and Peter Stutchbury. This tectonic expressivity is complemented in the work of fjmt by a strong and currently rather unique commitment to the creation of significant urban form. This predilection first becomes fully evident in its design for the Sydney Law School to be built on

the mid-19th-century Camperdown Gothic Revival campus of the University of Sydney, where one is still able to survey the skyscraper skyline of Sydney from a bucolic distance. Realized in a short six-year period between the competition design of 2003 to a handover in 2009, this complex, like Scientia, strives to reinforce the existing axes of pedestrian movement by extending the legacy of the Leslie Wilkinson addition to the initial campus carried out in the 1920s.

A primary feature of fjmt's subtle reorganization of the campus is the four-storey, somewhat Aaltoesque mass of the faculty office building mediating between the original Gothic Revival fabric and the picturesque expanse of Victoria Park to the east. A pedestrian axis linking the Anderson Stuart (Old Medical School) building to the park gates terminates in a broad flight of steps which crosses over the four-storey-deep earthwork of a massive podium and under the faculty offices takes its bearing. The asymmetrically inflected access corridors of this slab are transformed of this major east/west, north/south intersection. At this juncture they become glazed bridges suspended above the monumental stairway giving access to the park. It is just this play between the earthwork of the podium and the superstructure of the slab that would prompt the Australian critic Philip Drew to compare the new Sydney Law School to Utzon's Opera House:

There is a surprising connection with Utzon's Sydney Opera House; surprising, because the form of the Sydney Law School, like the Opera House, has been reduced to a dichotomy, a solid buried podium and suspended transparent superstructure… Richard Francis-Jones considered the Sydney Law School was 'an opportunity to redefine and reinterpret the architectural dialectic between city and campus: to extend the public domain and create a new opening of the university to the community, parkland and city beyond, with the study of law balanced carefully at this new threshold.' … Like the Opera House, the Sydney Law School begins with a broad flight of stairs that fold down from the forecourt off Eastern Avenue, to the greenery of Victoria Park. Much the same way the Opera House has its separate restaurant roof as a leading sculptural object out front, the Sydney Law School has, as its counterpart, a light tower rising 13 metres from the ground level that resembles Le Corbusier's 1960 light cannons at La Tourette….[6]

One of the most remarkable aspects of this curtain walled building is the stochastic play of the vertical timber louvres suspended in the air space between two layers of glass. These may be manually manipulated by the occupants to suit individual preference when necessary by overriding the servomechanisms that automatically control the angle of the louvres in relation to the sun. As the architect has put it:

…The gentle curve of the plywood louvre creates its own structural brace and rigidity while softening the daylight around its profile. The ventilating double skin system of enclosure draws in and controls natural daylight, mediating the environment to cool and heat as necessary, while creating reflections of the park, the landscape and the neo-Gothic sandstone façades over the varying grain of the curved timber screens….[7]

In addition to the academic offices housed in the office/slab, a large part of the law school is accommodated underground in a two-storey podium which, in addition to two levels of parking in the basement, carries four, 100-seat lecture halls, sixteen seminar rooms, a 5,000-square-metre library and a 300-seat main auditorium. All of this space is penetrated by light wells and by a monumental light cone clad in metal that serves to bring light down into the heart of the library. This cone also serves to ventilate the library volume by natural convection and is lit at night through at-grade skylights from the library under the forecourt. Sustainability is maintained as a fundamental precept throughout the design, from harvesting rainwater to the provision of an energy efficient infrastructure, passive thermal control and the use of environmentally sustainable materials. A system of natural ventilation is set up in the offices where high-level vents in the doubly loaded central corridor allow hot air to rise up through the linear atrium around which the offices are grouped. The free-standing, three-storey teaching building terminating the western end of this composition is similarly ventilated by a full-height atrium. Perhaps the only regrettable aspect of this design is the way in which a proliferation of diagonal paths between the neo-Gothic core and the new intervention has been allowed to over-complicate the surface treatment of the quadrangle.

Surry Hills

Completed in 2009, three years after the initial design, the Surry Hills Library & Community Centre may be seen as a diminutive intensification of the syntax first developed for the Sydney Law School. Programmed in close collaboration with the local community, this building succeeds at many levels at once; in the first instance, by virtue of being an exemplary small scale public building deftly integrated into its surroundings and, second, by being an equally exemplary exercise in sustainable engineering.

What is so remarkable about this hybrid work is the way in which its various public programs are all precisely articulated in relation to each other, so that at no point is a single modicum of space wasted or left underused. This measured

distribution makes itself manifest on the ground floor where the upper level of the library is plainly visible from the street through full-height panels of plate glass, presaged by a reading room café which serves as a natural buffer between the calm of the stack space and the bustle of the street. Immediately above this floor is the large function room (seating 125) which also faces out over the street, backed by a teaching kitchen in the middle of the plan and three moderately sized meeting rooms, two facing south towards the park through the atrium/conservatory; a truncated glazed volume which is fully integrated into the building at grade. The overall four-storey, cubic form of the building is capped by the children's nursery and day-care centre, together with an inner and outer play space having a capacity for 26 children. The basement is occupied by the lower level of the library, plus public computer terminals.

If one excludes the two-storey entrance hall which incorporates a party wall at the northern limit of the site and a pocket park to the south, the building may be said to employ a "thick wall" planning strategy along its northern, western and eastern faces, plus a four-storey, tapering conservatory volume facing the park. Virtually opaque on its western and northern elevations this prism is protected by adjustable wood-veneered louvres for the uppermost floors on its eastern face, plus plant material housed in the tapering full-height, double-glazed, atrium to the south. In many ways it is this, plus the decision to admit air into the building from above, that accounts for the "homeostatic" environmental balance established in the structure as a whole. Dan Mackenzie of the prestigious environmental engineering firm Steensen Varming would describe the "biomimicry" of the system in the following terms:

As in most respiratory systems, the point at which the air enters provides primary filtration and tempering. The air intake has been located as far above street level as possible to reduce the burden of pollutants from traffic and passers-by. It is also oriented to benefit from the natural driving force of the prevailing wind… The intake naturally tempers the air as it flows across a water-to-air heat exchanger coupled to five geothermal bores which draw energy from the earth (100 metres deep) to heat cold air, or cool hot air, as needed.

The tempered air is drawn down the building through the southern double façade, which helps to 'cocoon' the body of the building from the outside, even though the façade is transparent (providing connection between the interiors and the external park and vice versa). The transparency and connection further benefits from the southerly orientation (not requiring shading devices) and the planting, which, together with bedding biomass, provides the second stage

1 View of the Surry Hills Library & Community Centre southern façade and biofiltration atrium.

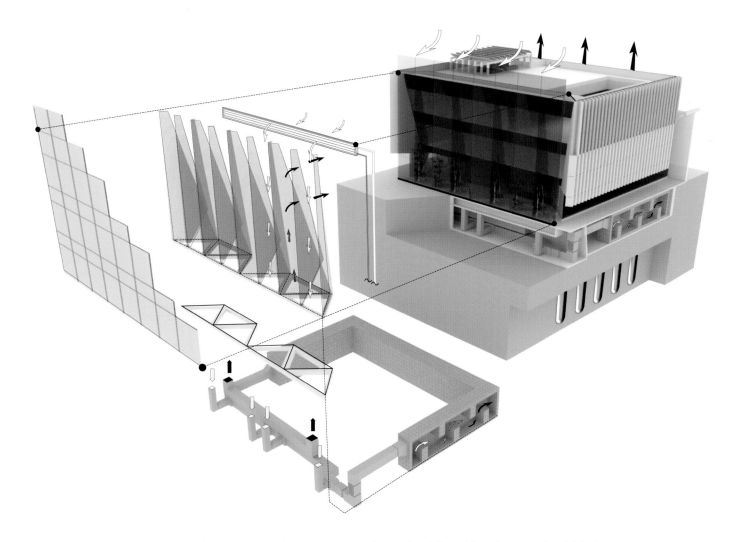

The Surry Hills Library & Community Centre:

Façade components—
Double skin façade cavity or "lungs" of the building cocoons internal spaces and provides transparent arteries to move through the building.

Geothermal coils.

Outside air intake—Clean air source located away from Crown Street to improve air quality. First stage cooling provided by geothermal coils to temper incoming fresh air.

Photovoltaic panels—Offset grid power demands. Panels also shade roof.

Green roof—Provides increased thermal mass and reduces heat gains to the building.

Relief air intake—Natural relief to outside.

Fan coil units—Trims fresh air to satisfy heating and cooling needs of the building.

Materials—Low VOC finishes. Low formaldeyde furniture.

Operable louvres.

Labyrinth—Air runs around the building perimeter through gabions walls that passively heat and cool the air.

Rainwater storage tank—Supplies toilets and landscape irrigation.

Geothermal heat exchanger—For passive tempering of incoming outside air to "bio-filter" by transferring energy from the earth to the building.

Bio-filter—Plants and biomass absorb carbon dioxide and release oxygen. Passive filtration and removal of air contaminants.

Labyrinth.

Refer page 208 for further detail.

of air filtration and the key to air quality improvement—the bio-filtration process, whereby the plants and biomass help to reduce external pollutants as well as increase oxygen levels. Air quality was a key initiative due to the nature of the building, which is used not only as a library and community centre (where occupant alertness can aid learning) but also as a childcare facility where the health of the community's children is of utmost importance. This is a key area of research, because even though there is general consensus that many plants are effective in improving air quality, actual quantified data is not readily available.[9]

Filtering, tempering and distributing the air in this building is further enhanced by fan coil units powered by photo-voltaic cells on top of the green roof, which in turn helps to reduces heat gain and boost thermal mass. These units drive the air down into a thermal labyrinth surrounding the basement level of the library. Capable of absorbing or radiating heat, the labyrinth also has the capacity to temper and distribute the air without entailing unnecessary ductwork. This labyrinth, recharged after the night purge, is able to store cool air in its mass for use during the day, thereby reducing the necessary level of refrigerant cooling by seventy per cent. It also

passively reduced the outdoor air temperature intake by ten per cent on the peak summer day. The experimental nature of this system led to the installation of oxygen and carbon dioxide sensors throughout in order to monitor the air quality. The latest results suggest that the concentration of oxygen is some ten per cent higher than in comparable buildings with conventional HVAC systems.[10]

The totally glazed atrium/conservatory on the southern face overlooking the pocket park is made up of tetrahedral tunnels of glass, which taper to nothing at the top of structure, with only plate glass sheets rising beyond the cornice in a rather exuberant display of hi-tech as an end in itself. Among the features that merit further comment is the servant-vs.-served pattern present in the double-height entrance hall including the soffit of the mezzanine and a folded roof plane above. By a similar token the main body of the building has servant zones comprising elevators, etc. on the northern and western faces respectively serving the library, the community centre and the child-care facility on the ground, first and second floors. Perhaps no one has written more perceptively of the latent political consequences of this work than the Sydney-based architect Laura Harding:

The Surry Hills community is ethnically and socially diverse.
Many of the locals who would be considered to have recently
'gentrified' the area were cautious about the inclusion of
high-quality finishes, fearing that they would be damaged,
while those from the Oasis Youth Support Network up
the road urged the architects to finish the building in a
manner befitting its public importance… Which raises the
question—why is the unrestrained luxuriance of private
housing defended with unrepentant zeal, yet an amply funded
public building condemned as social irresponsibility?

… Rather than willful symbolism, fjmt's intention has
been to invest the building's bespoke components with
architectural qualities that transcend their environmental
function—that contribute more holistically and specifically
to its urban character. Given the client's preoccupations,
this sensibility has liberated the building from what could
have been a fairly superficial overlay. In performance terms,
systems monitoring has shown that oxygen concentrations
in the buildings are five percent greater than average—by all
accounts a fairly superficial overlay. In performance terms,
systems monitoring has shown that oxygen concentrations
in the building are five percent greater than average—by
all accounts a fairly remarkable result. Time will reveal the
full worth of these results, but civic architecture seems an
entirely appropriate place for experimentation of this kind.

The subjugation of the public presence of architecture can
sometimes be an astute architectural response, but we must
take care that it is not enforced as a default position for
reasons of expediency and fear of community reaction. Public
urban architecture should be unapologetic and celebratory.
The fact that the Surry Hills Library and Community Centre
has drawn criticism for its attempts to do so is disappointing,
but makes it critically important. Public architecture should
be the subject of debate—but it should never have to
apologize for being well funded, forthright and ambitious.[11]

Socio-Plastic Form

At this stage of its evolution as a practice, four parti pris would
appear to crop up with a certain regularity in the work of fjmt;
first the small, compact prism as in the Surry Hills library; second,
the elongated slab block as in the law school for the University of
Sydney; third, the undulating roofwork as we will find this trope in
their proposals for the National Portrait Gallery in Canberra and
the Auckland Art Gallery; and, finally, the horizontally exfoliated
structure, first broached by fjmt in their proposal of 2001 for the
Museum of Contemporary Art in Sydney. What is exceptionally
compelling about the latter is the way in which eight exfoliated
screens in plan ultimately devolve into two major cinematic
volumes which when they are not being used for the projection
of films serve to frame the two primary monuments of the
Sydney Harbour panorama—the Sydney Harbour Bridge and
the Sydney Opera House. In partial allusion to the podium of the
opera house, the Moving Image Centre was projected on top
of a sandstone base affording stair access from Circular Quay
and direct access from George Street to the rear of the existing
Museum of Contemporary Art. The design provided for elevator,
stair and escalator access from top of this sandstone undercroft
to the twin auditoria above. The entire assembly would have
been capped by twin auditoria on the roof facing out across the
harbor to focus on the bridge and the Opera House. The baroque
parti of this remarkable design would be returned to by fjmt on
a number of occasions including their 2007 proposal for an
extension to Asplund's Stockholm City Library.

Res Publica

Apart from their honorific commissions involving relatively large
self-contained university and museological institutions, much
of the work of fjmt has been devoted to small-scaled urban
interventions such as the Max Webber Library, realized in the
Sydney suburb of Blacktown in 2005, or the new St Barnabas

built in Broadway, Sydney in 2012 which serves as both a religious space and a social centre, or the Bayside Police Station, built at Sandringham, Victoria in 2010. Something of the mediatory nature of these interventions may be gleaned from fjmt's varying statements of intent, for where the Max Webber Library was conceived as a place-form to compensate for the inherent "placelessness" of an adjacent shopping mall, the St Barnabas Anglican Church was conceived as an oasis of spiritual and secular calm within the bustle of downtown Sydney. At a more programmatic level the police station was designed to favour an open, interactive community-oriented approach to the maintenance of social order. As the architects wrote at the time of its completion in 2010, "We have sought to escape the existing architectural paradigms of the contemporary police station, characterized as they are by opacity, security, and fenced compounds."[5] Here, an effort was made to handle a police station as though it were a well-lit interface for a calm and constructive discourse between the police and the general public.

Exfoliation

Sometime around 2007, the fjmt practice clearly began to attain a particularly spatial audacity, combined with an exceptionally inventive integration of sustainable technology. Although such potential was already evident in the Sydney Law School and the Surry Hills Library & Community Centre, the synthetic creative power of the firm began to attain a particular exuberance with the larger works completed over the last five years in Australia and New Zealand. The first of these was the Owen G. Glenn Business School designed in 2003, which takes off from the exfoliated topographic paradigm first projected by the architects for the Moving Image Centre at the end of the '90s. In this instance, the exfoliated stratagem takes on the existing topography at a truly panoramic scale setting itself as a gigantic scenography comprised of transparent glass perforated metal and/or reflective screens, layered so as to conform to geometric hyperbolic trajectories in plan. The express purpose of this layered configuration is to extend and project the visual command of the structure at a geographic scale. In this instance, the building reaches out beyond the immediate confines of a pre-existing Oxbridge campus to touch the spread-eagled landmark features of the Domain in the first instance and Auckland Harbour in the second.

To integrate this concept into the site it was necessary to divide the institution into two different programmatic units, into the small-scale lightweight classrooms and offices and the large-scale heavyweight lecture halls. Appropriately enough, the architects arranged for the latter to be absorbed

into a massive earthwork/podium deftly inserted into the site, while allowing the former to be cradled within the seemingly dematerialized glass and metal screens projecting out as hyperbolic planes in plan from the unifying atrium in the heart of the work. Between these inherently static and dynamic elements, the one telluric and other aerial, the architects were able to create a public realm in the atrium linking the lecture halls in the basement to the classrooms suspended for five storeys above. Francis-Jones would characterize this design as being typical of his firm's concern for the creation and articulation of public space:

The public domain is something that as a practice we're very interested in. Generally speaking, with all of our projects we do try to create and define as much public open space as we can, and it's the same on this site. Before, there was basically a minimal carpark, an inaccessible gully and a road. Now, you have a large open square, places for gathering and Maori ceremony and generous foyers and atrium spaces.

Perhaps such an approach expresses a value judgement about a diminishment of the public domain in contemporary life. There is also a belief that in the academic environment these kind of unprogrammed spaces are most vital. It's no coincidence that we tend to think of a campus or university as being defined by quadrangles, lawns and open spaces— that's a great tradition. So I think we do bring a value judgement about the importance of public space to our projects. The university was also very focused on the quality of the circulation spaces, the movements of students and the public domain, and often pushed us in this direction.[11]

Hartoonian's perspicacious appraisal of this work takes the form of comment on the latent symbolism permeating the work as a whole. As he has suggested:

At a time when res publica, the most civic dimension of architecture, is on the verge of vanishing, it has to be challenging for an architect to invest in creating public enclaves. The main podium of the building, the design's move to accommodate terraces and the integration of horizontal and vertical movements culminating in the building's atrium are all part of spaces where students, visitors and the staff of the school interact with each other. It would not be stretching it too far to claim that running up and down from the building's stairs and elevators located in the atrium, students find themselves juggling with both the nuances of the market and the landscape of the Domain.[12]

One of the most ingenious aspects of this design is the way in which the podium, trapezoidal in plan, and rising for two floors above grade at the front and for a single floor at the

rear, is deployed so as to house nine lecture halls of varying capacity while affording easy access to the atrium above. The resulting counterpoint of the design is made explicit in the architect's description of the project:

These organic and flowing forms are suspended above, a solid podium that anchors the building and reinterprets the natural topography of the immediate sloping site. This counterbalancing podium form is joined spatially with the suspended ribbons at the atrium heart of the new complex, interconnecting the shared teaching spaces with the workplace, learning and social spaces of the business school. The fluid and open architectural expression provides a strong contemporary counterpoint to the traditional insular European buildings the characterized the beginning of the university.[13]

Surely the most dramatic aspect of this complex is the dematerialized "ribbons" that soar out into space as a concatenation of louvred, metal and glass planes the appearance of which constantly changes depending on one's viewpoint and the incidence of the sun. Elevated on steel-clad cylindrical columns this horizontal exfoliation is capped at its centre by an inclined glass that helps to bind the six-storey atrium within, along with its stairs and into the podium.

Exfoliation 3

This exfoliated plan will be totally transformed at the hands of the architects into their Concourse development realised in 2011 for one of the most dense retail areas in the whole of Australia; the Chatswood district in Sydney's northern suburbs. In this instance an enlightened municipality decided to insert a creative arts centre into the stronghold of consumerism. Although this policy of mediating commerce through culture was hardly given an easy passage, it involved much civic debate and consultation before a positive popular vote finally carried the day.

Once again, the design absolutely depends on the presence of a podium, only in this instance two large auditoria are situated on top of the podium rather than within it, with the result that honorific stairways lead up from a civic arena to serve the foyers of each hall. These halls are enclosed by manifolds whose dynamic sculptural presence is heightened by being faced in polished aluminium. These aerodynamic planes, with their subtly rounded edges, frame brise soleil grilles that, lined with Hoop Pine veneer, serve to represent the two principal auditoria, while a third timber grille spanning diagonally across the re-entrant corner between the two halls in effect represent the smallest auditorium set beneath the two auditoria. The warm plywood linings of each of these grilles respectively, five, four and three units high, echo a similar lining used to face not only the interior of the auditoria, but also the foyers which serve them. The theatre's fly tower is ingeniously incorporated within the all-encompassing roof structure so that the total mass is animated by the grilles and by the manifolds faced in aluminium. The alternating shallow and deep courses in this aluminium panelling refer to the coursed stonework deployed by Le Corbusier on the end elevations of the Unité d'Habitation, Marseille of 1952.

Darling Quarter

By way of contrast, Darling Quarter, Sydney, completed on a leftover site adjacent to Darling Harbour in 2011, is a curved galleria of a building separating the existing green amenity of Tumbalong Park from the heavy traffic of Harbour Street and Sydney's central business district that constitutes the eastern boundary of the site. The virtually continuous nine- to six-storey-high structure paralleling Harbour Street is rendered as a kind of thick-walled galleria. This space with six office floors on either side is lit by elongated fan shaped skylights let into the roof of what is otherwise a continuously curved radial form. Much like G.H. Wyman's Bradbury Building

realized in downtown Los Angeles in 1893, the balcony corridors accessing the offices are served by stairways, bridges and freestanding elevator stacks with fully glazed elevator cabins. The sweep of the galleria provides for a continuous public promenade at grade with fixed seating and tables on the axis of the galleria. The park frontage is similarly treated as a continuous small-scale retail street covered by a cantilevered portico, which is "feathered" out on its leading edge with timber louvres. The five-storey curtain wall above is shielded with automated horizontal timber louvres against the penetration of western light.

Darlington

The School of Information Technologies for the University of Sydney completed in the Darlington area of the city in 2006 may be seen as a synthesis of the architectonic concepts developed for both the Owen G. Glenn Business School and Darling Quarter. Although this is only a four-storey infill structure on a very restricted urban site with a considerable slope from one end to the next, it has been treated as a gateway building serving both to represent the existing engineering campus and to link it back into the community. This treatment entails a continuation of a traditional walkway that is widened out into a foyer with a glass roof as the building disgorges onto Cleveland Street. The building screens itself from the noise pollution on this congested street through a glass and metal-fritted screen façade that follows the straight line of the existing street. This screen is held clear of the fenestration where the uses are particularly sensitive to noise. The opposite face the building is curved as it is integrated into the context of the campus. This curved front with anti-glare slot windows and a stainless steel skin is reminiscent of the dynamic radial block forms favoured by Erich Mendelsohn in the '30s.

Folded Roofworks

If dematerialized screens in metal and glass in plan embody the "baroque" syntax, which has come to fore in recent large scale designs by fjmt, much the same ethos also informs their serial concrete and steel folded plate roof constructions in section. This sectional syndrome appears as a dominant trope in the 2005 competition entry for the National Portrait Gallery in Canberra. Here we again encounter an opposition between earthwork versus roofwork with woven infill, constituting the essential tectonic substance of the work. The architects were to interpret the symbolic significance of this form on a long, somewhat romantic line in the text that accompanied their submission:

The proposed form and rationale of the gallery is a metaphor of the natural and urban landscape that is the Australian setting for the human figure with the architects creating an analogous 'frame' for the human figure. Sinuous roof forms represent the canopy of the sky and clouds, the podium evokes interpretation of the ground or contours of the land, and the vertical timber volumes, slots and spaces draw reference to the bush, forest and other places for the appearance of the human figure.[14]

In the National Portrait Gallery project, wide-span folded plates made up of post tensioned, prefabricated concrete components are supported by tall in-situ reinforced concrete cylindrical columns that are marginally wider at mid-point than at their extremities. This roofwork with clerestory top lighting between the folded plates obviously owes a debt to Jørn Utzon whose career was inseparable from the mid-century modernization of Australia and the realization of the Sydney Opera House. While this inspiration is implied by the serial circular geometry from which the curved profiles of the folded plates in the Canberra project are generated, the crowning form of the roof as a whole is to be found early in Utzon's career in one project after another.

Among the exceptionally elegant aspects of this competition design is the crowning canopy formed by the first folded plate along the entry front and the manner in which the glazed foyer at the ground floor is withdrawn along this front so as to welcome the visitor to the reception, the temporary exhibition space and the main lecture hall at grade while the permanent collection and the administration are located immediately above.

A New Datum

The use of a folded roof in their Auckland Art Gallery Toi o Tāmaki of 2011 enabled the architects to make a simultaneous allusion to both the Maori people and the unique fauna of New Zealand. Premiated in 2004 as the result of an international competition, this roof initially took the form of a saw-tooth roof spanning clear over the existing gallery. This was subsequently transformed into a repetitive version of the canopy employed in the Scientia complex, fabricated in this instance out of a timber-boarded "vault" applied to a light steel frame, with each folded canopy being poised on top of its own tapering timber column. What was opportune about this ingenious component was the way in which the architects were able to reiterate its form in order to achieve a floating roof, sailing effortlessly over the large space in the centre of the original building to become, with equal ease, the roof over the new extension comprising a café at grade with offices on the first floor and a more ample

1 Soffit detail with Albert Park beyond, Auckland Art Gallery Toi o Tāmaki.

library combined with another café above. This tessellated roof not only provided for a new entry into the art gallery but also for a sculpture forecourt and an equally monumental access to Albert Park, which drops down to the basic datum of the city at this point.

The gallery represents a new creative datum for fjmt in as much as herein they attained a particularly subtle balance between roofwork and earthwork; a tectonic, dialectic, so to speak, which ever since the realization of the Sydney Opera House has been so much a part of the Australian imagination. When it comes to responding to the challenge of both climate and landscape it is surely a fact that in New Zealand, as in Australia, the indigenous ground, along with the flora and fauna that it still engenders, takes priority over everything else. This was already the case with the new Parliament House in Canberra designed by mgt wherein a biaxial berm of a megaform swept in from two sides to virtually overwhelm the crystalline core at its heart.

This dialectic between the earthwork and roofwork has also been a constant theme in the successor firm of fjmt as we may judge from the priority given to the podium in one work after another, irrespective of whether the counter principle is a prism or an exfoliated roof. In this regard, it is obvious that without an amply accommodating earthwork, the roofwork would have no solid ground on which to rest and this is just as much a point of departure for the Toi o Tāmaki, to give the Auckland art gallery its Maori name, as it is for any other major civic work by fjmt.

In the Auckland Art Gallery this dialectic between the telluric and the aerial comes to be enriched and inflected by a number of other contrasting features operating at the same time. In the first instance, of course, there is the pre-existing building, this somewhat incongruous 1887 exercise in French classicism; while in the second, there is the outside grandeur of Albert Park and its exotic canopy of pohutukawa trees that have always been bearing down on this piece of Eurocentric eclecticism. To this nature/culture opposition fjmt has now added the elegant third term of a tessellated roof made up of a series of connected canopies, the complex "folded" soffits of which are lined with Kauri, a rare New Zealand wood which has been salvaged from fallen trees in the midst of beleaguered rainforests.

These "nautical" canopies, suspended at different levels, now float not only over the portico earthwork backing into the park, but also over new art galleries added behind the heavy masonry shell of the existing museum. In conscious opposition to the mansard roofs of the existing building, the tessellated canopy roof in Karuri wood extends over these

1 Richard Francis-Jones, "The (Im)Possibility of Slowness: A Note on Globalisation, Ideology and Speed in Contemporary Architecture" in *10x10: 10 Critics 100 Architects* (London: Phaidon, 2000), 433–4.

2 Richard Francis-Jones, "Architecture Not Language—A Note on Representation," *UME* 2 (1997): 50–1.

3 John Crosling, "Revealing Academia," *Architectural Review Australia*, Summer (1999): 84–91.

4 Richard Francis-Jones, Chancellery & Business School: Architects Statement. Sydney, NSW, September 2004.

5 Gevork Hartoonian, 2004, "Landscape, The Fabric of Architecture," *Architecture Australia*, 93/1 (2004): 64–71.

6 Richard Francis-Jones, "Force for Change: Architects Statement," *Architectural Review Australia*, 119 (2011): 73.

7 Philip Drew, "The Bridge That Gathers," *Architectural Review Australia*, 111 (2009): 72–83.

8 Richard Francis-Jones, Sydney Law School: Architects Statement, Sydney, NSW, October 2003.

9 Dan Mackenzie, "So How Does It Work?" *Architecture Australia*, 99/2 (2010): 101–104.

10 Russell Fortmeyer, "Library Down Under," *GreenSource*, May (2010): 71.

11 Laura Harding, "Surry Hills Library & Community Centre," *Architecture Australia*, 99/2 (2010): 41–49.

12 Richard Francis-Jones, National Portrait Gallery: Architects Statement, Sydney, NSW, November 2005.

13 Richard Francis-Jones. Interview with John Walsh. Auckland, February 2008.

14 Ibid.

15 Ibid.

galleries so as to bond the old and the new indissolubly together; this fusion that extends beyond the roof forms to encompass the circulation itself. This intention was made quite explicit by Francis-Jones in a recent interview with John Walsh in which he explained that the visitor "…is connected to a series of galleries, and then you move out and you're connected to the park, and then you go back and are offered views into another gallery from a higher level or through to an atrium. All of this helps to orientate visitors. I wanted to make navigation through the complex an easy process. There's a series of loops in the design of this building, which gives a kind of circulation matrix that is always connecting with the outside or another room…."[15]

Lightness of Being

The design, detailing and fabrication of the canopies themselves returns one to the very beginnings of fjmt practice, above all to the Scientia gateway building at the University of New South Wales. However unlike the symmetrical repetitive dematerialized roof structure of Scientia, the carved symmetrical and asymmetrical wooden canopies that constitute the tessellated roof of Auckland are assembled from the following components; a hyperbolic timber frame the soffit of which is lined with laminated Kauri wood plus an underlying steel frame caped by an inclined weather-proof deck. As in the Scientia these canopies are each carried on tapering columns, faced in Kauri wood, with hinged metal joints at the top and bottom of the shaft. This hi-tech, timber tour de force with outriding aileron at the leading edges of each canopy, not only roofs the space throughout but also embodies the primary profile of the building.

Despite Francis-Jones's insistence that architecture cannot be meaningfully regarded as a language, one is nonetheless aware of the evolution of a particular architectonic syntax within the overall trajectory of the work; one which one has to recognize as having decisive Australian roots in part via the influence of Utzon's perennial roofwork versus earthwork paradigm as exemplified in the Opera House and in part through the corrugated, metal woolshed/verandah tradition of Glenn Murcutt's hyper-environmental approach. This affinity goes beyond the Sydney circle to include an implicit recognition of the virtues of Sean Godsell's timber latticework architecture or, let us say, of dematerialized flying roofs dramatically exemplified in the work of Lindsay and Kerry Clare. What sets the work of fjmt apart however is their particular commitment to the creation of urban form; one which is focused to an equal degree about the axial pathways of the pre-existing civic fabric and the topography of the attendant landscape.

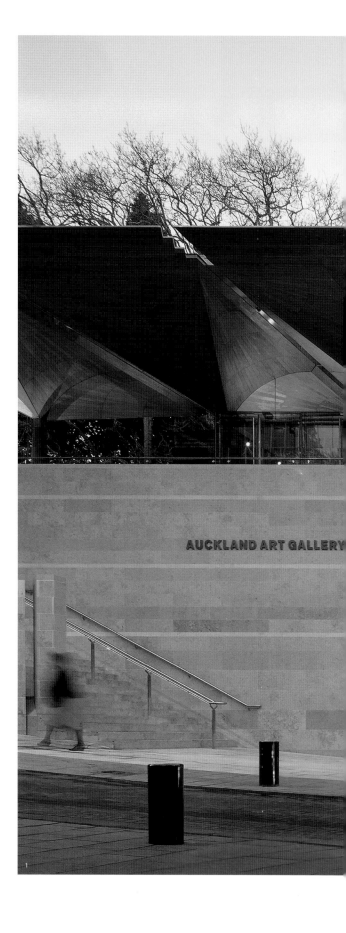

1 View from Kitchener Street showing entry and north atrium, Auckland Art Gallery Toi o Tāmaki.

Crown Street façade detail, Surry Hills Library & Community Centre

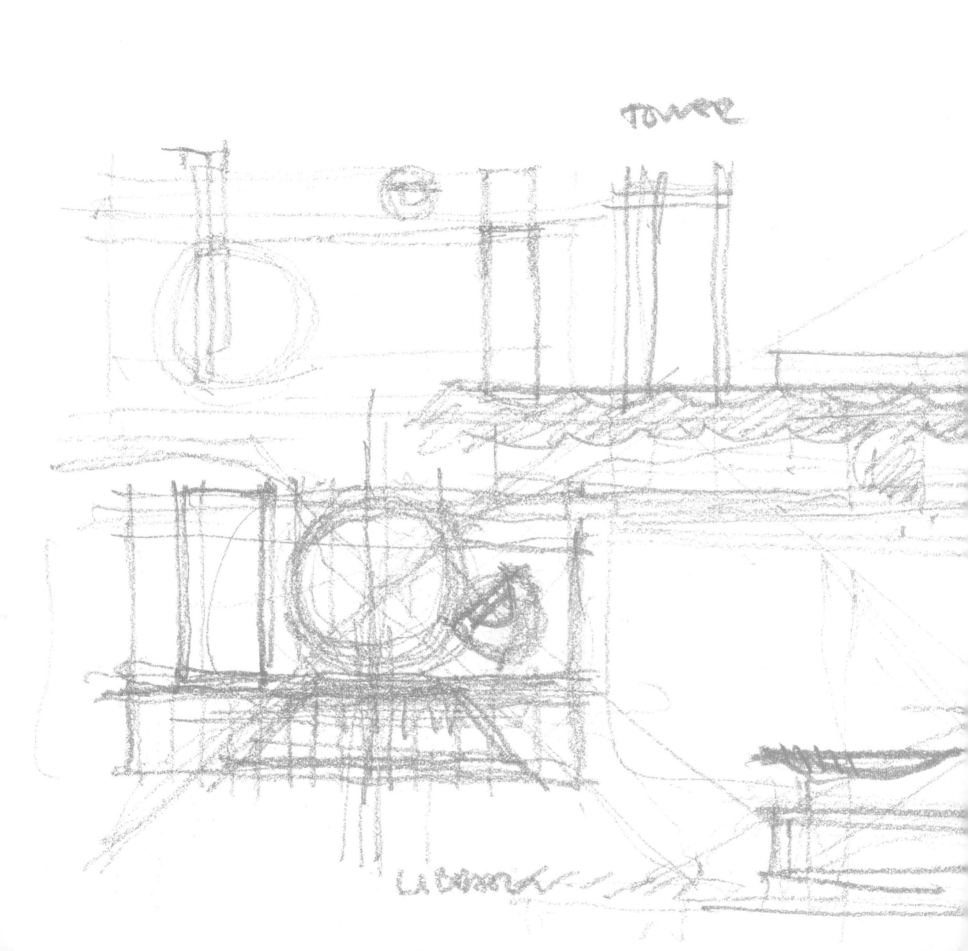

tower

libra

Architecture as the Mediation of the Universal and Specific

Richard Francis-Jones

I
Architecture and the Human Condition: Universal and Specific

An authentic contemporary connection to place is deeply problematic. The sense of interconnected inhabitation developed through centuries of close and intimate settlement in the land, myth and ancestry was lost with the embrace of modernity and all it offered. We are absorbed with all the great rewards that modernity brings to our lives but at the same time a sense of melancholic loss for what cannot be regained remains.

Modernity offers us the world, a breathtaking expanse of technological possibilities and freedom but leaves us with a sense of perpetual displacement. It seems only tenuous connections can be made within the speed, breadth and sweep of modernity. We are left with a sense of homelessness, a longing for an interconnection with and place in the world, our community; an inseparable cultural bond that grounds us.

The grounded pre-modern connection to a specific locale, place and culture interwoven in the specific is lost through displaced modern consciousness. This is the reality of a condition that cannot be adequately compensated for by nostalgia or the beguiling obsession with the new. But perhaps we can seek a more universal sense of interconnection, not the specific connections of a lost pre-modern culture but the more general and difficult connection of the universal; an authentic interconnection with the world which is individual, direct and not mediated by the conditioning of the specific.

With the development of a contemporary sense of universal connection with the world, it may be possible to begin authentic re-connection to the specific and to a locale. These connections will be subtle, as our modern condition is one of displacement and our interconnection is primarily universal, but this does not make it less profound, and perhaps ultimately makes it more so as it is free from the myth and distortion of socio-religious culture.

The universal is the basic shared phenomenological human condition of being together on this earth, under this sky, framed and orientated through landscape and architecture. Experience and interpretation of the reality of this basic condition can ground us within the flux and noise of a contemporary placelessness.

Perhaps an authentic architecture can begin through restating and interpreting this condition; making metaphorical connections to our phenomenological condition and framing our relation with the world; positioning us in relation to the earth, sky and landscape. Abstract relations that simultaneously project forward through form and technology to reframe our relation to the world, and at the same time, reach back to connect us to what is unchanging in our world.

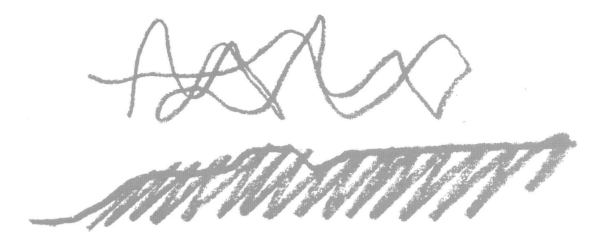

II
Elements of the Universal:
Skyplane and Groundplane

Irrespective of the specifics of culture, history or site, is the basic existential condition of being in the world, on the earth and under the sky; between groundplane and skyplane.

We carve and dig into the ground, piling up the earth and clay.

We reach up with posts and frames, stretch and weave glass and fabric in planes and vaults.

We shape and figure the space between the plane of the sky and the plane of the ground, distorting both in attempts to secure a place.

Skyplane: Roof canopy

Wallplane: Fabric and weave

Groundplane: Platform topography

…The building brings the earth as inhabited landscape close to man and at the same time places the nearness of neighbourly dwelling under the expanse of the sky.

Martin Heidegger
In *Hebel: der Hausfreund* (Pfullingen, 1957), 13

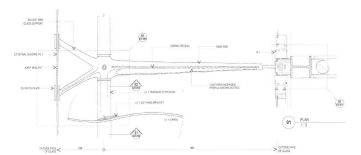

Authenticity and the Tectonic

The formal development and explorative potential of contemporary construction materials and systems technology have played a central role in shaping the direction of architecture over the last century. This innovation and transformative influence continues to this day.

The materials with which we build are central to our work and ongoing architectural investigations. Materials, after all, are fundamental to the very medium that is architecture and integral to the tectonic nature of authentic architectural representation. We are very interested in contemporary developments in materials, technology and exploration of the formal potential offered by these systems. In particular, technological advancement in the structural, thermal and dynamic visual performance of glass and composites creates new opportunities. A more transparent, responsive and kinetic architecture, calibrated to human preference and aspiration, is developing.

Equally, we are interested in the persistence of building materials and the associated depth of human relations with the material of the earth with which we have built for thousands of years. This is the phenomenological and poetic relation with materials; the tectonic assembly of constructs into meaningful alignments, the materials that figure and frame our relation with the world and our changing place within it.

There is a collective memory embodied within the stone, clay, wood and the material fabric of a place and its transformation through human settlement and struggle. These natural materials, lifted directly from the earth, are full of depth, texture and life. They have borne witness to the prolonged human drama, and are the very tools by which we attempt to resolve our place in the world. We have grown close to them and the memory they embody of a lost interconnection with the world. This is the potential depth and significance that lies within the architectural use and expression of natural materials.

These are the dual material interests that are explored in our architecture: the formal, spatial and environmental potential of contemporary material technology, and the possibility of poetic depth in the expressive use of natural materials. Both interests are explored through a contemporary tectonic expression of materials and assembly, within a dialectical understanding of architecture, a dialectical exploration of alienation and place; transparency and solidity; lightness and weight; the visual and the tactile; the specifics of locale with the reality of the global.

The increasingly interconnected globalised nature of contemporary culture and industry is reflected in the procurement of building materials and systems manufacture from all across the world for even modest and simple projects. Accordingly, seeking a relation to locale primarily through local materials and industry, in a direct sense, is ever more limited and ultimately synthetic. More partial, abstract and dialectical relationships to a specific locale that acknowledge our globalised condition are the only authentic possibility.

IV
Intuition

Within the frenetic world of professional practice, and the instrumental development and construction industry where time is constantly denied, how does the architect launch the architectural project and through it, thoughtfully respond to contemporary theoretical issues? Ironically, it is perhaps through the avoidance of thought, through thoughtless action.

The drawing of the first line across the site intersects the site with the programme and at this moment simultaneously explores, discovers and uncovers the project that in some ways is already there.

Thought and theory are sometimes impediments to understanding, or at least understanding that comes directly through action. Certainly they are impediments to intuition, and intuition is perhaps the primary means through which the architect engages, via the architectural project, with the pressing cultural and theoretical issues of our time.

Intuition, in some respects, is the opposite of thought. It goes around the cognitive limitations of thought, and through intuition the limitations of time can be overcome as intuition is immediate requiring no time; time and thinking may in fact block this creative insight.

Intuition is an existential quality beyond the rational. It is rooted in our connection to the world we inhabit; it is our feeling rather than our knowledge. It is a manifestation of the interconnectedness of all things. Remarkably, it is the means for a holistic response to the vastly complex nature of our human condition. And it is a response less from us than through us.

But this first intuitive line drawn across the site, this formal concept, must be transformed, constructed and assembled from materials and systems to become architecture. And this will require direct engagement with the market and industry, with all its limitations, its possibilities and its technology.

Intuition must be reinforced with rigour, constancy, and discipline with a deep sense of collaboration. A collaboration that will find the concept evolved, transformed, protected and realised.

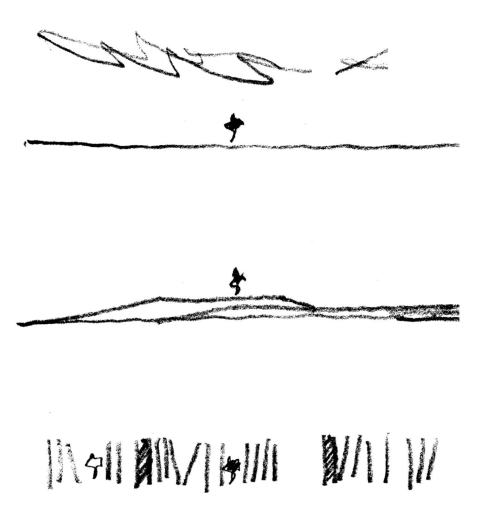

V
Absorption

In architecture, representations of reality are postulated and explored through the formal relations of the building and the reality of its making. Not the surface application of an idealised image, but through the spatial organisation, formal order, structure, construction and specific relation with the site and interpretation of the programme. Thus, the representational nature or meaning in architecture does not depend on its stability, function or the efficiency of the means of its production, but on the way in which all of these have been limited and subordinated or transformed by purely formal requirements. Purpose is therefore not a restrictive condition that compromises our art, but an integral element of specific representation.

Architectural representation becomes the making of critical frames through which to understand our experience of the world, a formal means, of cognitive effect, with an ethical and social purpose.

But it is also important to understand the limits of this representation. The architectural framings of the world are not, for example, political and never will be. This is beyond the limits of architecture. They only frame the events that occur around them and which are staged within them, accommodating comedy and tragedy with equal indifference.

However, this indifference may only be in relation to what is transient. These architectural frames can embody something more essential behind appearances, something more fundamental and enduring. They can place or position us in relation to the world in which we live. This is, in a sense, the idea of the sublime that began in the eighteenth century—the absorbing and overwhelming power of the natural landscape.

When we look out over the ocean at the horizon, there is a calming, meditative effect. We are placed in relation to the world in a way that is immediately overwhelming, emphasising our insignificance in relation to the vastness of the ocean or the stars. But at the same time we are comforted, we are pleased to be such a small part, our egos recede and we feel momentarily connected.

Architecture can similarly adjust our experience of the world and our place within it. We are made aware of the conditions of our lives by constructing alternative frames within which things are set in a slightly different order. These are the critical frames through which we ultimately attempt to reconcile our place in the world.

Milling space ceiling detail, St Barnabas Church

Diversity, mix, equality, integration and the preservation of cultural and historic values are not natural by-products of present market-based trends. To surrender the concept of planning the city as a whole and to assume that the major decisions about our future will continue to be made in the private market is to abandon the principles of equality, justice and democratic decision making to which the best of planning has always adhered.

Peter Marcuse
"Density and Social Justice," *Columbia Documents of Architecture and Theory* 3 (New York: Rizzoli, 1993), 83

The right to the city is far more than the individual liberty to access urban resources: it is a right to change ourselves by changing the city. It is, moreover, a common rather than an individual right since this transformation inevitably depends upon the exercise of a collective power to reshape the processes of urbanization. The freedom to make and remake our cities and ourselves is, I want to argue, one of the most precious yet most neglected of our human rights.

David Harvey
"The Right to the City," *New Left Review* 53 (London: LNR, 2008): 23–40

City represents the most significant effort on the part of human civilization to a complete transformation of the natural environment, the most radical shift from the state of nature to the one of culture by creating a "microclimate" particularly right to the development of some fundamental relationships for human life.

Vittorio Gregotti
Il Territorio dell'Architettura, Feltrinelli, Milano. 1966

City

City
Sydney

What is exceptionally compelling is the way in which eight exfoliated screens in plan ultimately devolve into two major cinematic volumes which when they are not being used for the projection of films serve to frame the two primary monuments of the Sydney Harbour panorama; the Sydney Harbour Bridge and the Sydney Opera House.

— Kenneth Frampton

Museum of Contemporary Art

This project proposes a dynamic engagement of art, city and moving image. The natural topography, harbour and traces of earliest settlement have inspired a form and are characterised by ribbons of steel and glass, light and movement.

The museum building (originally the Maritime Services Board headquarters, constructed in 1952) is on the western shore of Circular Quay, one of Australia's most significant and important historic cultural sites. The new Sydney Harbour Moving Image Centre is sited adjacent to and integrated with the museum, which is also extensively refurbished and expanded.

A series of glimmering planes are to be inserted into the existing sandstone masses and will extend in sinuous organic form to open towards the harbour and its great monuments. These fins of metal and glass form linear horizontal shafts through which the building breaths, drawing in cool fresh air at a low level and expelling at rooftop; these energy fins are thus the veins and arteries that serve the main volumes and spaces.

The ribbon-like planes are suspended above a new stepped sandstone podium that forms a great pubic terrace or platform, offering views across the harbour and a grand, welcoming entry.

Above the foyer, drawn up through escalators that moderate and control movement, is the Moving Image Centre. Space is compressed and expanded though the curvilinear forms into a series of episodes, framing and engaging the city with the spaces of the centre. The curved blades orientate the main public cinemas and rooftop theatres directly towards the city's icons, the Harbour Bridge and Opera House.

Within these spaces, the audience is thus confronted with a literal window, framing the city and its icons. A moveable screen descends in front of this "window to the city," replacing and juxtaposing the actual city view with the infinite view of the moving image projection. A great public rooftop incorporating two paired open-air theatres, frames the grand stage of Circular Quay and Sydney Harbour.

1787

1790

1820

1929

40

1960

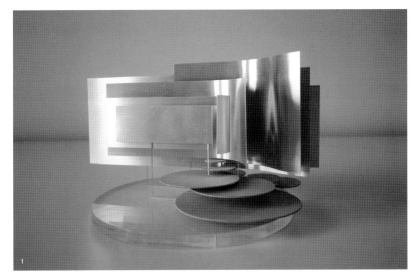

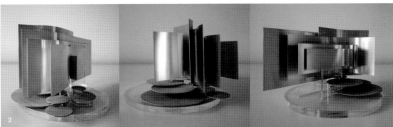

1,2 Concept model. 3 The layered façade orientates the public cinema and roof top theatre towards the Harbour Bridge.
4 Geometric setout; planes of the layered façades.
5 Site plan illustrates primary urban alignments to Circular Quay, Opera House and Harbour Bridge.
6 Historical morphological analysis.

4

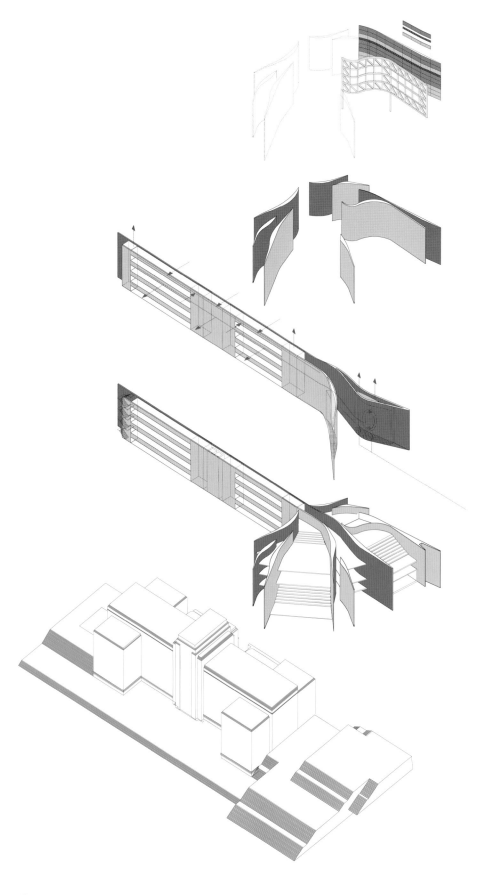

Structure and cladding
Braced steel lattice walls
Aluminium cladding
Transparent translucent glazing
Ventilation grills and louvers

Blades
Structural spatial envelope
Blades free from the existing
Organic opening to harbour

Spine
Services spine
Central blades penetrate existing building
Define support and circulation
Energy environmental control
Wet areas lift stairs services
Energy fins
Fresh air intake
Exhaust air
Heat exchanger
Stack

Spine and blades
Articulated new insertion of organic light-weight blades
Metal and glass
Spine transforms existing building
Blades open to the monuments of the city

MCA + podium
Platform of sandstone
Base for existing building
Orientates to quay
Grand public terrace
Topography

The Mint

The Mint project is the transformation of one of Sydney's oldest and most precious historical sites on Macquarie Street into a new, meaningful public place formed and characterised as much by the carefully inserted contemporary buildings as the conserved and adapted heritage structures.

The vacant and almost ruinous Mint Coining Factory and associated buildings have been transformed into the campus-like headquarters of the Historic Houses Trust. Contemporary architectural forms have been carefully inserted to accommodate a major public auditorium, exhibition areas, foyer and bar, while existing buildings have been adaptively reused to create a significant new resource centre for the public, and new work environments for the staff.

These clearly defined public rooms and facilities are gathered around a central courtyard, which is given new life and form as a significant public space of the city. While the contemporary architectural forms have been carefully designed to form direct and clear relations with the existing buildings in terms of scale and proportion, they are uncompromisingly new. They have sought to create a new architectural layer on the site, designed in the innovative and "forward-looking" spirit that underpinned the original 1850s constructions.

This "layered" approach of placing new and old in a bold transforming relationship is apparent in the general organisation of the project, and in the design of the new courtyard. The strict symmetry of Trickett's original plan, with its central pavilion and identical wings, has been transformed into an asymmetrical axis about a pair of related pavilions of opposite/dialectical character, new and old, light and heavy, stone and glass. The outcome is a rich and complex assembly of form and spaces through which the layers and events of the site can be read and interpreted.

The Mint is of exceptional cultural significance. It contains one of the oldest buildings in Sydney: the southern wing of Governor Macquarie's Rum Hospital (1811–16) and important remains of the Sydney branch of the Royal Mint (1855–1926). Its raison d'être was that seminal event in the history of New South Wales: the discovery of gold.

The new built forms have been developed to reinforce and interpret the geometric alignments conceived in 1854 by Joseph Trickett, while at the same time introducing a new point of symmetry that relates to the primary public access and contemporary use of the site. The strict symmetry of Trickett's plan with central pavilion and identical wings has been transformed into an asymmetrical axis about a pair of related, pavilions of "opposite/dialectical" character, new and old, light and heavy, stone and glass.

1 Bar
2 Engine House
3 Theatrette
4 Reception and workspace
5 Superintendant's Office
 (now the Caroline Simpson
 Research Collection)
6 The Mint
7 Coining Factory
8 Courtyard

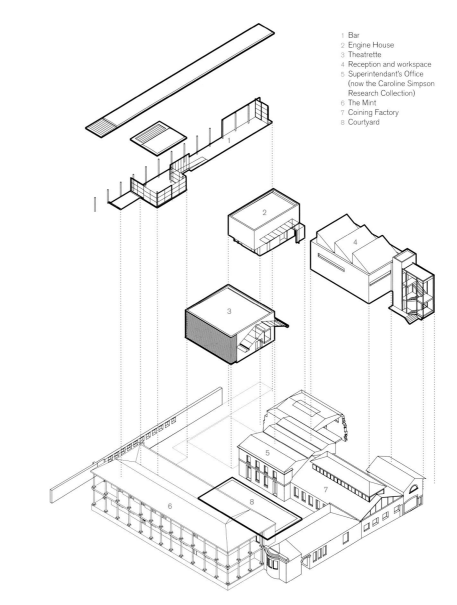

Axonometric: Built form elements

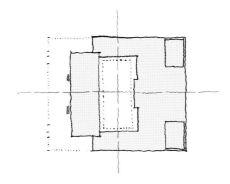

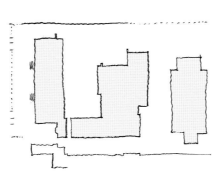

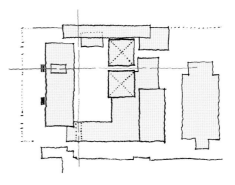

Sketches: Form evolution   A Joseph Trickett's symmetry 1854   B Extant buildings 2002   C Symmetry transformed 2005

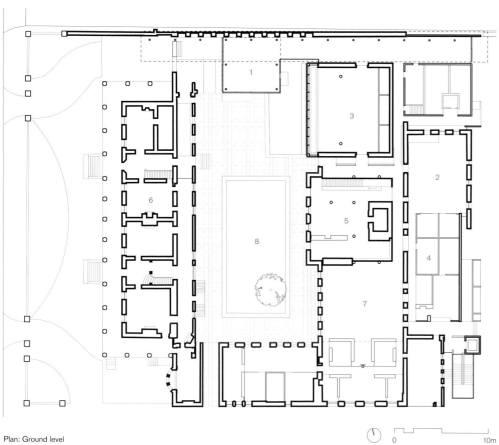

Plan: Ground level

1 Bar
2 Engine House
3 Theatrette
4 Reception and workspace
5 Superintendant's Office
  (now the Caroline Simpson
  Research Collection)
6 The Mint
7 Coining Factory
8 Courtyard

1 The Mint courtyard

1 Engine House
2 Theatrette
3 The Mint
4 Courtyard

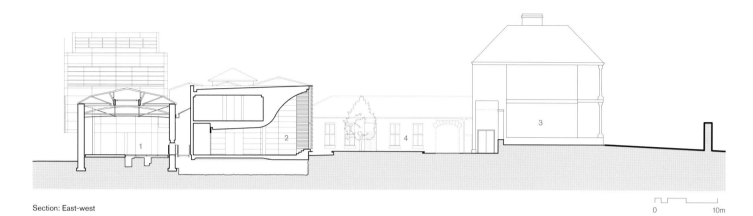

Section: East-west

0   10m

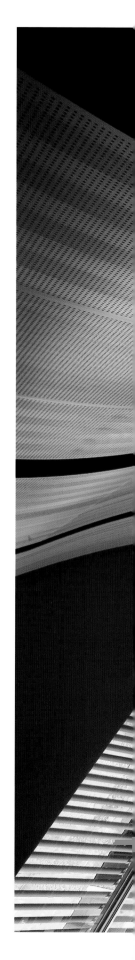

1 The theatrette interior.
2, 3, 4 The new transparent Theatrette forms a partner to the historic stone Superindent's office.
5 The automated timber louvre panel-lift door of the theatrette in varying positions.

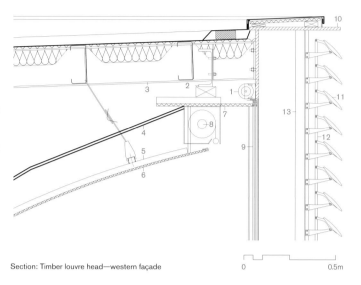

1 Sashless window motor unit
2 Pelmet beam
3 Steel roof support rafter
4 Facetted services
  trough beyond
5 Suspended precurved
  steel angle
6 Curved acoustic timber
  veneer ceiling
7 Concealed fixed access panel
8 Projector screen
9 Operable sashless window
10 Fabricated steel fascia angle
11 Timber louvre system support
12 Louvre frame
13 Fabricated steel mullion

Section: Timber louvre head—western façade

0   0.5m

1, 2 The operable timber louvres and awning system of the theatrette.

1. Insulation provides a thermal barrier.
2. In summer motorised high level louvres provide relief air path for displacement air (removal of internal heat gains and pollutants). In winter louvres remain closed when external temperatures are < 19°C in order to retain heat.
3. Penetration of high angle summer sun and subsequent heat gain is reduced by external shading devices. In winter, low angle sun penetrates to aid heating.
4. Integrated joinery units function as air displacement outlets, shelving and partitions. Air either heats or cools by tracking to heat sources. The air forms a plume of cool air around the heat source that rises as the temperature increases, thus removing heat.
5. Underfloor systems provide background radiant cooling in summer and up to 100W/m² radiant heating during winter.
6. Thermal mass of building reduces winter heat loss and provides an effective barrier against external environment.
7. Concealed sheet metal and flexible duct work delivers heated air to joinery units (100% outdoor air).
8. In summer ceiling fans encourage air plumes to rise, drawing hotter air away from occupants and in winter, encourage mixing of room air to maintain a constant environment.

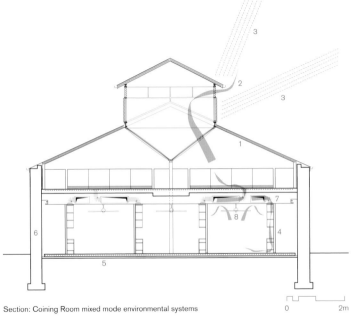

Section: Coining Room mixed mode environmental systems

0   2m

1 View across the refurbished coining factory cast and wrought iron roof to the contemporary structure beyond.
2 Frameless glass display case suspended within existing opening. 3 The ceiling lightly touches the ruinous building fabric.
4 A suspended timber floor provides views and access to historic fabric and archeology below.
5 Notations from steel framed glazed panels applied to the existing wall fabric preserve the broken profiles of existing openings. 6 The layers of ruinous fabric juxtaposed against the contemporary insertions.

Balfour Park

Balfour Park is an urban renewal project at the southern gateway to the city and involves the redevelopment of the former Carlton & United Brewery. fjmt was invited to provide a concept design for this important and extensive urban site.

Fundamental to our approach is the creation of a rich network of public places (parks, gardens, squares and residential streets). These are integrated with the existing village and city networks and overlaid with a rich mix of facilities (such as shops, cafés, galleries, offices, educational facilities, apartments, houses and terraces).

At the centre of the scheme is a significant new public open space—Balfour Park—formed through the resolution of Balfour Street and Jones Street geometries and uniting the communities from either side of the Broadway division. A sequence of new squares reinforces the open-space network, and these squares are strategically positioned in relation to the heritage brewery buildings and precinct entry points.

The heritage buildings accommodate a variety of community uses and house other public facilities like galleries, restaurants and cafés. These uses are encouraged to permeate into the open spaces, blurring the "borders" and enriching public places.

The proposed housing accommodates a range of living and lifestyle options underpinned by a commitment to sustainability.

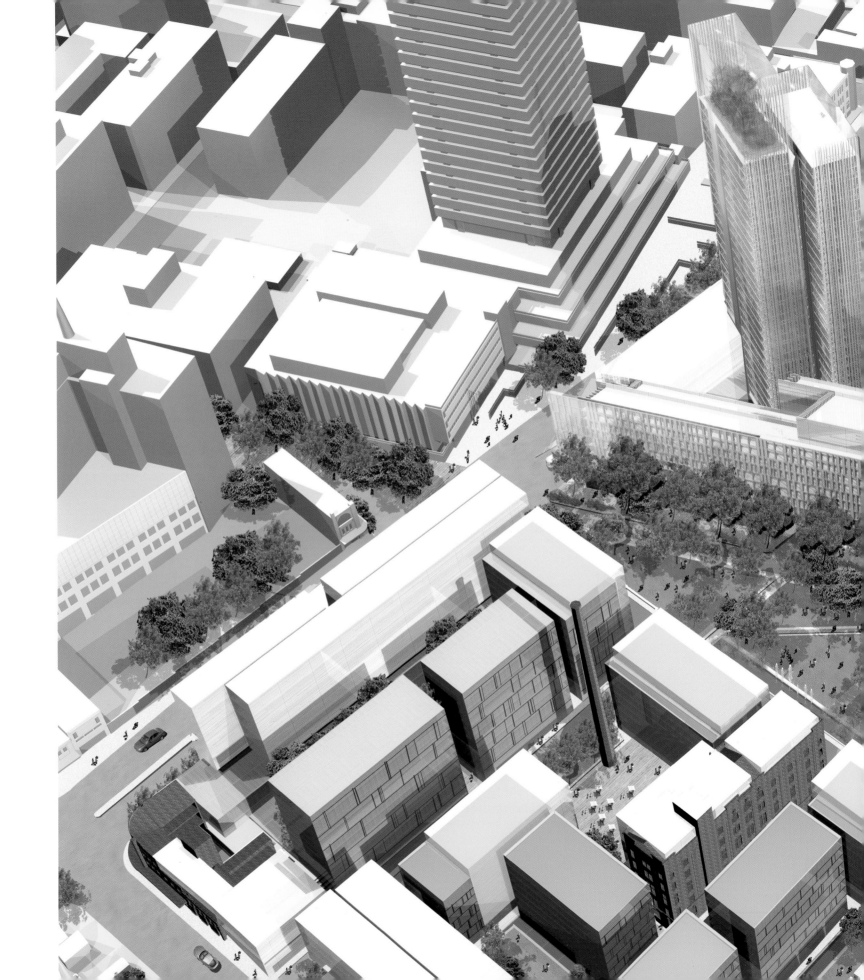

1 A network of parks, squares and streets integrated into the fabric of the city.
2, 3, 4 Concept model.

A The serpentine building form unites the street geometries giving definition to Balfour Park.
B Vistas from the Broadway approach and from Railway Square framed by new towers and existing University of Technology building.
C Public spaces created around significant heritage items.

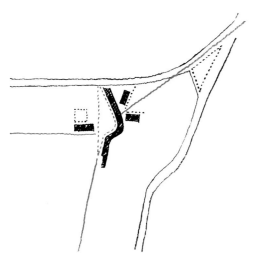

A Building form

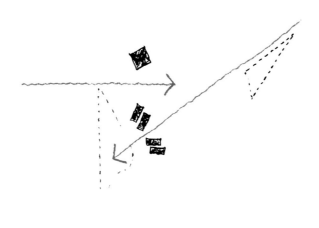

B Vistas

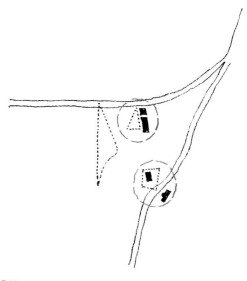

C Public spaces

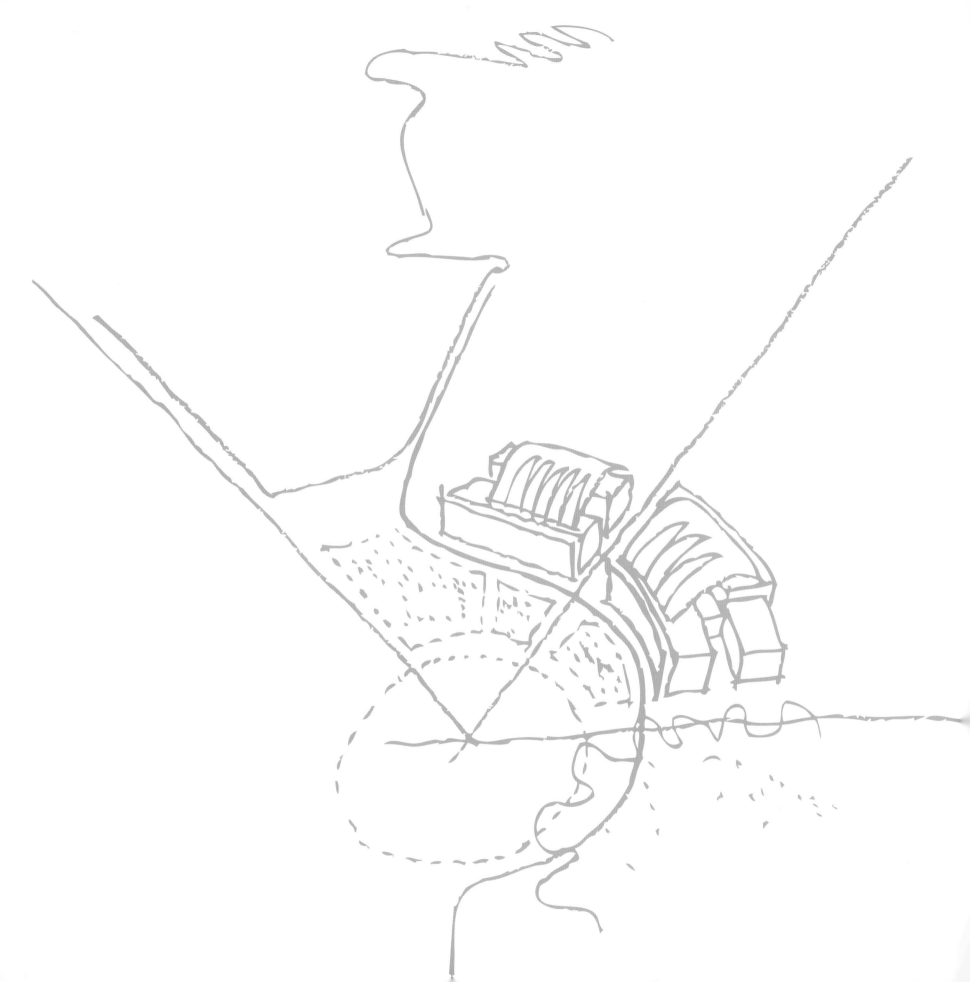

Darling Quarter

Darling Quarter is a true integration of urban design, architecture, and landscape architecture toward the creation of a public place within the city.

We have sought to enhance the joy and beauty of Darling Harbour, one of the most popular public places in Australia, and to do so in a way that imbues it with a sense of quality and permanence.

Darling Quarter is where the western edge of the city and the park meet and is celebrated in a series of defined public spaces, including a pedestrian boulevard, parklands, gateway, children's playground, and activated edges lined with cafés and restaurants. It is a place for everyone, for city workers at lunchtime and in the evenings, families, children, the young and old, visitors and locals.

This is a very different type of office building in a very special location. It is an architecture of human scale, natural materials and of a warmth of character appropriate to this very public parkland location. The long gently curving façade defines and enhances the public realm with a warmth and transparency unusual in commercial buildings. The mullions are made of natural timber and irregularly spaced like rows of trees in a forest. Between these deep, profiled posts are adjustable timber louvres that control heat and glare, automatically adjusted in relation to the position of the sun. Importantly, this composed use of natural timber in layers behind very transparent glazing also creates a soft and warmth backdrop to the tree canopies of the parkland.

The curves of Tumbalong Park and a ribbon-like connection with the Darling Harbour waterfront determined the primary geometry of the architectural form. Split at its centre, the new buildings frame and define a new pedestrian street, the civic connector, that links south Darling Harbour via Bathurst Street to Town Hall and the very centre of the city.

The different scales of the east and west wings of the project respond to and reflect the varying scale of the park and city, united and resolved through the curved roof that draws natural light to the interior. These long forms of timber and glass, capped by the gentle curves and the scalloped apertures of the roof, create a background to the parkland and a foreground to the rising city beyond, uniting the two in a new public place, Darling Quarter.

Above the restaurants, cafés, bars and promenade are the work environments of the building, centred around day-lit atriums. Lobbies on Harbour Street and escalators bring visitors and workers to the dramatic atrium floors. The asymmetry of the workplace floors and atriums, edged with stairs, bridges, breakout areas and glazed lifts, creates a stimulating and collaborative campus environment.

An important aspect of the project's design innovation and sustainability is not simply the "green" score that reaches the highest levels of sustainable accreditation, but the focus on occupant well being and the creation of an enabling, supportive, human and ultimately inspiring place to work, generate, and exchange ideas.

1 Darling Quarter reconnects the Darling Harbour Parkland to the city centre. **2** Built form elements.

A Public domain and landscape: the primary volume is generated through the extended radius of Tumbalong Park and the northern tangental extension to the waterfront.

B Connections and vistas: two urban lines further refine and divide the built form; a ribbon like promenade from the waterfront and a new pedestrian street connecting the centre of the city to the park.

C Threshold and edge: The built form articulated as vaulted roofs above central atriums combine to define a new pedestrian street and public promenade.

1 Paired workplace platforms and atrium
2 Glass and timber louvred façade and timber awning
3 Vaulted roof profile

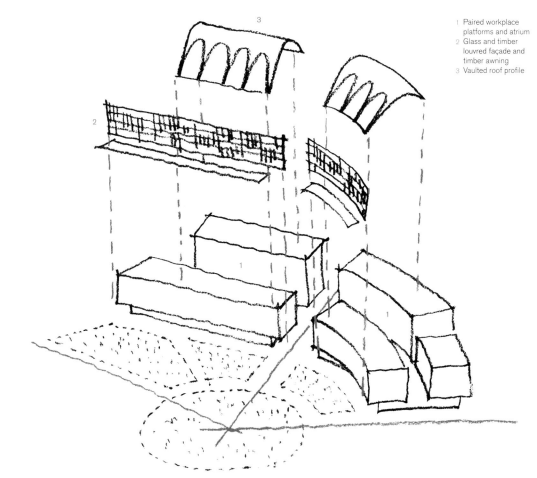

Axonometric: Built form elements

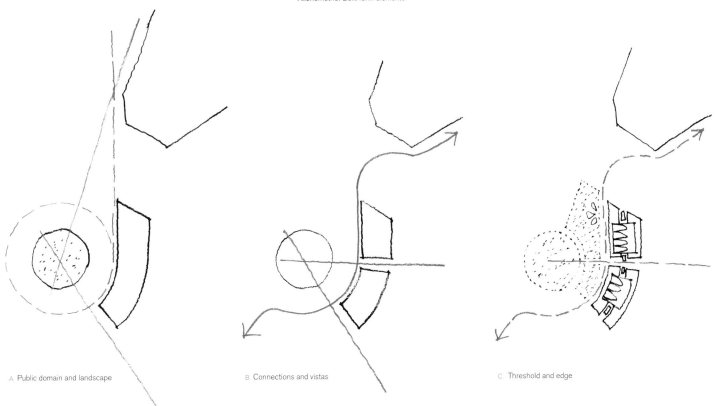

A Public domain and landscape

B Connections and vistas

C Threshold and edge

Plan: Site

1 Commercial office
2 Playground
3 Community green
4 Retail terrace
5 Pedestrian boulevard
6 Pedestrian street
7 Tumbalong Park

0   50m

1 Darling Quarter is
where the western edge
of the city and Tumbalong
Park meet.

1 The western façade
facing the park enhances
the public realm with a
warmth and transparency.
2 Timber mullions are
irregularly spaced with
automatically adjustable
timber louvres controlling
heat and glare.

1 High visible light
transmittance insulated
glazing unit
2 Timber louvre blind
3 Solid timber mullion
cladding
4 Curtain wall mullion

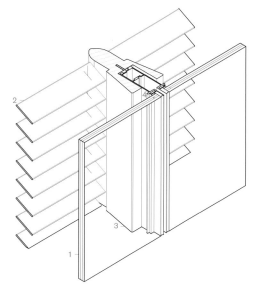

Axonometric detail: Articulated façade

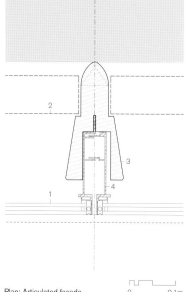

Plan: Articulated façade

0   0.1m

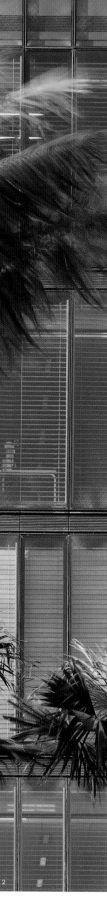

1 Natural light penetrates deep inside the floors, contributing to occupant well-being. 2 The asymmetry of the workplace floors and atriums, edged with stairs, bridges, breakout spaces and glazed lifts creates a stimulating and collaborative campus environment. 3 The tapering profile of the atrium roof creates a light filled, open and collaborative work environment.

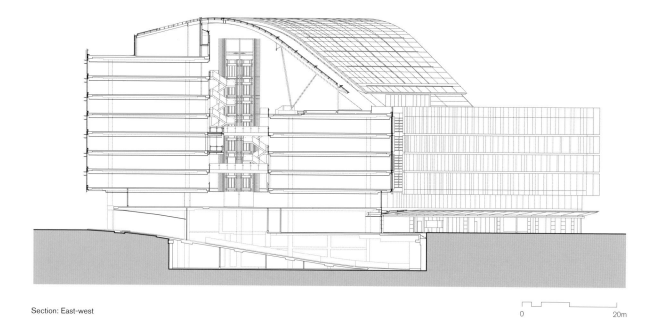

Section: East-west

0   20m

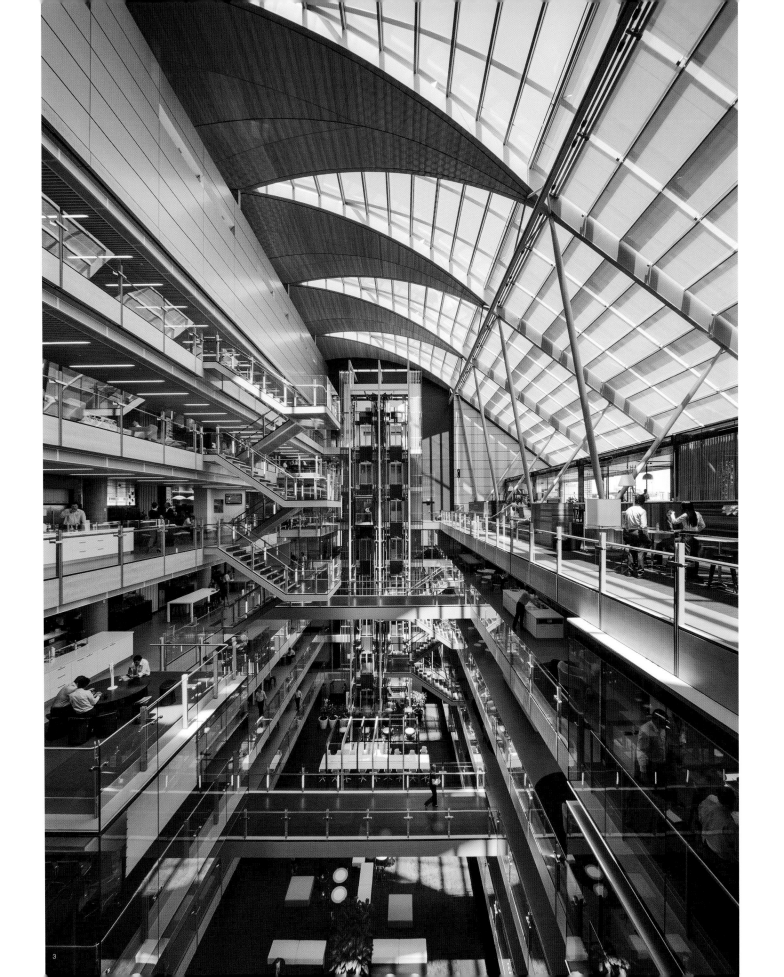

1 The long gently curving façade defines and enhances the urban promenade. 2 A programmable LED system is integrated within the façade to create dynamic light effects. 3 Kiosk and toilet facilities are provided beneath the timber organic forms of the shade canopies. 4,5 The warm timber façade creates a gentle background to community green and waterplay. 6 The park façade forms a unique backdrop to children's playground.

Layers of glass, zinc and polished aluminium form a curvilinear profile of the bridge **3** The unique sinuous form of the footbridge connects the parkland to the city centre.

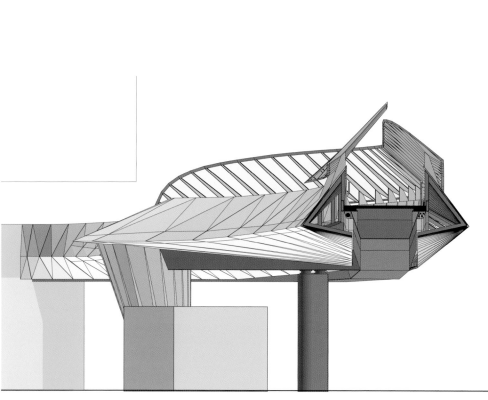

Section: Pedestrian footbridge

0   2m

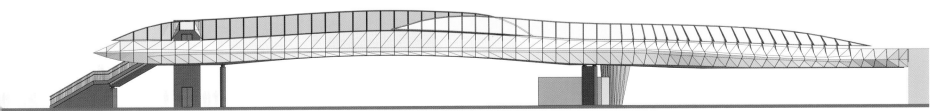

Elevation: Pedestrian footbridge

0   5m

St Barnabas Church

St Barnabas church and adjacent community hall, located on Sydney's busy Broadway, were destroyed by fire in May 2006. A Sydney institution for over 145 years, efforts to rebuild the church began almost immediately. The architecture of the new church complex seeks to respond to the qualities and great opportunity of this special site in the city, and equally importantly, to the great sense of openness, welcoming and joy that characterises St Barnabas.

The new church offers a peaceful oasis of gathering and worship within the busy noise of the city. It provides a balance of open courtyard, landscaped gardens, informal and formal, fixed and flexible spaces. At the centre of the church is the informal social-heart gathering spaces and the calm peaceful space of worship.

The gentle rising curved volumes of the worship space characterise and focus the appearance of the church in the city. The worship space, with its folding floor that wraps up around the congregation and opens up to soft cloud-like ceilings, is conceived like an open-hand under the sky; a warm, protective, generous and light-fill space. Complementing the worship space is the counter-curved form of the foyer and social-heart that rises in a gesture of welcome and invitation to the central landscaped courtyard.

Separating these curved forms and courtyard from the street are the linear sheltering frame and canopies that define the entrance streetscape and steps up to the courtyard. These fine frames of off-form concrete open to the street though large windows that accommodate the shop and meeting spaces beneath the awning canopies that project out over the footpath.

The forms of this church are structured, assembled and finished in simple, modest materials, concrete, compressed cement sheet, steel and glass.

St Barnabas
ANGLICAN CHURCH
wholesome
wholesome
natural health market
The Broadway
Shopping Centre
P

1 The gentle rising curved volumes of the worship space characterise and focus the appearance of the church in the city. **2, 3** Sectional concept model.

A Concept sketch studies of the spacial sequencing of garden, courtyard, gathering and worship.

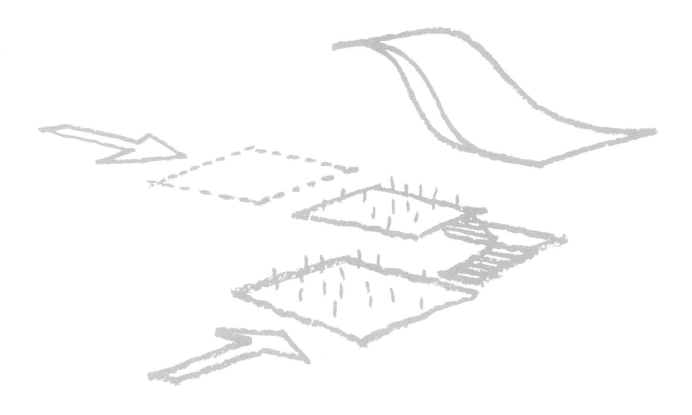

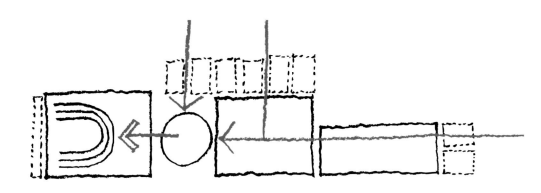

A Concept sketch

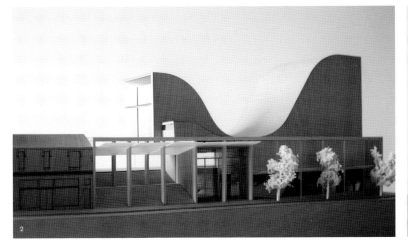

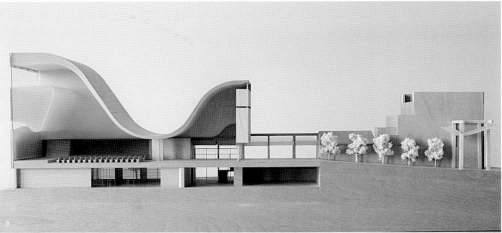

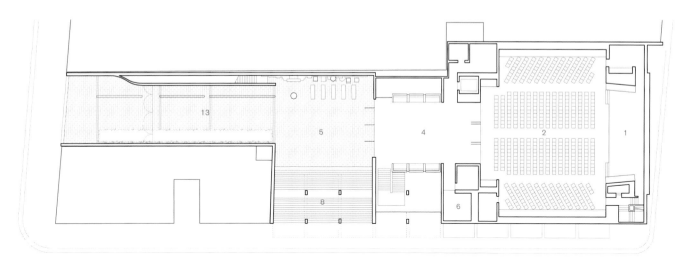

Plan: Level 1 (Broadway)

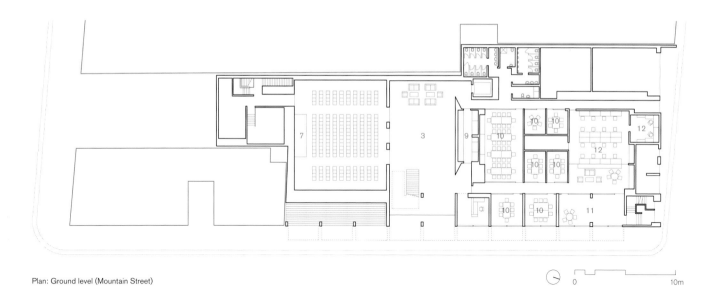

Plan: Ground level (Mountain Street)

0   10m

1 Stage
2 Worship space
3 Lower gathering space
4 Upper gathering space
5 Forecourt
6 Crying room
7 Multipurpose hall
8 Mountain Street stairs
9 Kitchen
10 Meeting room
11 Music room
12 Office
13 Garden entry from Broadway

1 Elements salvaged from
the original church and the
illuminated cross of the
new elevation characterise
the courtyard.

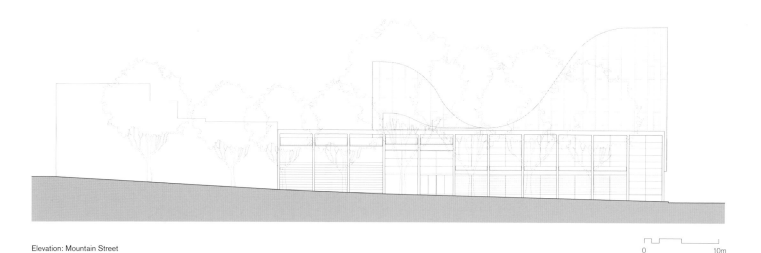

Elevation: Mountain Street

0   10m

1 The curvilinear profile of the worship space rises above and acts as a counterpoint to the trabeated street form.
2 Wide stairs and canopies connect the courtyard with Mountain Street.

1 Upper gathering space
2 Lower gathering space
3 Mountain Street

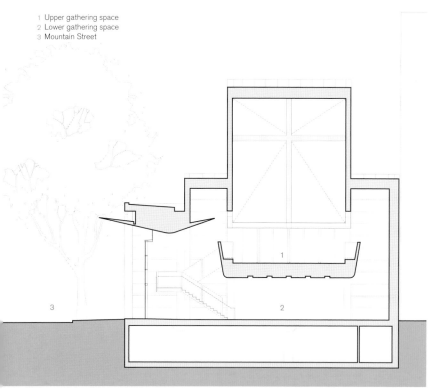

Section: East-west

0   5m

1,2 Below the bridge-like form is the gathering space which connects Mountain Street with the office space and multi-purpose hall. 3,4 The cross transforms into a three dimensional form within the gathering space.

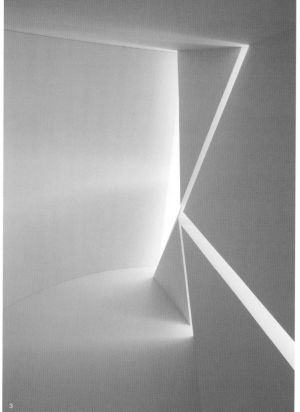

1, 2, 3, 4 Indirect light
reaches the worship space
from above and either side
of the congregation.
The floor curls up fusing
with the walls, providing
a space of informal play.
5 The worship space with
profiled ceiling integrating
indirect vertical daylight.

1	Stage
2	Worship space
3	Upper gathering space
4	Lower gathering space
5	Forecourt
6	Multipurpose hall
7	Kitchen
8	Meeting room
9	Office
10	Garden entry from Broadway
11	Mountain Street

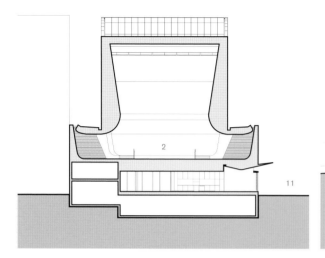

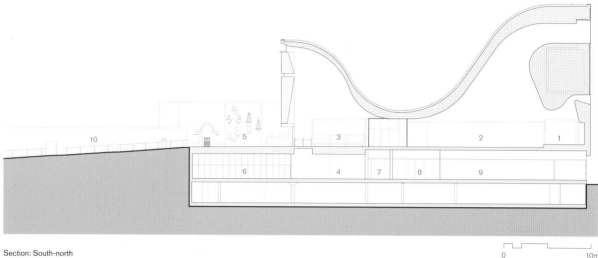

Section: West-east

Section: South-north

0   10m

1 The worship space caters for a modern congregation including amplified music, contemporary band configurations and words projected onto the ceiling volumes. The stage allows for large numbers of people to participate in the service.

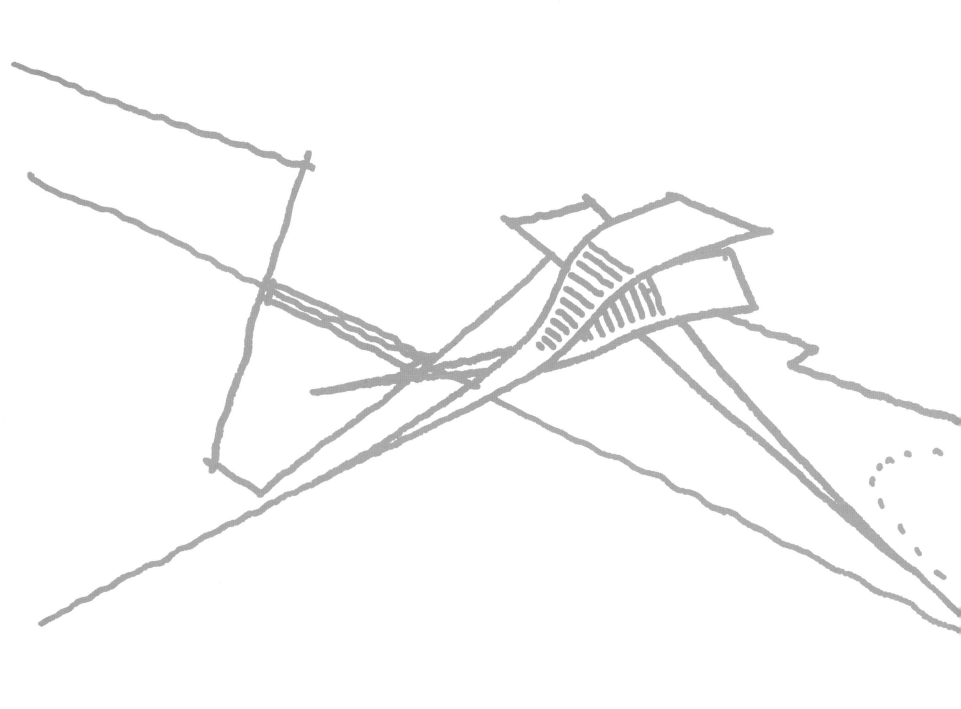

Open House: Barangaroo Cultural Centre

Conceived as part of the Barangaroo urban renewal project, the Open House is a cultural facility that will become a public focus for this new, high-density, mixed-use community that extends the city to its western waterfront.

Theatre, live music, comedy festivals, public art installations, improvised performances, open lectures and global conferences will all be staged at the Open House.

The Open House is as much landscape as it is building. Its design is an architectural interpretation of both the natural and industrial waterfront landscape that makes Sydney so distinct. It will be constructed from weathered timber and concrete. Steps and seating will be made from tallowwood layered within a white concrete curved form. Automated timber louvres will protect and shade the glazing from the afternoon sun and light reflected by the water.

The Open House will be self-supporting in terms of energy, water and waste; it will be entirely self-sufficient.

The Open House is designed to be a focal point, a talking point, a meeting point, and a place that encourages the free exchange of ideas, demonstrating Sydney's intrinsic diversity.

1 Folded planes follow
the line of the new street
extension and opens to the
harbour through an artificial
topography. 2 Folded
ground plane wraps over
exhibition, function room
and learning areas that
are further sheltered by
automated louvres of
recycled timber.

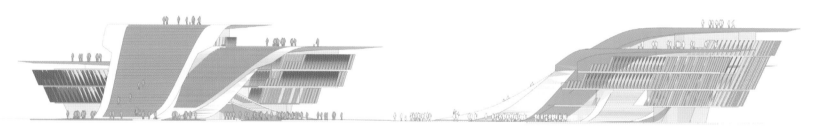

103

City
Newcastle

Newcastle Museum

Newcastle Museum is composed of a series of reused, late-turn-of-the-century brick railway workshop structures located within the Honeysuckle waterfront urban regeneration precinct. This project involved the complete refit of these important heritage buildings with new facilities and exhibitions as well as the construction of a new welcoming "Link" building that interconnects all the disparate areas of the redesigned museum.

The concept for the new museum was to create a cohesive complement to the heavy brick structures through a lightness of form and touch. The new building elements were conceived as a series of floating cloud-like roof forms that hover in between the heavy masonry of the existing workshops. These white cloud-like forms draw in natural light, and shade and protect visitors and exhibits, while also creating a new sense of entry and central orientation for the museum circulation.

Below the floating roof forms is the Link structure in steel and glass that accommodates the foyer, temporary exhibition and circulation areas. This structure is joined to the adjacent workshop buildings via a series of metal tube-like forms that create extended threshold transition zones into the differing exhibition volumes. Interconnected in this way are the Blacksmith's and Wheel Shop (1880), the Locomotive Boiler Shop (1887), and the New Erecting Shop (1920).

The Link is a fully glazed volume protected by the lightweight cloud-like canopy structure that floats between the existing buildings. The glazed façades are offset from the existing heritage walls, enabling the walls to be both protected and revealed to view.

A new entry and courtyard with a gently raised lawn create an ingress from the railway station and contribute to the bridging of the line that has long divided the city from its waterfront.

1 Courtyard/station entry
roof profiles suspended
above the glazed Link
pavilion.

1 The roof profiles and glazed pavilion foyer are separately articulated but interconnect the existing workshop buildings.
2 Exhibition spaces are clearly visible through the transitional threshold of the Link pavilion.

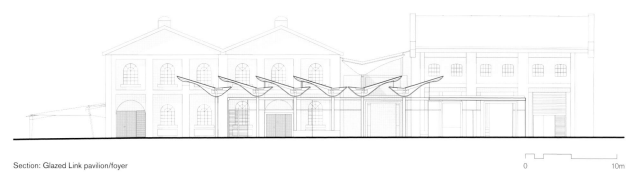

Section: Glazed Link pavilion/foyer

0   10m

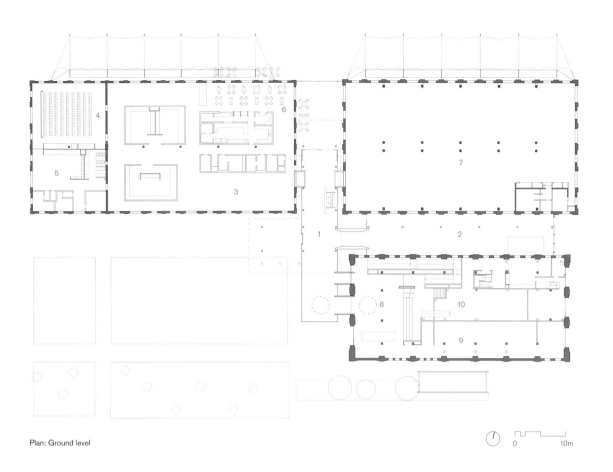

1 Foyer/Link pavilion
2 Temporary gallery
3 Newcastle Story
4 Theatrette
5 Education centre
6 Café
7 Super Nova exhibition
8 The BHP exhibition
9 Xstrata Coal exhibition
10 Museum services

Plan: Ground level

0   10m

1, 2 The generous internal volumes of the workshops can be adapted for a variety of temporary or permanent displays. **3** The roof profile of the temporary gallery is independently supported between the heritage workshop buildings.

1 Continuous steel angle
2 Glazing
3 Steel plate outrigger
4 Galvanised mesh screen
5 Purlins
6 Sarking and insulation
7 Box gutter
8 Metal deck roofing
9 Angle support beam
10 Fabricated roof framing
11 Fabricated steel column head
12 Set plasterboard curved ceiling
13 Circular steel column
14 Internal downpipe

1 Merewether Street, where the roof of the temporary gallery is recessed between the heritage workshops.
2 Temporary gallery construction photograph illustrating layered nature of the roof. 3 Steel framing for the insertion of the tube-like threshold forms between the heritage fabric. 4 Entries to each major gallery space are identified by industrial tube-like threshold forms which provide orientation, signage and identity.

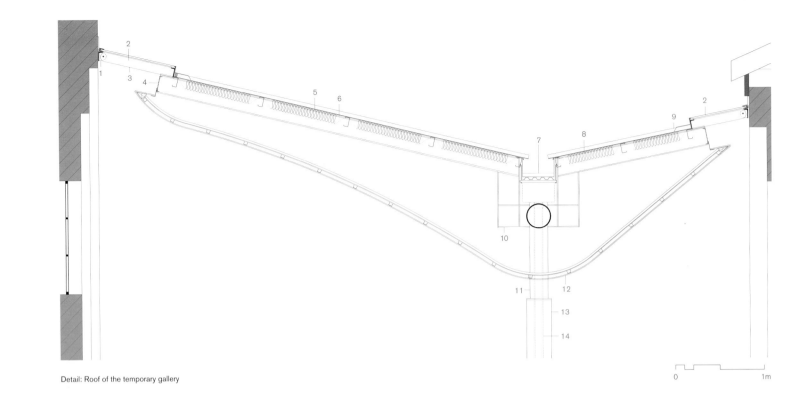

Detail: Roof of the temporary gallery

0   1m

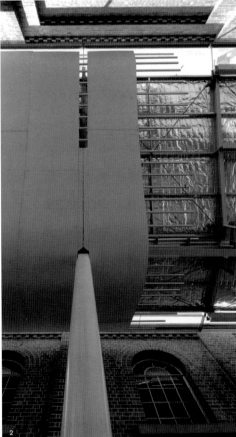

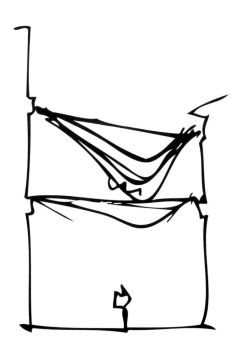

City
Melbourne

117

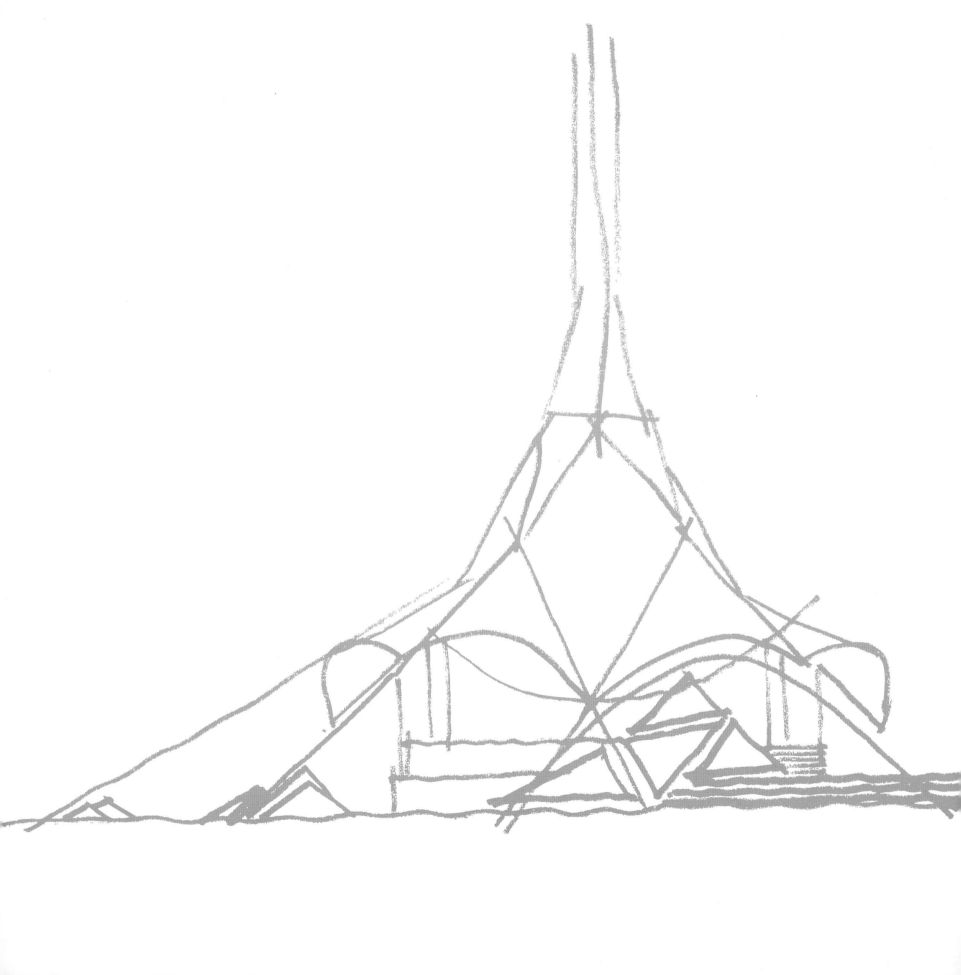

Southbank Cultural Precinct

The Southbank Cultural Precinct masterplan includes an upgrade and extension to the Arts Centre facilities designed by Roy Grounds, a significant new public domain with a pedestrian emphasis, and the creation of the Sturt Street Cultural Spine to integrate the precinct with Southbank Promenade, the city and other cultural facilities.

A series of three new building forms are proposed as strategic insertions into the precinct to address key elements of the project objectives. These new insertions are carefully positioned and conceived in relation to the urban design, architectural and functional requirements and complement and contrast Roy Grounds's three existing built forms. The new insertions are conceived as crystal-like glazed structurally geometric forms that bring light and view deep into the solid concrete structures and excavated spaces of the existing Southbank Cultural Precinct.

The new inserted built elements are positioned to define, enliven and activate the public spaces of the precinct. Each insertion is related to each key public open space and addresses these spaces with entrances, foyers, cafés, food outlets and other open space infrastructure. Each insertion contributes to and enables the "street-life" activation and sense of place of the public domain of the precinct. The new insertions, through their transparency, uses, and associated technology of lighting and art-data projection, reinforce the theatrical, performance, and celebratory character of the precinct.

1 The new Sturt Street Cultural Spine integrates the precinct with Southbank Promenade, the city and cultural facilities along Sturt Street. 2, 3, 4 Each of the geometric crystalline insertions is related to one of the key public open spaces. 5 Precinct model, Sturt Street Cultural Spine.

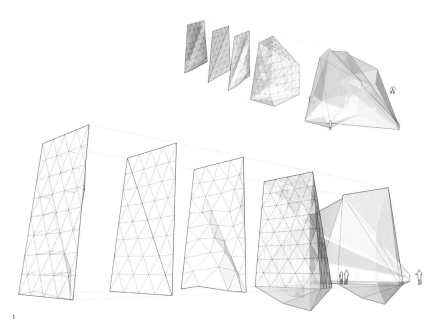

1 Exploded axonometric showing components of each crystal form. 2 Each of the three inserted crystalline forms relate to specific programme transformations for access improvements and activation of the public domain. 3 Diagram illustrating the layering system and the crystal forms.

The crystalline forms are an integrated architectural system of enclosure, structural support, passive/active environmental control, and energy generation.

The structure of the crystalline forms is a diamond-based web-frame of steel integrated with the framing support for the glazing panels. Photovoltaic panels are integrated in to the glazing where maximum benefit can be achieved and to enhance shading of the interior.

Suspended from the structural frame are a series of 'cloud-like' shade elements. These suspended elements assembled from repetitive perforated metal panels provide local shading as necessary for the interior spaces. Between these panels and the glazing surface a linear plenum is created that forms an integral element of the environmental control system. This plenum is ventilated at the upper level via automated operable glazed units to release hot air and reduce heat load in summer months and closed to enhance natural heating in winter.

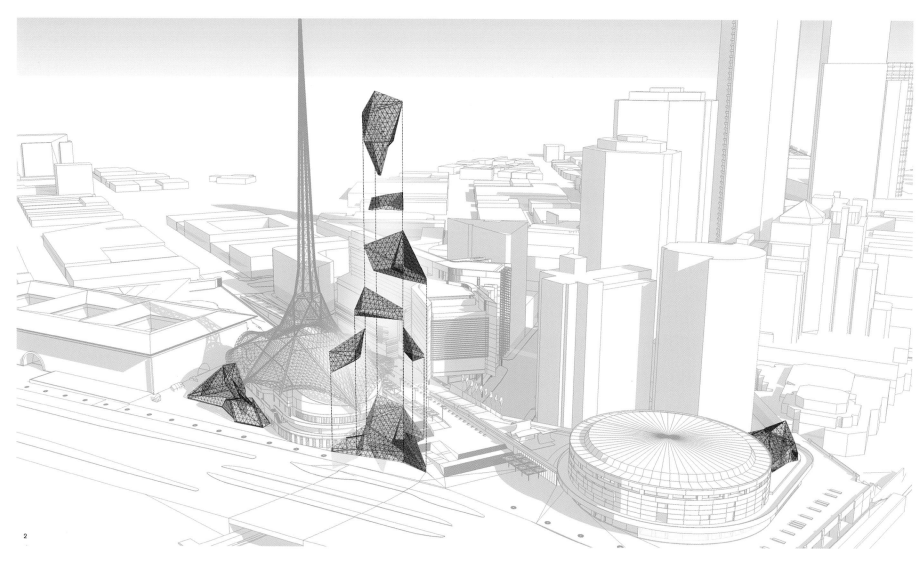

1 Glazed unit panel
2 Triangulated structural frame
3 Automated operable ventilation panels
4 Ceiling baffle 'cloud'
5 Air plenum

Apex form

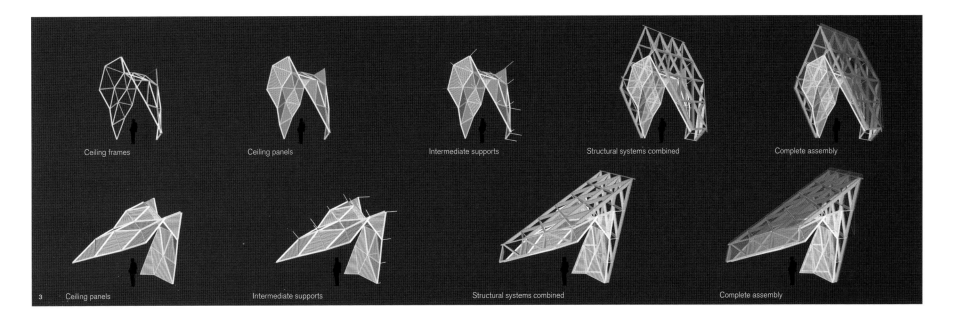

Ceiling frames   Ceiling panels   Intermediate supports   Structural systems combined   Complete assembly

3   Ceiling panels   Intermediate supports   Structural systems combined   Complete assembly

City
Hobart

125

Tasmanian Museum & Art Gallery

The Tasmanian Museum & Art Gallery is the second oldest museum in Australia and its collection mandate is the most diverse of any in the country. Its campus at Constitution Dock on Hobart's waterfront includes a rich collection of heritage buildings including the Commissariat Store (1808-10), the Private Secretary's Cottage (1815) and Custom House (1902).

This masterplan project will expand the museum through new additions and adaptive reuse as well as extend the public open space and museum forecourt. The redevelopment will be the single largest and most significant cultural development ever undertaken in Tasmania.

The scheme interweaves heritage buildings, new contemporary elements and archaeology to create a rich and unique experience for visitors. A series of new elements have been integrated into the existing heritage fabric to create a coherent museum complex.

A new louvred and glass roof is suspended on fine timber columns to enclose the central courtyard. The intentional randomness of the columns within the courtyard allude to the trees of the original waterfront landscape while the multi-layered timber louvre, steel and glazed roof reinterprets the tree canopies and provide environmental control of the courtyard space underneath. The operable curved timber louvres on the underside of the roof enable natural light to be manipulated at different times of the day and throughout the year, transforming the character of light and shade in the courtyard.

Two new box-like timber volumes are carefully placed in relation to the heritage elements. The first frames the new entrance into the courtyard with a café underneath the suspended volume and a gallery/lecture space above. The second box is locked into position between the Private Secretary's Cottage courtyard and street-front opening out to Sullivans Cove and connects the extensive new gallery spaces with the public waterfront. These suspended timber forms are akin to fine jewellery boxes protecting their contents, and along one side a series of spiral wood louvres behind glass rotate to reveal Hobart's waterfront.

Two new courtyards are formed by this juxtaposition of new and existing elements: the Central Gallery with its glazed lantern roof and the Private Secretary's Cottage courtyard. Both atrium spaces improve orientation and circulation for both the new galleries and heritage galleries.

Finally, a new public open space is created that also forms a forecourt to the new Watergate museum entrance. The ground plane of this new public square has been delineated by a series of folded strips that have been generated from the existing built fabric geometry. The topography of the site both artificial and natural is transformed to provide a dynamic civic square that offers a range of opportunities and scales for intimate and large gatherings.

1 New temporary gallery
   and back-of-house
2 Main link/circulation spine
3 Original escarpment
4 Bond Store
5 Queens Warehouse
6 Commissariat
7 Central courtyard
8 Café and theatre
   (Watergate building)
9 Dunn Place
10 Archaeology and integrated
   exhibition space
11 Custom House
12 Central gallery

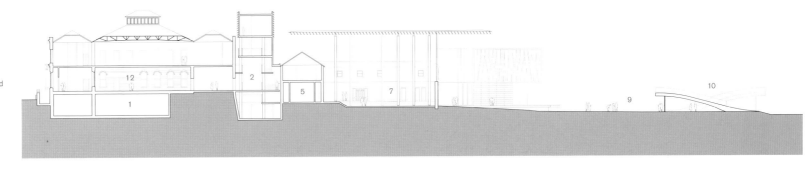

Section: West-east

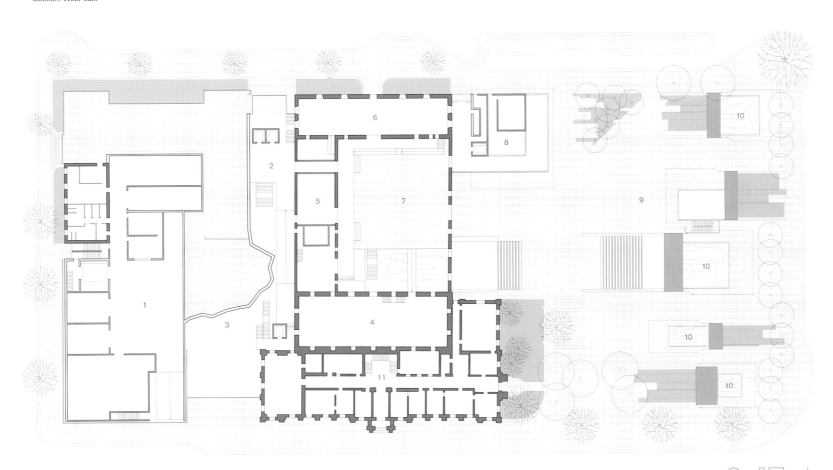

Plan: Ground level

0   10m

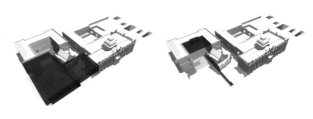

A Dunn Place

B Watergate building

C Central courtyard roof

D Link building

E New gallery building

F Lantern roof

129

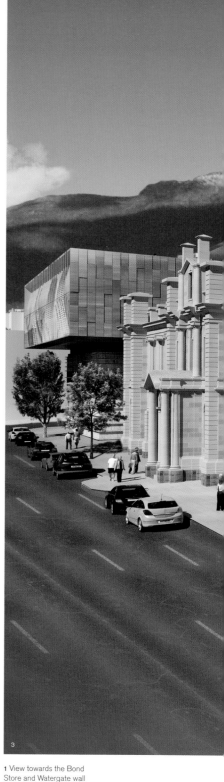

1 View towards the Bond Store and Watergate wall within the new central courtyard. 2 View from Constitution Dock. 3 View from Davey Street of new forecourt entry and Dunn Place.

135

City
Canberra

Among the exceptionally elegant aspects of this competition design is the crowning canopy formed by the first folded plate along the entry front and the manner in which the glazed foyer at the ground floor is withdrawn along this front so as to welcome the visitor to the reception, the temporary exhibition space and the main lecture hall at grade, while the permanent collection and the administration are located immediately above.

— Kenneth Frampton

National Portrait Gallery

This proposal for the National Portrait Gallery in Canberra outlined a vision for a building and open-space complex that turns to address Reconciliation Place and the lake.

The emphasis is as much on the people visiting the gallery as the portrait subjects and works within the collection: a celebration of the individuals who have made a major impact upon Australia, as well as the social collective which has been shaped by their contributions. More than a mere building, it is a combination of external open space as much as a traditional gallery interior, capable of accommodating a range of functions and events. The gallery was to be sheltered and protected, open and engaging, unique and representational, and welcoming to all.

Much like the frame of an artwork, which defines the subject and how the artist intends the subject to be viewed, the architecture will similarly frame the collection, views and vistas to the landscape, and the visitors themselves. Based upon classic traditions of human proportion and anthropomorphic form, elements are collected below emblematic roof profiles that unify and gather all the disparate components of the gallery.

The proposed form and rationale of the gallery is a metaphor of the natural and urban landscape that is the Australian setting for the human figure, with the architecture creating an analogous "frame" for the human figure. Sinuous roof forms represent the canopy of the sky and clouds, the podium references the ground and contours of the land, and the vertical timber volumes, slots and spaces draw reference to the bush, forest and other places for the appearance of the human figure.

The preliminary design solution is an architecture that derives from fundamental and accessible elements and essences, and yet is entirely specific and unique in interpreting the vision of the gallery within this special site. The design therefore is the creation of an Australian architectural setting for the human figure and human representation. It is a building that is itself like a portrait, or rather a portrait frame for the combined "collection"—namely, the artwork and visitors.

A Roof—sky. A series of roof forms create an undulating, hovering canopy above the gallery, unifying all parts of this open and inviting public institution under a powerful emblematic form. The light coloured forms seem to reach up to the sky and draw daylight into the galleries. The roof, analogous to the canopy of the cloud over the landscape, creates a place for the human figure—the vertical within the horizontal—and has associations with light forms of clouds and sky. Yet this roof form is as much determined by the daylit performance of the gallery environments, carefully reflecting indirect and controlled light onto the portraits.

B Gallery—figure—forest. Gathered under the generous roof are the galleries and museum spaces. The primary gallery volumes are a series of eucalypt-clad forms with varying vertical panels, evoking the trunks and branches in the Australian bush. Occasional vertical light/window strips penetrate the forms, within which the human figure may appear either as an image of one of the portraits (a rendition to announce the exhibition to those passing by) or the silhouette of a gallery visitor who, for a moment, becomes like one of the artworks and a live portrait. These strip openings, like the gaps between trees in the bush, allow light and vistas into the interstitial spaces of the galleries.

C Framing of the human figure. The gallery visitor will view carefully curated portraits of Australians juxtaposed not only with them, but with the landscape. This will offer meaning and insight so that they themselves, as visitors, will be equally framed by the architecture, and brought into the composition of the collection and the landscape. As the visitor meanders through the galleries, they will view each other as well as the portraits. They will be framed by the architecture, almost becoming part of the architecture; themselves juxtaposed with the Canberra landscape. Much like the frame of a canvas, which defines the subject and how the artist intends the subject to be viewed, the architecture can similarly frame the collection, views and vistas to the landscape, and of visitors themselves. It is an architecture revealing a deeper understanding of our culture through the way it frames and orientates us in relation to the place, each other and, ultimately, our world.

D Podium—ground. The podium resolves the differing site levels and adjacent landscape spaces. It also subtly elevates the gallery in the tradition of metaphorically raising and honouring the institution, thus asseting its eminence and enhancing the sense of arrival. Fundamentally, the podium gathers the surrounding external spaces and interconnects them with the galleries. In doing so, the podium, through its material and groundplane character, becomes analogous with the ground itself: the horizontal plane upon which the human figure stands; the ground of human representation; the ground frame of the portrait. All who visit, idle and move across this gathering groundplane are framed and connected and become participants in the vision of the gallery.

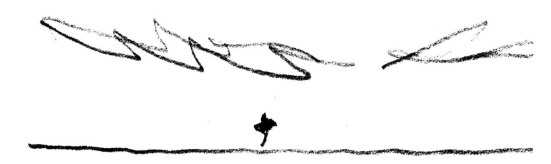

A Roof—sky

B Gallery—figure—forest

C Framing of the human figure

D Podium—ground

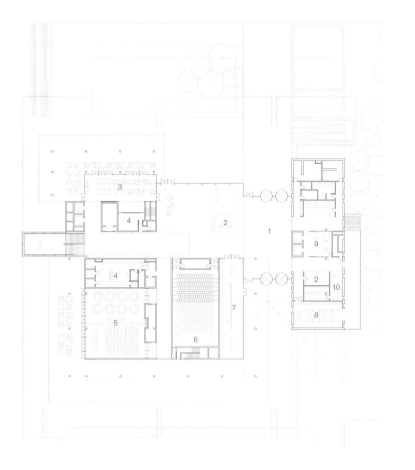

Plan: Podium level

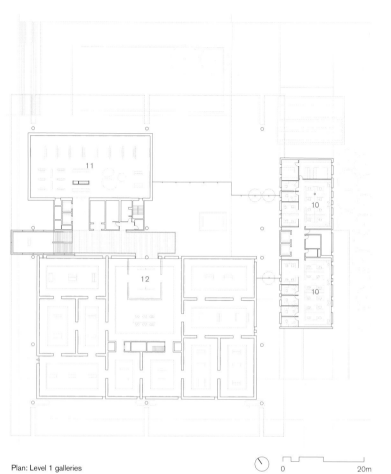

Plan: Level 1 galleries

1 Entry
2 Reception/cloaking
3 Café
4 Kitchen
5 Function room
6 Lecture theatre
7 Gallery shop
8 Education activity room
9 Administration reception
10 Staff offices
11 Temporary exhibition
12 Historical collection

0   20m

1 North elevation showing the building's relationship to the landscape and the Lake Burley Griffin waterfront.
2 Central atrium foyer.

City
Auckland

The exfoliated stratagem takes on the existing topography at a truly panoramic scale setting itself as a gigantic scenography comprised of transparent glass perforated metal and/or reflective screens, layered so as to conform to geometric hyperbolic trajectories in plan. The express purpose of this layered configuration is to extend and project the visual command of the structure at a geographic scale... beyond the immediate confines of a pre-existing Oxbridge campus, to touch the spread-eagled landmark features of the Domain in the first instance and Auckland Harbour in the second.

— Kenneth Frampton

Owen G. Glenn Business School

fjmt + Archimedia (architects in association)

Our inspiration for this project was drawn directly from the fusion of natural landscape, urban form and the history of cultural exchange and flow that characterise this beautiful site at the edge of the campus, overlooking Auckland Harbour and the Domain.

Prior to modern development, this landscaped valley used to be known for the Waipapa stream that flowed directly into the harbour, and it was near this stream that early European settlers traded with the Ngāti Whātua tribes. An equal inspiration was the university's ambition to create a new centre for learning and innovation; a welcoming place of knowledge exchange and collaboration for future leaders.

Architectural forms open through a series of organic flowing ribbons in a gesture of invitation, outreach and optimism, gathering the energy of the site into a major new public square. These layered glass and stainless steel planes are carefully composed to orientate and join the forms and internal volumes of the new building to significant landscape elements. The central atrium and internal gathering space is directed out between the two largest ribbons to connect with the natural landscape of the Domain, while the northern figural "head" is turned to look directly towards the harbour and Rangitoto Island while terminating the axial vista of Wynyard Street.

These organic and flowing forms are suspended above a solid podium that anchors the building and reinterprets the natural topography of the sloping site. The counterbalancing podium form is joined spatially with the suspended ribbons at the atrium heart of the new complex, interconnecting the shared teaching spaces with the business school's workplace, learning and social spaces.

At the centre of the complex are two interconnected spaces that create a sense of collegial and scholarly community. The first is a welcoming forecourt, or open square, that is defined by the gentle curve of the embracing forms. The second is the central atrium that vertically connects all levels of the complex and is the collegial focus. The social hub bridges suspended within this atrium become platforms for informal gathering and exchange; they are busy points of interaction and look out to the beautiful natural landscape of the Domain.

1 Built form and spatial relationships. **2** Concept model.

A The northern figural "head" looks towards the harbour and island.
B Central form and internal gathering space is connected with the Domain's natural landscape.
C A series of organic flowing ribbons orientate the new building and entry foyer.

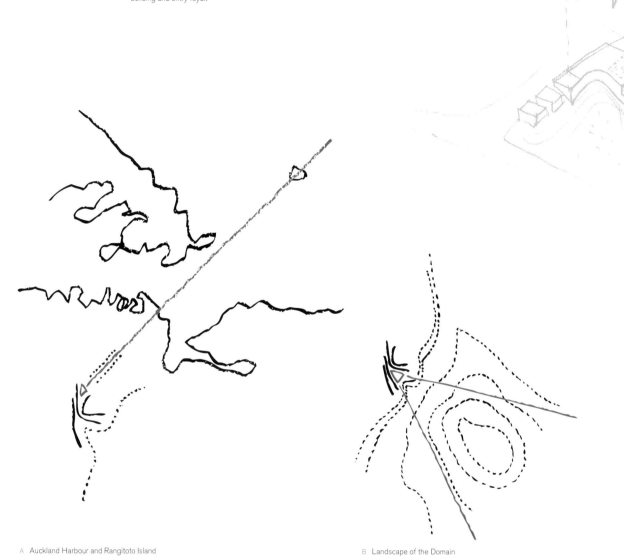

A Auckland Harbour and Rangitoto Island

B Landscape of the Domain

C Central courtyard and internal entry foyer

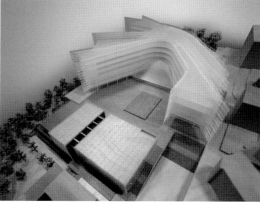

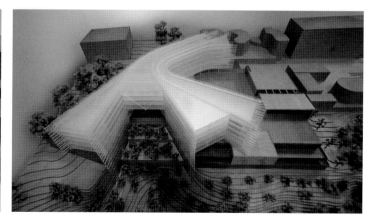

1 Entrance foyer
2 Atrium
3 Lecture theatre
4 Caseroom
5 Computer lab
6 Breakout space
7 Open plan workspace
8 Cellular office
9 Meeting room

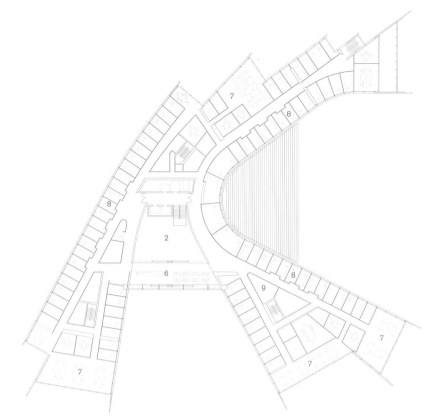

Plan: Level 4 (typical)

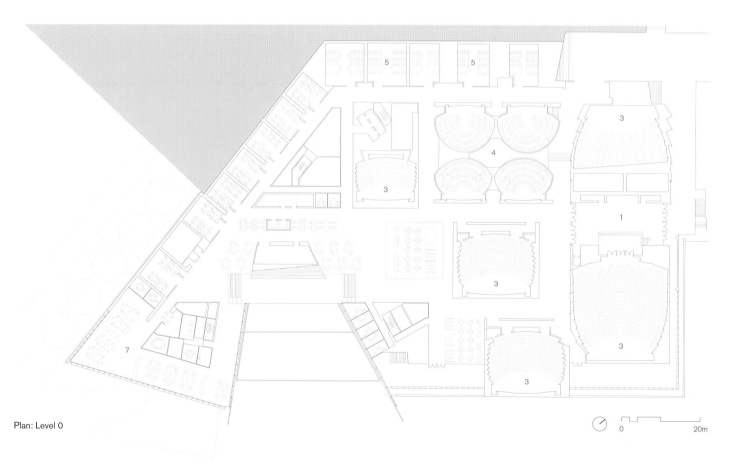

Plan: Level 0

0   20m

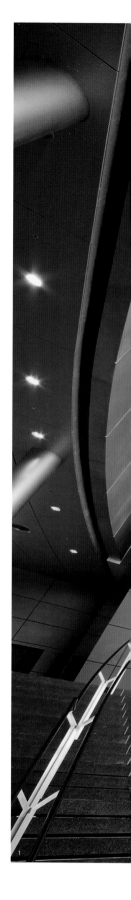

1 The central atrium vertically connects all levels of the building.

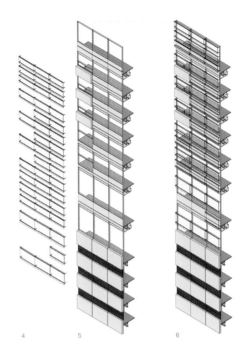

| 4 | 5 | 6 |

Facade system components

1 Layered glass and stainless steel planes incorporate a suspended external, glazed shade panel of titanium interlayers. **2** Louvred planes to the raised café and terrace enclosed by glazed windows. **3** Upper mezzanine workplace lounge is accommodated within the foyer roof profile. **4** The foyer breakout seating and collaboration space overlooking the central courtyard. **5** A detail view of the incorporated structural shade louvres which provide support and protection to the glazing.

1 Stainless steel structural louvres.
2 Profiled glazing to curvilinear skylight.
3 Primary steel structure.

4 Glazed, titanium strip sunscreens.
5 Stainless steel panel, ventilation louvres and glazing.
6 Combined system.

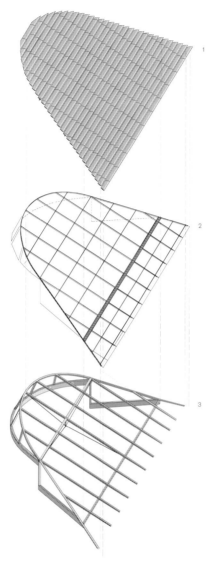

Entry roof exploded axonometric

In conscious opposition to the mansard roofs of the existing building, the tessellated canopy roof in Karuri wood extends over these galleries so as to bond the old and the new indissolubly together; this fusion that extends beyond the roof forms to encompass the circulation itself.

— Kenneth Frampton

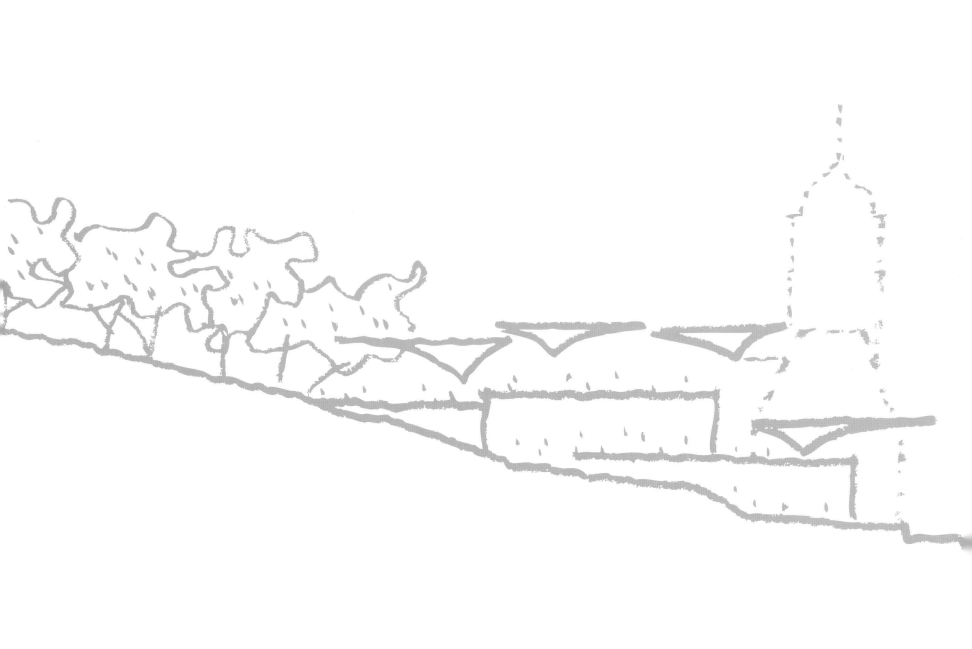

Auckland Art Gallery Toi o Tāmaki

fjmt + Archimedia (architects in association)

The new Auckland Art Gallery Toi o Tāmaki is an extensive public project that includes the restoration and adaption of heritage buildings, a new building extension, and the redesign of adjacent areas of Albert Park.

The architecture has developed from a concept that relates as much to the organic natural forms of the landscape as it does to the architectural order and character of the heritage buildings.

The new building is characterised by a series of fine tree-like canopies that define and cover the entry forecourt, atrium and gallery areas. These light, profiled forms are inspired by the adjacent canopy of Pōhutukawa trees and "hover" over the stone walls and terraces that reinterpret the natural topography of the site. The ceilings of the canopies are assembled from carefully selected Kauri, profiled into precise geometric patterns and supported on slender and tapering shafts. These emblematic forms give the gallery a unique identity that is inspired by the natural landscape of the site.

Between the stepped stone podium and hovering canopies, an openness and transparency is created to allow views through, into and out of the gallery circulation and display spaces and into the green landscape of Albert Park. In this way the gallery opens to the park and adjoining public spaces in an inviting and engaging gesture of welcome.

The entry sequence into the gallery follows a progression from the street forecourt, under a generous and welcoming canopy, through into a lower foyer to emerge via a broad stair into the large, light-filled atrium. The atrium provides a central orientation and display space for all visitors. Gallery circulation extends from the main atrium in a clear series of loops interconnecting all gallery spaces via the smaller southern atrium that mediates the junction with the existing Wellesley Wing.

A diverse range of exhibition spaces and rooms are created, both fixed and flexible, formal and informal, heritage and contemporary, naturally lit and artificially lit, open and closed, high spaces and lower spaces.

1 The redevelopment creates a strong connection between the gallery, Albert Park, and Auckland city.
2 The pōhutukawa trees in the adjacent Albert Park.

A Concept sketches illustrating the terraced podium and roof canopies and its relation to the existing building and landscape.
B Sketch outlining the progression of the roof profiles, atrium and terraced podium interrelationship.

 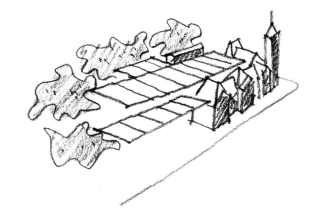

A Podium and canopy concept sketch

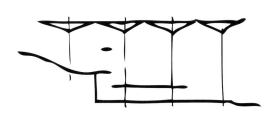 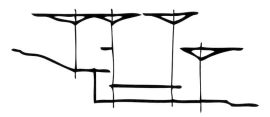 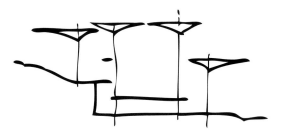

B Canopy concept progression

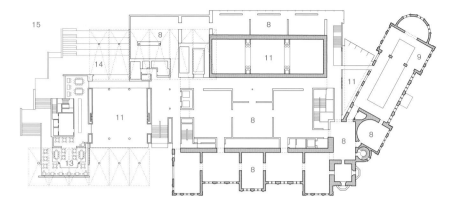

Plan: Level 1

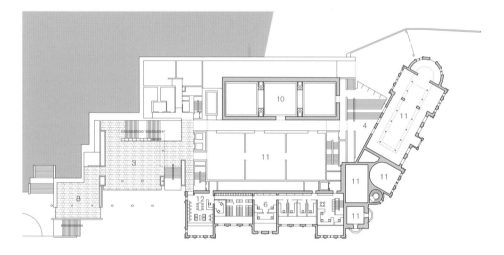

Plan: Mezzanine level

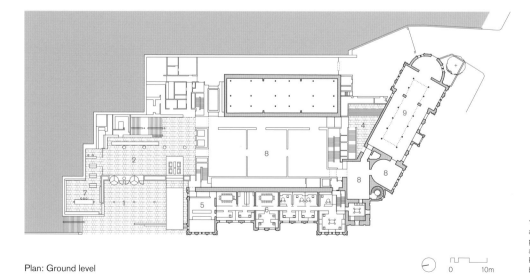

Plan: Ground level

1 Forecourt
2 Foyer
3 North atrium
4 South atrium
5 Administration reception
6 Office
7 Shop
8 Gallery
9 Wellesley Gallery
10 East Gallery
11 Void
12 Library
13 Café
14 Amphitheatre
15 Albert Park

1 View from the external amphitheatre. The transparency of the north atrium allows views from Albert Park into the gallery and beyond to Kitchener Street.

1 The light-filled north atrium provides a central orientation for visitors. Choi Jeong Hwa's *Flower Chandelier* was specifically designed for the space.
2 Kauri roof canopies cantilevering over the eastern sculpture terrace at the Albert Park interface.
3 The café in the north-west corner of the gallery within the extension of the roof canopies.

1 Foyer
2 North atrium
3 Members lounge
4 Amphitheatre
5 Forecourt

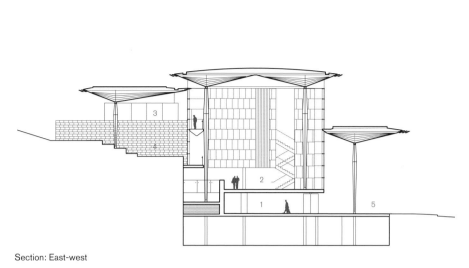

Section: East-west

Elevation: North

0   10m

1 The triangular ceiling of the south atrium is set back from the heritage building via a perimeter of skylight. **2** Bridge through the south atrium connecting the Wellesley Gallery with the main building. **3** The south atrium frames a vista to the tree canopy of Albert Park. A stepped informal amphitheatre is created for school and educational groups as well as performances.

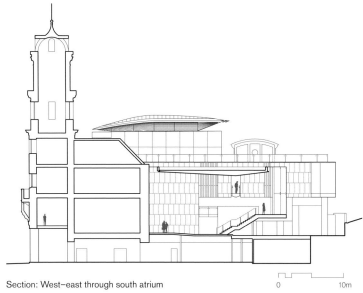

Section: West–east through south atrium

0   10m

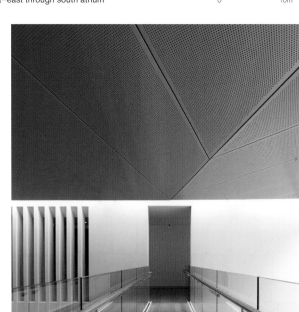

1 Integrated engraved
artwork by Arnold Manaaki
Wilson on the tree forecourt
entry column shaft.
2 Custom design bench
of bent and profiled Kauri
designed by the architect.
3 North atrium in gallery
function dinner mode.

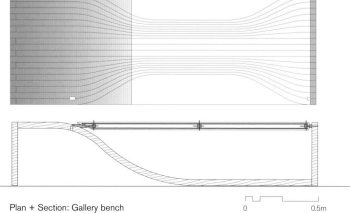

Plan + Section: Gallery bench

0   0.5m

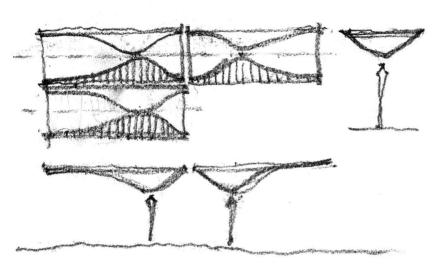

Early concept sketch of the Kauri canopy

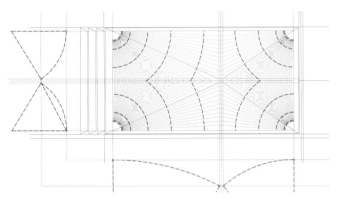

Plan + projected profiles: Kauri soffit setout

1 The slender, tapering Kauri columns support the Kauri canopies also conceal services and drainage. **2** The ceilings of the canopies are assembled from carefully selected Kauri, sourced only from fallen forest stocks, profiled into precise geometric patterns.
3 A synthesis of computer-aided design, skilled joinery techniques and traditional boat building technology was used to fabricate the Kauri canopy.

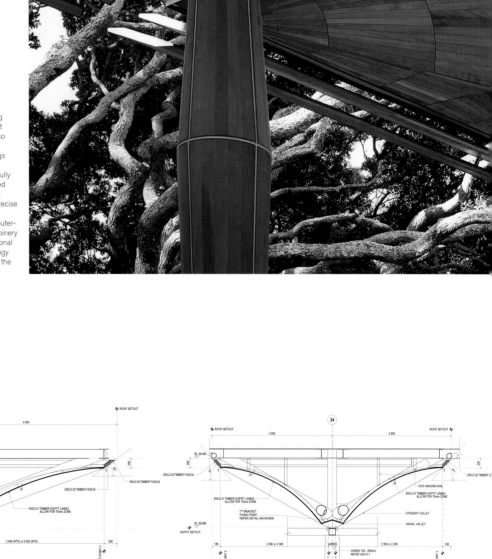

Detail sections: Kauri roof canopies

173

City
Stockholm

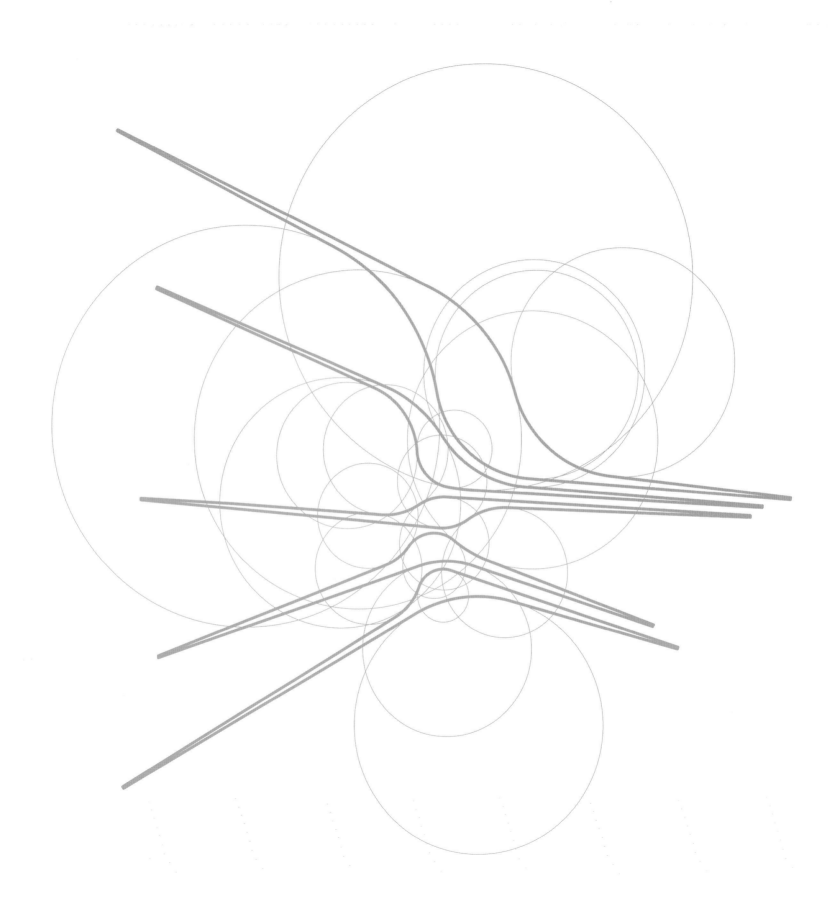

Stockholm City Library

A series of organic urban forms seek a resolution and synthesis between the urban conditions, natural topography, landscape and the monumental object form of Gunnar Asplund's great library.

Sinuous ribbons of layered glass and metal hover over a stone podium, creating a new public place. The ribbons form a folding plane, extending the contours of the Obervatoriekullen topography. At the new building's heart are a series of organic leaf-like glazed atria, opening toward the new square and existing Asplund building, and presenting visitors with an exciting and unfolding vision of the whole library within.

Through a series of folding forms related to the contours of Obervatoriekullen, a new Library Square is formed complementing Library Park and creating an extended landscape ground/podium for the Asplund library. The geometry of Odenplan is extended and invited into the new Library Square through the folding curvilinear form. The direct vista from Odenplan of Asplund's library is revealed with a clear pedestrian path and vista from Odenplan to Library Park. A new Library Square is created through the sinuous folding forms embracing and deferential to Asplund's library and energised through the life, display and activities of the new library—a welcoming place for public gathering, festivals and civic events.

Through this organic, carefully aligned new urban form, a resolution and synthesis are sought between the urban conditions, natural topography, landscape and the monumental object form of Gunnar Asplund's great library. The curvilinear forms and transparency of the new building have been developed in a careful dialectic with the Asplund library. Layers of geometric and formal relation create a complement and completion, yet at the same time a landmark new public building and place for the twenty-first-century library of Stockholm. At the heart of the new building is a series of organic leaf-like glazed atriums that open towards the new square and existing Asplund building.

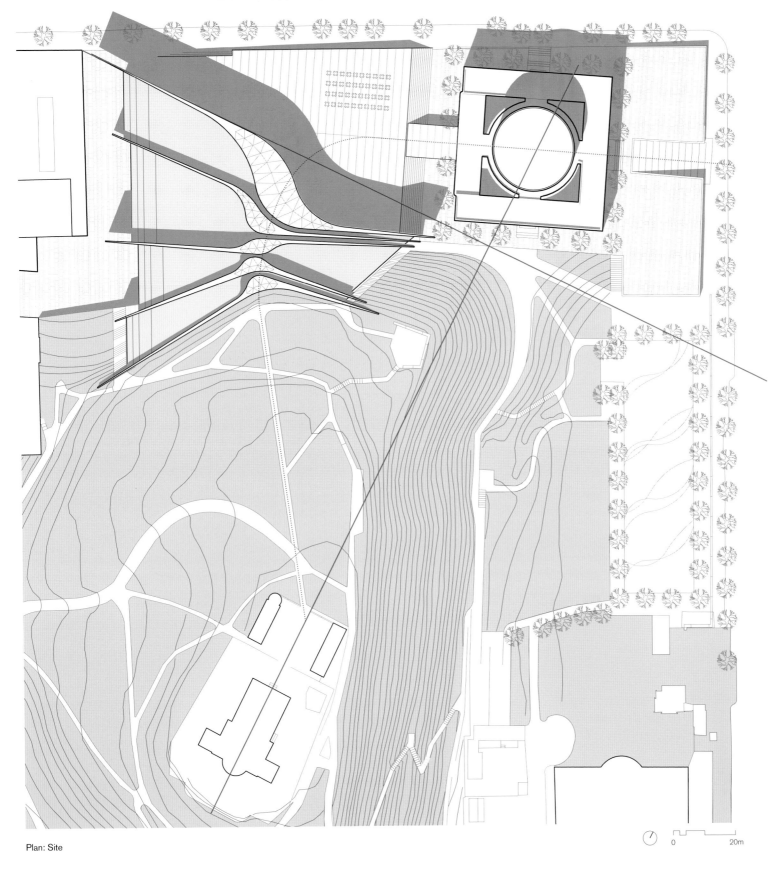

A. The Odenplan geometry is extended and invited into the new Library Square through the folding curvilinear form. The direct vista from Odenplan of Asplund Library is revealed in juxtaposition with the existing Annex Three to create a clear pedestrian path and vista from Odenplan to Library Park.

B. A new Library Square is created through the sinuous folding forms embracing and deferential to Asplund Library and energised through the life, display and activities of the new library. A welcoming place for public gathering, festivals and civic events.

C. The folding curvilinear form geometrical synthesises the urban alignment of Odenplan and the landscape contours of Obervatoriekullen. Each "ribbon" of the new form relates to and extends the contours and topography of Obervatoriekullen and embraces and integrates the existing Annex Three.

D. The organic series of leaf-like glazed skylights to the new building are a complement to the rotunda of Asplund Library and created a geometric and circulation line of connection that curves the main entry axis of Asplund Library through the new atriums and entry, through Obervatoriekullen to the Observatory entrance.

E. At the heart of the new library are the series of organic leaf-like sky-lit atriums that bring natural light and orientation. These unifying volumes are visually connected with the new public square and the Asplund building to accommodate the arrival, foyer circulation display and learning zones within exciting and overlapping platforms and spaces.

F. The first ribbon/fold leaf-like form swells to accommodate learning zones within curved floors at various levels, while the remaining ribbons order the subject areas collection into scaled spaces interconnected with the Annex Three creating spaces for display, exhibition, children, young people with study areas near natural light and overlooking the secure conservatory gardens.

Plan: Site

0   20m

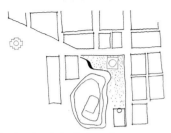

A Odenplan axis and urban landscape form

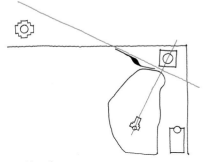

B Library Square

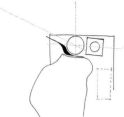

C Topography and form

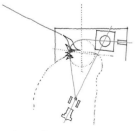

D Circulation line of connection

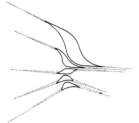

E Atrium circulation and light

F Function and flexibility

1 Leaf-like glazed sky-lit
  circulation atriums
2 Support services pods
3 Ribbon fold forms of glass
  structure and metal
4 Subject area collection and
  study spaces
5 Landscaped conservatory
  study gardens
6 Public square
7 Restaurant
8 Foyer

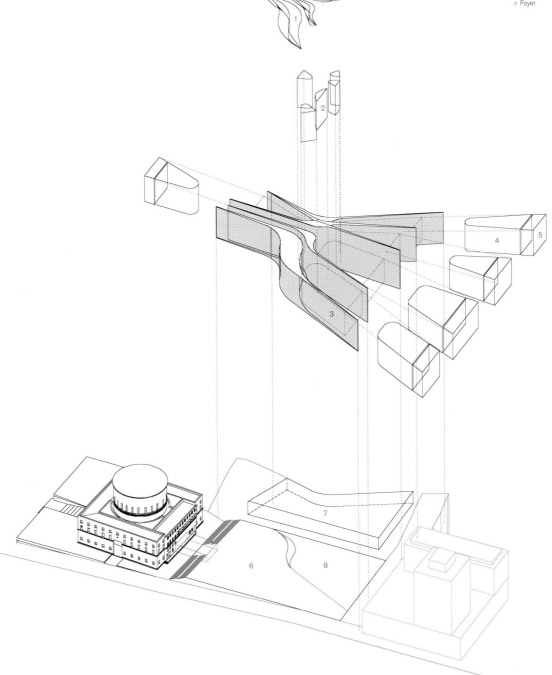

Roof louvre detail, Craigieburn Library

Architecture is not simply a circumscribed field of buildings, houses or offices.
It's not like painting or creating determined objects that circulate but buildings
in which everyone lives… Every citizen has something to say about architecture.

Jacques Derrida
"Invitation to a Discussion," *Columbia Documents of Architecture and Theory* 1 (New York: Rizzoli, 1992), 23

Nothing can be defined or derided on the basis of its origin. The important thing
is what is done with it and how far a community identifies with something that
symbolizes its favourite way of dreaming, living, dancing, playing or loving.

Eduardo Galeano
Niels Boel "Eduardo Galeano: The Open Veins of McWorld," *UNESCO Courier* January (New York: UNESCO, 2001)

Make a welcome of each door and a countenance of each window.

Make of each place, a bunch of places of each house and of each city, for a house
is a tiny city, a city a huge house. Get closer to the shifting centre of human reality
and build its counter form.

Aldo van Eyck
"Place and Occasion, Right Size, The Interior of Time," *Forum* 1962–3

Community

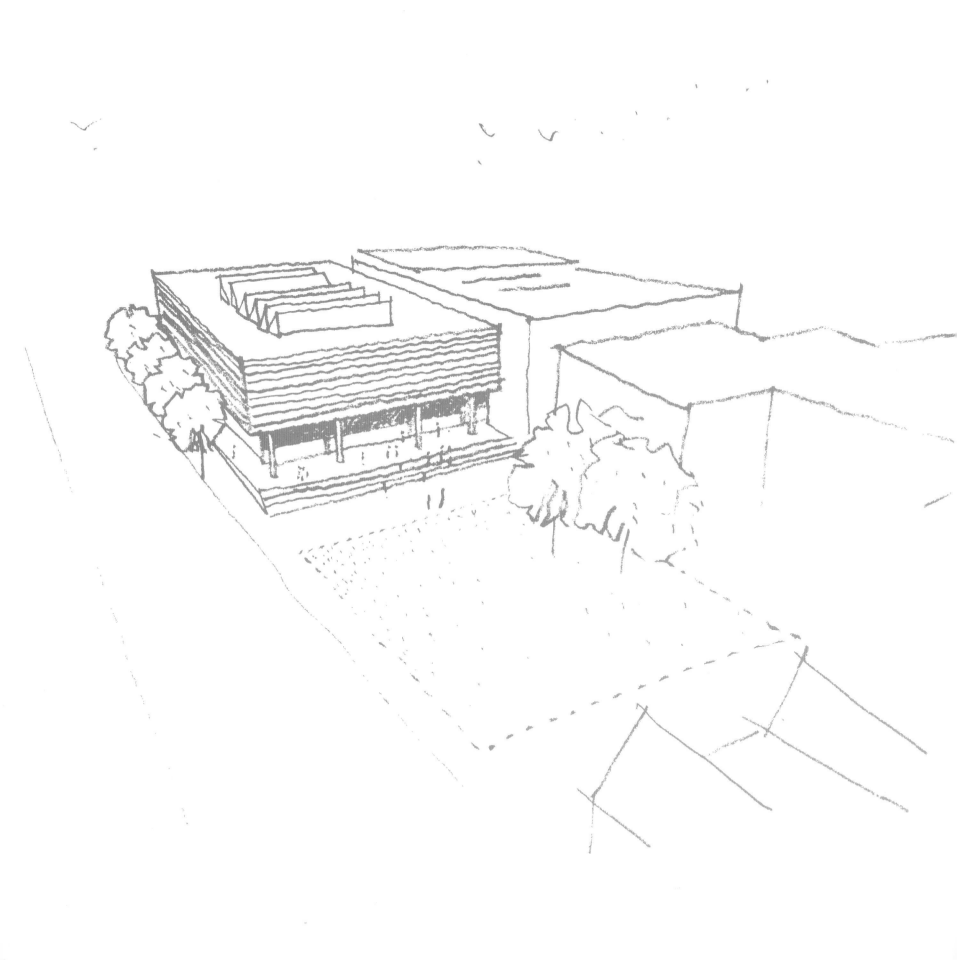

Max Webber Library

Blacktown is the most populous local government area in New South Wales. A recent large-scale retail development subsumed streets and absorbed much of the life of this important urban centre.

We approached the making of the new library as an opportunity to resist the increasing commercialisation of the city, by creating a "civic dam" to the expanding shopping centre and creating a truly public place for the entire community.

The new library is conceived in two parts: a solid volume in terracotta, containing the book stack and forming a solid block against the shopping centre and carpark; and a glass and louvre volume lifted up above a podium to define and characterise the new public space. This transparent volume of glass contains the library's reading, study, collaboration and children's spaces, sheltered and shaded by automatic louvres, which track the path of the sun.

At the centre of the library space is a circular void and stair, lit from above through a profiled timber ceiling. This central focus of the library balances the natural day lighting and view to create a sequence of interconnected spaces that offer variety and richness to the visitors.

The building is intended to be both a compliment and contrast to the shopping centre and associated visual noise. It is open to the street, transparent and inviting, but also seeks a visual quietness to simply "stand" and mark the street corner and open space as public and accessible to all.

The Blacktown community quickly embraced their new library, with over 400-per-cent increase in patronage in the first year.

Located in the western suburbs of greater Sydney, Blacktown is a regional city outside Sydney that is often neglected in terms of public facilities. The project created an opportunity to re-establish and reinforce the public realm within a city environment dominated by the shopping mall, carpark and visual pollution of advertising. Creating a sense of place and embodying the public values and aspirations of the community in juxtaposition of the non-place of the ubiquitous "shopping mall" and associated zones for consumption. Sited next to a giant shopping complex this project affirms the public domain through defining a new square and creating a bulkhead to the commercialisation through an architecture of simplicity and silence.

1 Sited next to a large shopping centre the project affirms the public domain through defining a new square. **2** Looking towards the central stair and elliptical void to the "light clouds" above.

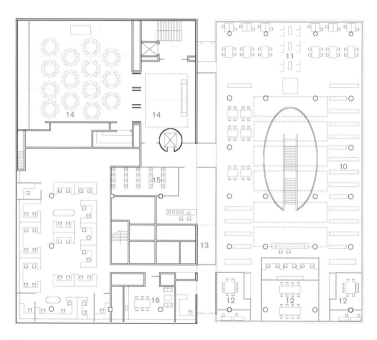

Plan: Level 1

1 Foyer
2 Café
3 Customer service
4 Book returns
5 Newspapers, magazines
   & new acquisitions
6 AV collection
7 Children's area
8 Amenities
9 Lending collection
10 Reference collection
11 Study area
12 Group study/
   meeting rooms
13 Local history
14 Multi-purpose room & lobby
15 IT seminar/ training
16 Staff area
17 Catalogues
18 Storage
19 Self-check

1 A solid volume forms
a stop to the expanding
shopping centre, while an
open, transparent volume
defines a new public space
and invites entry.

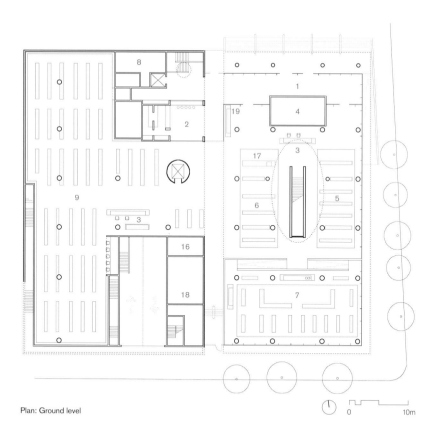

Plan: Ground level

0   10m

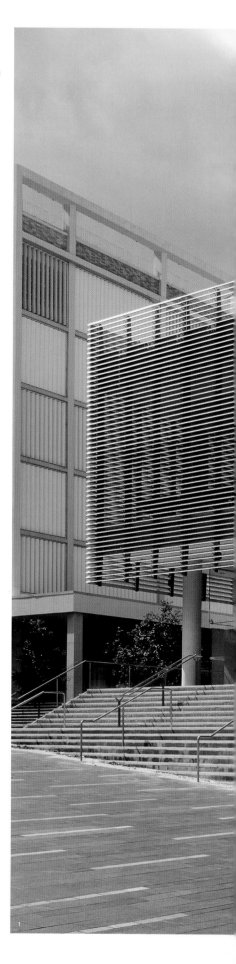

1 The open library façade as seen from the corner of Flushcombe Road and Alpha Street. 2 The automated and glare-control sunshade louvres of the first floor study area. 3 Natural light is reflected through a series of profile baffles and skylights to gently reveal and enhance their forms and materiality, and to create a glow and lightness within the whole library.

What is so remarkable about this hybrid work is the way in which its various public programs are all precisely articulated in relation to each other, so that at no point is a single modicum of space wasted or left underused.

— Kenneth Frampton

Surry Hills Library & Community Centre

Located in the heart of Surry Hills, a dense inner city "village" of Sydney, this so-called hybrid building is many different things in one: a library/resource centre, a community/neighbourhood centre, and childcare centre all integrated into one modest building accessible to all. On the southern edge, the Collins Street road closure is converted into a modest public park with a raised grass platform. This new space extended the function of the building and reasserts it as a public place.

The brief was developed in close consultation with the local community. The key approach emerging from these discussions was based on the community wanting a single facility everyone could share: library, community centre, and childcare all in one. In this way the building became a truly shared place where the whole community could meet and use it in different ways.

The library is over two levels (ground and lower-ground). The community centre on level 1 comprises a function facility, meeting rooms, teaching kitchen and offices. On level 2, the childcare centre accommodates 26 children and includes an outdoor landscaped play area.

Transparency became an architectural theme, creating an inviting and welcoming building, accessible and open to public view. At the same time it was important the building not only expose what is accommodated within, but that it represented and embodied the values of the community.

From early studies, four integrated formal elements emerged: a new simple open space; a prismatic glass environmental atrium; a suspended "U"—shaped timber form; and a transitional foyer space.

The tapered glass atrium evolved in response to the ambitious sustainability objectives of the project, and to the sense of layered transparency. The series of glass prisms creates an open, transparent façade, akin to a doll's house, and addresses the new open space, making all the different activities of the centre visible and displayed, encouraging participation.

The timber "U" form embraces the prismatic environmental atrium and orients towards the south and the new little park. The "solid" sections of the timber form are made of automated louvre systems that filter and control sunlight and view. This warm timber form is lifted above the ground to create transparency and accessibility.

The foyer space is a lower transitional form mediating the scale of the building against adjacent shops while creating a welcoming, transparent entry. Suspended cloud-like roof profiles bring daylight into this space and extend out above the street to mark the entrance.

The new centre has been designed with the aim of being a benchmark for sustainable, low-energy-use buildings while still maintaining the functionality of a public building. A combination of innovative design strategies and technologies were utilised to make this possible.

The design sought to establish a contemporary sense of place, providing an open and inviting public facility with a strong connection to its setting. We have sought to create a certain "monumentality," significance, and dignity to this important public place, and the community values it embodies.

1 The building is located on Crown Street, the main street and community focus of Surry Hills. **2** Concept model.

A The primary cubic volume is raised to open out at ground level to Crown Street and the adjacent park.

B The cubic volume is transformed into a U-form embracing and opening to the park.

C A tapering triangular glazed bio-filtration atrium mediates the opening to the park.

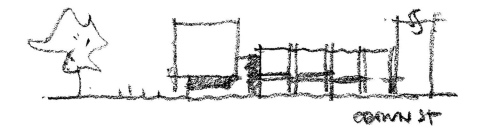

CROWN ST

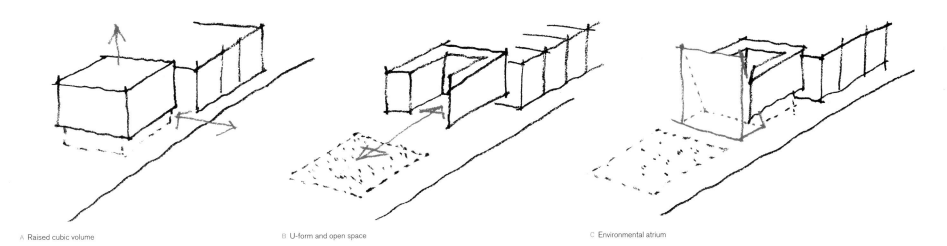

A Raised cubic volume

B U-form and open space

C Environmental atrium

1 The transparent
environmental atrium
viewed from across the
new Collins Street reserve.

1 Lobby
2 Administration
3 Environmental atrium
4 Void
5 Children's play space
6 Cot room
7 Heat-and-serve kitchen
8 Staff room
9 Teaching kitchen
10 Function room
11 Balcony
12 Neighbourhood centre
13 Meeting room
14 Language laboratory
15 Library collection
16 Loans desk
17 Catalogue counter
18 Library reading room
and café
19 Collins Street reserve

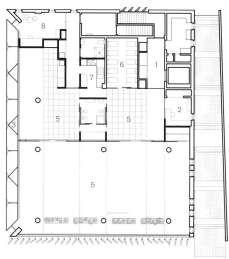

Plan: Level 2 (childcare centre)

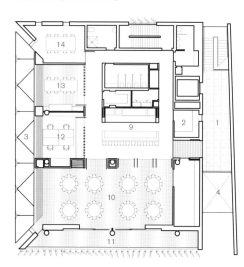

Plan: Level 1 (community centre)

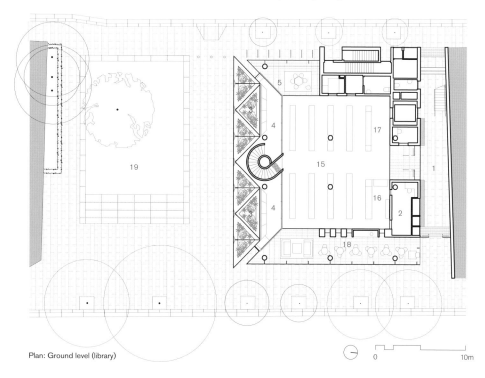

Plan: Ground level (library)   0   10m

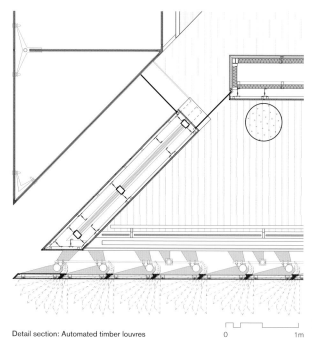

Detail section: Automated timber louvres

0   1m

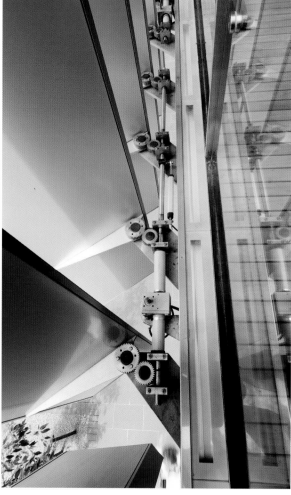

1, 2 The automated custom louvre system tracks the position of the sun. Louvre operating arms and motor are exposed and integrated. **3** Surry Hills Library and Community Centre presents to the streetscape as a finely crafted wooden box.

Section: Entrance lobby

0   2m

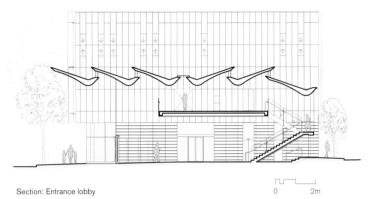

1 Australian artist
Robert Owen working
on the mezzanine ceiling
panels in his studio.
2 View of lobby ceilings
with white profiled light
reflectors and integrated
artwork by Robert Owen.
3,4 Suspended cloud-like
roof profiles bring daylight
into this space and extend
out above the street to
mark the entrance.

1 Pre-fabircated powder coated 2mm aluminium sheet
2 Beam 100x100x6 -detail shown dotted beyond.
3 6mm flexible plasterboard ceiling lining.
4 Fineline XT series louvre arm and patch
5 Fineline XT series mullion
6 Rondo furing channel
7 Precurved rondo top cross rail
8 Ceiling hanging system
9 R2 blanket insulation, vapour barrier over purlins
10 C10019 purlin at 600 centres
11 Fabricated 1.6mm sheet stainless steel box gutter
12 Ventilated rain screen "Prodema" façade cladding

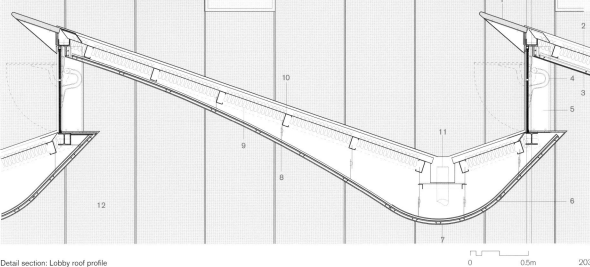

Detail section: Lobby roof profile

0   0.5m

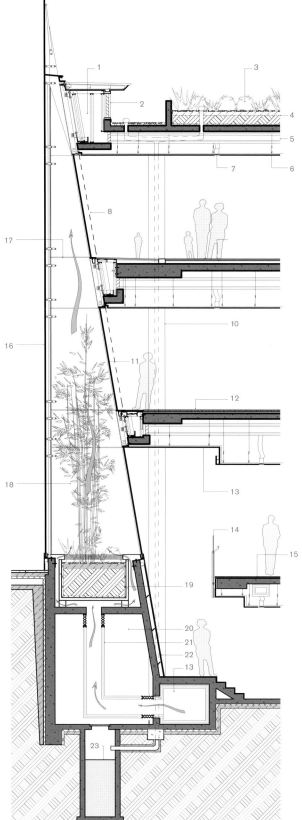

1 Mechanical air plenum, with acoustic baffles.
2 Environmental atrium air intake.
3 Green roof planting. Drought resistant, maintenance free indigenous species.
4 450mm organic soil zone.
5 Rigid mechanical ductwork.
6 Exposed two-way ceiling grid system with "CSR Gyprock Focus E-T15" ceiling tiles
7 "Holoake PMF series" air grilles
8 "Silent Gliss Tess 100" electrically operated tensioned roller blind system
9 Outdoor playspace impact absorption surface. Finish, 15mm Softrax® wetpour rubber wear layer, 60mm Softfall® base, 80mm sand cement, screed to fall, 160mm post tensioned "Green Star mix" concrete slab
10 In-situ concrete column with ice white "Pandomo" polished render finish
11 25.62mm laminated and toughened glazing, interlayer impregnated with mirror reflective polyceramic frit
12 "ASF Horner PR2" timber sprung floor, with American rock maple FSC certified, 160mm post tensioned "Green Star mix" concrete slab
13 Timber veneer over joinery board concealed fixed with expressed joints. Veneer to match "Prodema" cladding
14 19mm laminated and toughened glazing patch fixed to 316 stainless steel linish no 4 staunchon
15 15mm "Petra Crema" limestone tiles, 60mm sand cement screed, 160mm post tensioned "Green Star mix" concrete slab
16 26mm laminated heat strengthened glass
17 Hi-modulus black structural silicon
18 Atrium planting
19 GRC planter
20 Mechanical plant room
21 Rigid mechanical ductwork
22 Supply air ductwork from thermal labyrinth
23 Stormwater pumpout pit

Detail section: Environmental atrium

0   2m

1, 2 Views into the main library and children's space illustrating the light filtration of the landscaped atrium.
3, 4 A white concrete spiral stair leads into the lower ground reading room.
5 Ground floor reading areas open directly to the busy urban Crown Street.

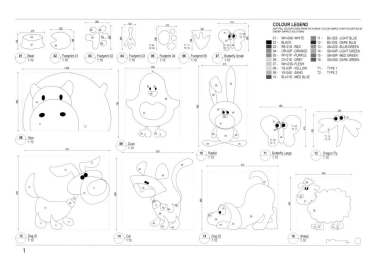

1 Detail documentation for the play area animal inlays "follow the footprints." **2** Children overlook Crown Street through the automated shape louvres. **3** Footprint inlays lead to the animal. **4** Children gather at the edge of the environmental atrium. **5** The outdoor children's play space with automated fabric shade system retracted.
6 Low morning sun on the Crown Street façade.

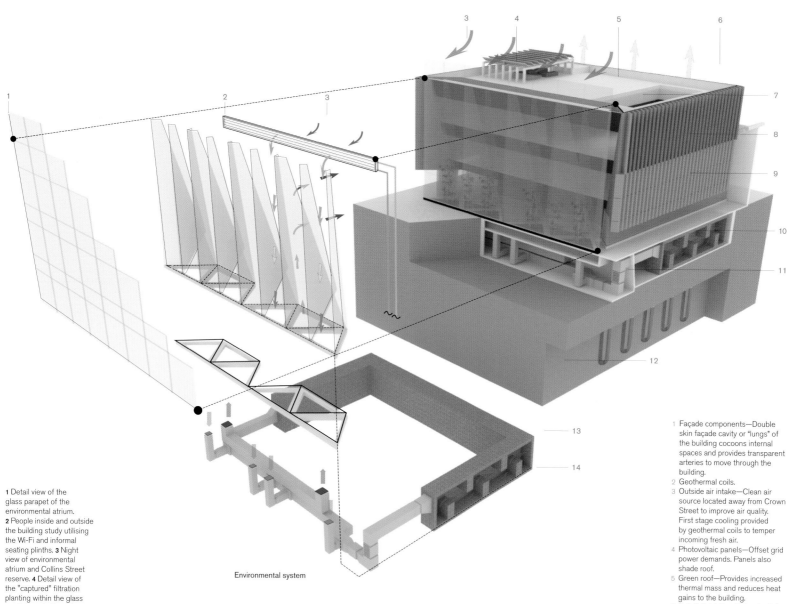

Environmental system

1 Detail view of the glass parapet of the environmental atrium. **2** People inside and outside the building study utilising the Wi-Fi and informal seating plinths. **3** Night view of environmental atrium and Collins Street reserve. **4** Detail view of the "captured" filtration planting within the glass ventilation shafts of the environmental atrium.

1 Façade components—Double skin façade cavity or "lungs" of the building cocoons internal spaces and provides transparent arteries to move through the building.
2 Geothermal coils.
3 Outside air intake—Clean air source located away from Crown Street to improve air quality. First stage cooling provided by geothermal coils to temper incoming fresh air.
4 Photovoltaic panels—Offset grid power demands. Panels also shade roof.
5 Green roof—Provides increased thermal mass and reduces heat gains to the building.
6 Relief air intake—Natural relief to outside.
7 Fan coil units—Trims fresh air to satisfy heating and cooling needs of the building.
8 Materials—Low VOC finishes. Low formaldeyde furniture.
9 Operable louvres.
10 Labyrinth—Air runs around the building perimeter through gabions walls that passively heat and cool the air.
11 Rainwater storage tank—Supplies toilets and landscape irrigation.
12 Geothermal heat exchanger—For passive tempering of incoming outside air to "bio-filter" by transferring energy from the earth to the building.
13 Bio-filter—Plants and biomass absorb carbon dioxide and release oxygen. Passive filtration and removal of air contaminants.
14 Labyrinth.

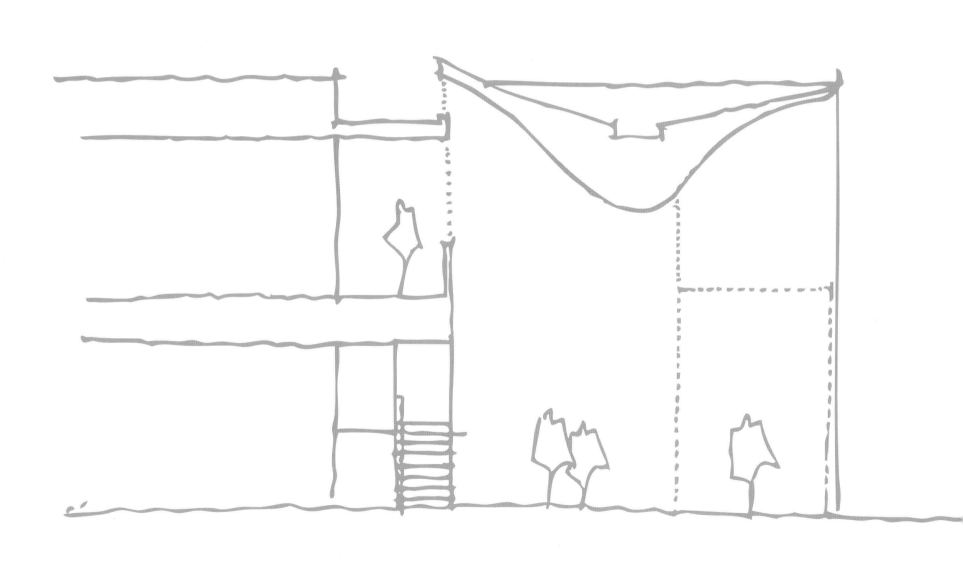

Bayside Police Station

We have sought to escape the dominant paradigm of the contemporary police station, characterised as they are by opacity, security and fenced compounds. Instead, an emphasis is placed upon the police station as a truly public community building: inviting, accessible and part of the civic fabric of the neighbourhood.

The same strict technical and, in particular, security requirements must be achieved to create a safe working environment, all within the very tight cost constraints for this typology. Our intention is to reinforce the Victoria Police's vision of a more open and interactive approach to contemporary policing.

The more public elements of the station are composed within an overarching formal frame, addressing the primary street and lifting the scale of the building to the adjacent Masonic Hall. This profiled concrete frame is like an abstraction of a portico, enlarging the entrance and sense of invitation while positioning the public meeting and control rooms in a tight composition and opening them to natural light from above. The work spaces, meeting rooms, sally port, holding rooms and gymnasium within the station are gathered around a central top-lit atrium, lined with timber. The atrium is the central circulation spine, a place for informal meetings and special events with a stage created by the switchback stair, but also an honorific space of contemplation to the nature of community policing. Within this top-lit space is an integrated exhibition/artwork displaying the historical progression of the local police from the turn of the twentieth century through to the present time.

An emphasis has been placed upon the expressive and tectonic development of natural materials within the primary public spaces of the station. The atrium is lined with Victorian Ash panels and lit from above, with light reflected around curved, cloud-like baffles. The perimeter of the main station volume is a layered system of glass operable panels, a captured linear landscaped garden, and a wall of continuous metal louvre grilles that provide environmental mediation and security.

1 Portico detail. **2** Victorian Ash profiled timber light baffles of the atrium. **3** Ribbed pre-cast panelling form the façade of the secondary element. **4** Metal grille shades and screens the main glazed façades.

A Concrete portico and terracotta boxes layer the primary U-form from the street. Profiled light deflectors are suspended above the central atrium while metal mesh and landscape screens from secondary façades.

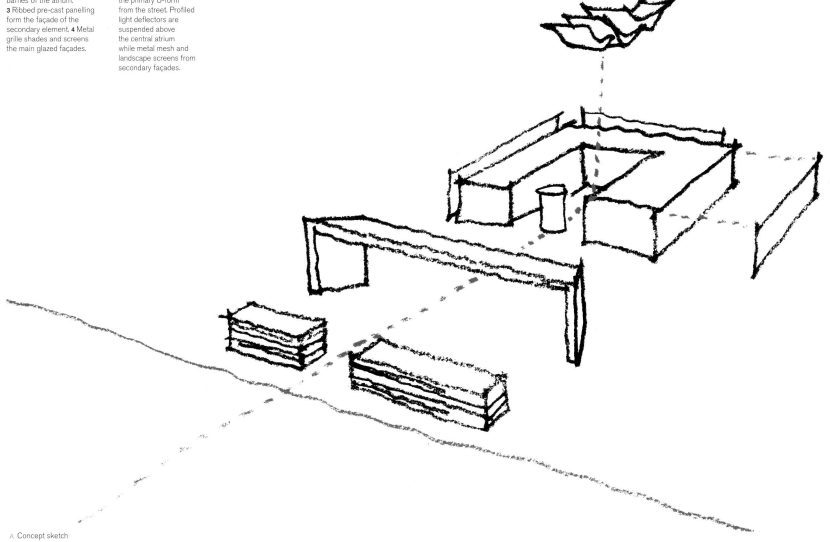

A Concept sketch

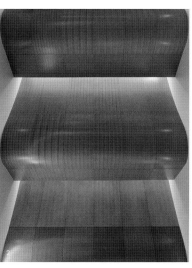

1 The atrium is lined with Victorian Ash panels lit from above, with light reflected around curved cloud-like baffles. **2** The central atrium, which functions as a visually porous, light-filled void in the heart of the station. **3** In a clear break with the bunker-like police station of the past, Bayside's public face is defined by a soft and natural materiality of terracotta tiles and the curved Victorian Ash lining to the portico.

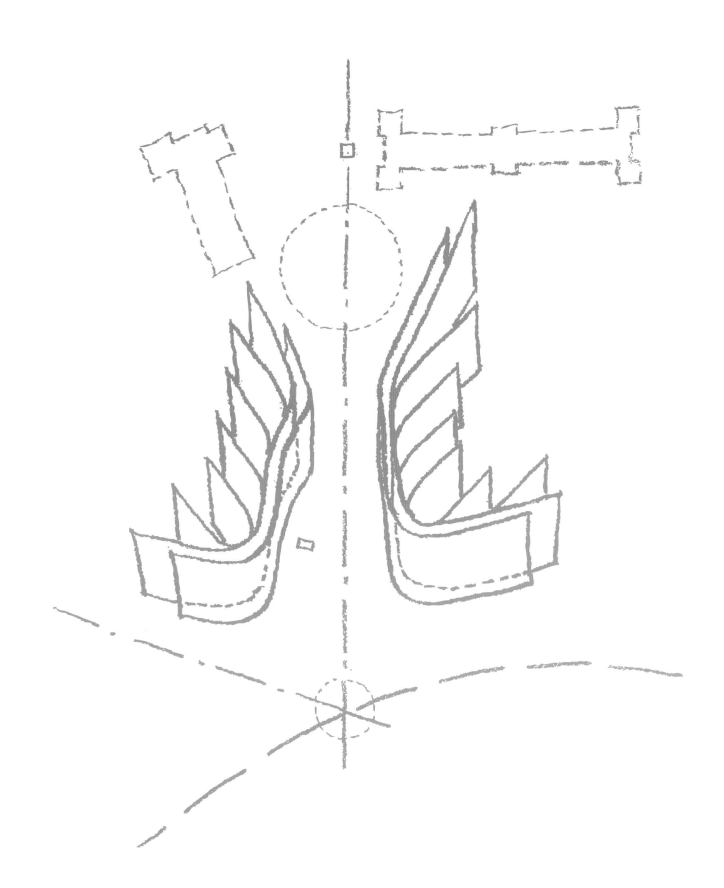

Little Bay Apartments

This pair of related apartment buildings forms an entrance to a new residential community located on the historic former Prince Henry Hospital site, a site that includes many heritage buildings and overlooks the beautiful waterfront of Little Bay.

The design proposals for these two buildings—Manta and its sister Alaris—have been drawn from an analysis and reading of the particular qualities and characteristics of their locality and context. Their sinuous forms compress and then open out in a strong entrance sequence to the Prince Henry site, reinforcing the corners at the intersection of Pine Avenue and Anzac Parade, then stepping down and peeling back to reveal a new public space and the elegant façades of the historic Flowers Wards, the heritage landscape and coastal vistas beyond. The new north-facing open space and ground level retail accommodation create both a communal focus and commercial heart for the Prince Henry community.

Behind the screened façades raised above street level, three to four levels of apartments are oriented toward the easterly views, the city and Botany Bay. A random pattern forms the primary street walls, while providing shade and privacy to generous private open space and interiors beyond. The orientation of the apartments and avoidance of overlooking is a direct result of building form and internal planning initiatives. In particular, the overlooking of primary living areas and external private open spaces, as well as the number of apartments facing each other across Pine Avenue, is minimised. External shading systems and staggered vertical blades further augment the performance of the buildings.

In the context of budget-constrained floor area, apartments are designed to maximise efficiency. The majority of plans provide media areas, minimise circulation space and maximise liveable space. They are positioned to take advantage of prevailing breezes and promote cross ventilation, including single-oriented apartments, which are augmented with solar stacks. Each living space aligns with a generous private open space, which together with garden terraces and communal landscaped areas create amenity for residents, as well as attractive foregrounds to views.

Foyers, dispersed along the buildings' primary address, are clearly marked by dramatic awning structures and lightboxes featuring interpretive heritage imagery provided by the adjacent Nursing and Medical Museum. They create a site-specific experience for residents and visitors, affirming Prince Henry's past at its most public interface.

ALARIS 2-8, PINE AVE
By Stockland

Significant existing features including the gatehouse, Flowers Wards, pathology building, clock tower and the Norfolk Island pines in Pine Avenue surround the two sites and are recognised in the design for their cultural and morphological value.

Manta and Alaris create two sinuous forms which flank the entry to Prince Henry along Pine Avenue, open to a new public space and reveal the elegant façades of the Flowers Wards and the landscape and coastal vista down Pine Avenue.

1 The two new apartment buildings frame the entry to the community and define a new public square.
2 View from Pine Avenue back toward the new public square and southern apartment building.
3 Prince Henry Hospital circa 1935.

A Buildings compress and open to create a clear sense of entry and arrival to the Prince Henry community.
B New public domain framed by Flowers Ward, clock tower, former pathology and new building façades.
C Composition of existing features and new building elements maximises public and private amenity.

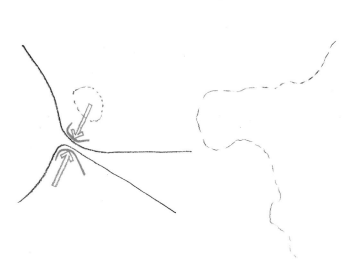

A Compressed entry

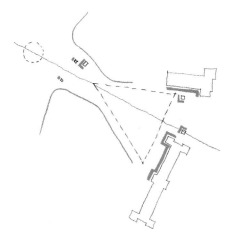

B Public space definition

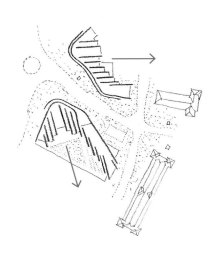

C Apartment view and orientation

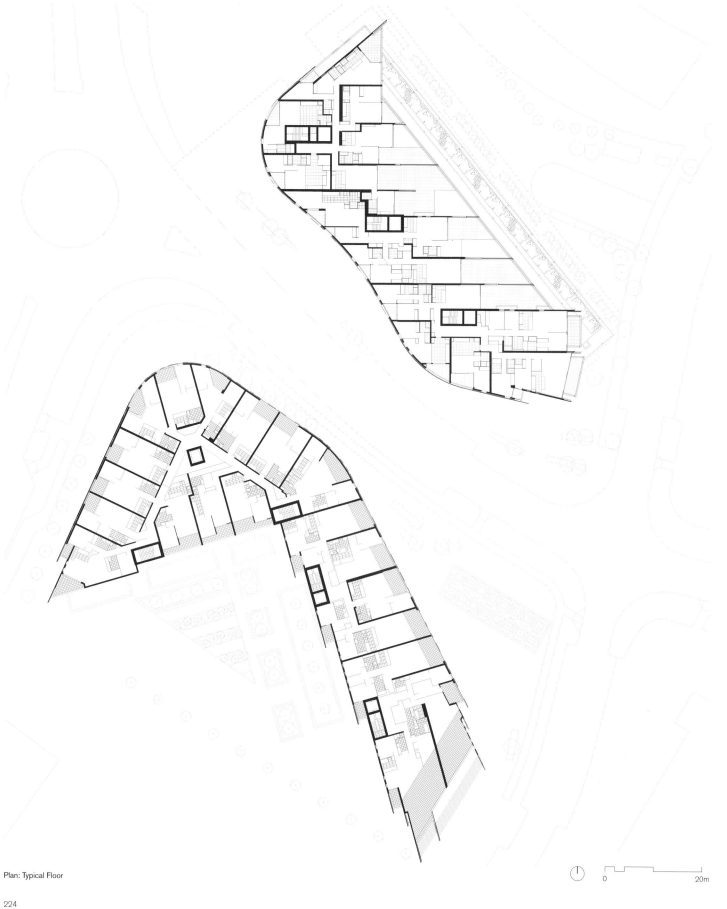

1 The curved form of the two apartment buildings frame the entry to the new residential community while creating a new public square lined with shops and services.

Plan: Typical Floor

0   20m

1,2 The seperating walls
of the "stepped-plan"
apartments of the northern
building are extended in
a series of louvred panels
to frame views to the
ocean and ensure privacy
between residences.

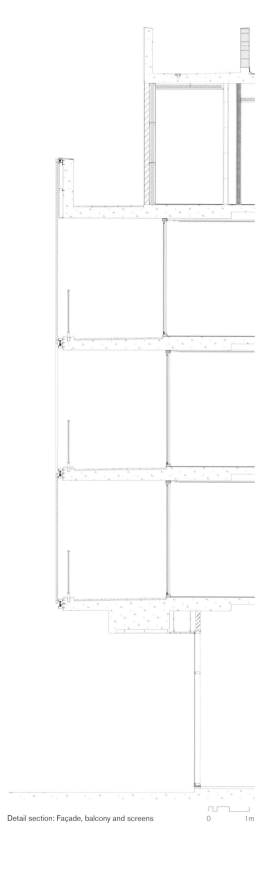

Detail section: Façade, balcony and screens

0   1m

1 The layered façade system of louvres, precast panels, sliding shade screen and terracotta panels. **2,3** The layered walls of precast concrete and vertical louvres frame views to the ocean and ensure privacy between apartments. **4** The layered façade systems are revealed and extended at the building edges with the grey precast concrete and vertical louvres behind the adjustable screen and terracotta.

In this instance an enlightened municipality decided to insert a creative arts centre into the stronghold of consumerism. Although this policy of mediating commerce through culture was hardly given an easy passage, it involved much civic debate and consultation before a positive popular vote finally carried the day.

— Kenneth Frampton

The Concourse

Chatswood is the third largest retail centre in Australia, behind the Sydney and Melbourne CBDs. It is dominated by large, internalised retail complexes and intense retail activity. It was into this context that the City of Willoughby decided to make a public place devoted to creativity, learning and debate as a relief to the compulsion to purchase. After over ten years of debate and intense consultation which culminated in a popular vote, the project for a civic place was realised. A public open space, where there is no pressure to purchase, is at the centre of a complex of artistic performance venues, library and community function rooms—The Concourse.

The complex was conceived as an organic sculptural form opening, embracing, and defining a new public place that is raised on a stone platform. Ribbons of polished aluminium wrap and enclose the timber-lined performance venues, creating silent surfaces amid the noise of retail and opening the foyer spaces to the street and square through filtering brise-soleils of plywood.

Below these hovering ribbons that hold the concert hall and theatre volumes, the other facilities are accommodated within the terraces and platforms of the stone podium. This stone base is an interpretation of the stone ridge that stretches from the city into the northern suburbs, which formed the spine of settlement.

The lowering of many of the facilities under the podiums resolved a series of challenging brief requirements and the overshadowing issues of southern orientation. The built form, which could have occupied the full footprint of the site many times over, offers over 5,000 square metres of accessible open space with significantly improved northerly aspect. One of the largest and busiest municipal libraries in Australia is also achieved on a single level.

The Concourse consists of a matrix of interwoven performing-arts facilities. Vastly contrasting functional requirements work harmoniously and in close proximity to each other, including a 1,000-seat concert hall, a 500-seat theatre, rehearsal spaces, exhibition, multi-purpose hall and function rooms.

The concert hall is conceived as a "boat-like" interior of timber "floating" in a dark spot-lit space where the focus is on the performance stage within a "sea" of sound.

The theatre provides a venue to foster the local performing arts communities. It provides professional full-stage and fly-tower facilities and the seating stretches around and above the stage such that the audience embraces the performers.

Most important has been the creation of a true public space that is now the focus for the civic and cultural ceremonies and events of the people of Willoughby.

1 The Concourse creates a new public square along the main Victoria Avenue mall from the railway station. **2** Concept model.

A Concept sketch showing the relationship between the aluminium ribbon enclosures and the timber performance volumes: "shells within shells."

B Evolution of the pod/enclosure concept.

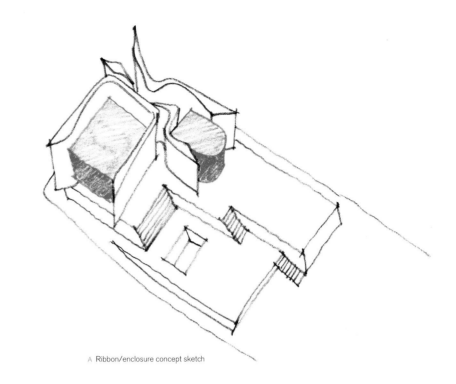

A Ribbon/enclosure concept sketch

B Pod/enclosure concept sketch

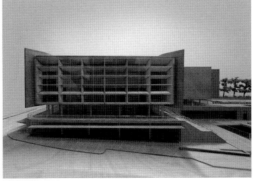

1 Concert hall
2 Foyer
3 Theatre
4 Water court
5 Raised landscape
   platform
6 Retail
7 LED "urban screen"
8 Terrace
9 Library foyer
10 Library stack
11 Library administration
12 Quiet study
13 Meeting rooms
14 Rehearsal studios

Plan: Roof

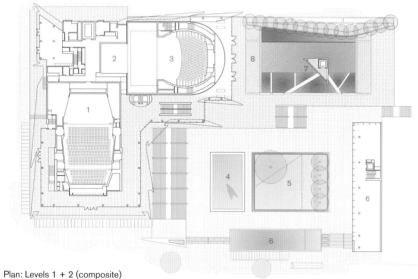

Plan: Levels 1 + 2 (composite)

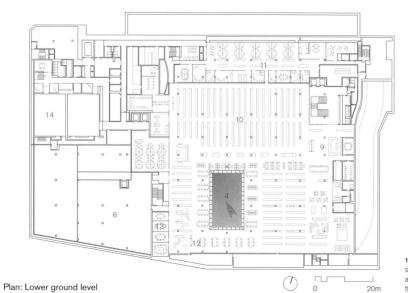

Plan: Lower ground level

0   20m

1 View from the public
square across the library
and water court towards
the central foyer.

1 Polished aluminium sculptural ribbons enclose the key volumes including louvred green room and plant area. 2,3 Detailed views of the profile polished aluminium ribbons, louvres and shade screens. 4 The open glass and timber brise soleil of the concert hall overlooks the street life of Victoria Avenue.

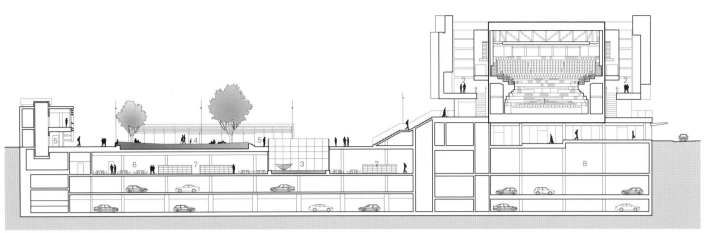

Section: East-west through library and concert hall

0   10m

1 View of the concert hall with full orchestral choir and audience. 2 Detail view of timber profiled lining and integrated fibre optic lighting. 3 View from balcony looking towards stage and choir seating. 4 A centrepiece of the performance venues, the concert hall has balcony and choir seating and accommodates 1,000 patrons.

1 Concert hall
2 Foyer
3 Water court
4 Raised landscape platform
5 Retail
6 Library foyer
7 Library stack
8 Rehearsal studio

1 Foyer
2 Theatre
3 Terrace
4 LED Urban Screen
5 Civic hall
6 Library foyer
7 Quiet study

1 Central foyer profiled ceiling, a timber brise soleil and integrated artwork by Warren Langley. 2 View of 500 seat from the stage. 3 Theatre audience on the terrace during intermission. 4 The curved profile of the theatre is visible through the timber brise soleil from the terrace raised gardens.

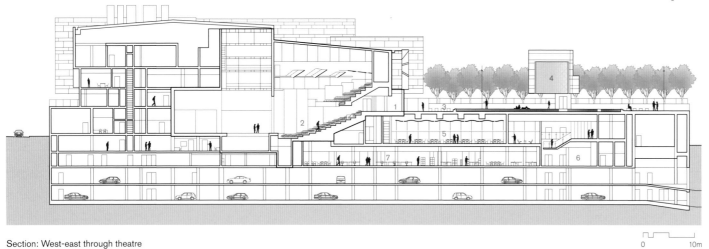

Section: West-east through theatre

0   10m

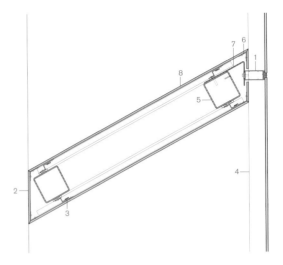

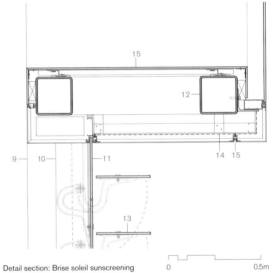

1 Aluminium transom
2 Aluminium plate
3 Z-clip conceal fixed to back of panel
4 Timber lining beyond
5 Steel truss
6 Cold formed steel angle bracket
7 Bent plate
8 Plywood panels
9 Steel column
10 Aluminium louvre mullion
11 Fixed top pane
12 Steel framing
13 Louvre in open position
14 Light gauge framing
15 Weep hole

Detail section: Brise soleil sunscreening

0   0.5m

1 Detail view of externally glazed timber brise soleil allowing natural light into the foyer spaces.
2,3,4,5 Construction images of the foyer brise soleil shade system. 6 Layers of aluminium ribbons peel back to reveal the timber performance venue forms and foyers within.

245

Craigieburn Library

Incorporated in 1994, Hume City is a fast-growing municipality north of Melbourne. This rapidly expanding community required a library, learning centre and gathering space to serve as a public community focus. The selected site was open in character and surrounded by an expanding series of new housing projects and retail development.

We envisaged the project to become the built focus of public life for the Craigieburn community and also sought to connect the architecture with the landscape that is being rapidly transformed by residential expansion.

The native vegetation and indigenous materials of this landscape are being replaced with imported brick, concrete and tiles that characterise new housing development. In contrast, the project utilises locally sourced earth as the primary building material, establishing a high-sustainable, green agenda and setting a new benchmark for the growing township of Craigieburn.

The building is conceived as a series of interlocking pavilions of varying height and scale that step down from the entrance and a two-storey, central library reading space to the low scale of the children's library. Each pavilion extends into the landscape through louvred roofs that create a series of northern verandahs.

The cruciform circulation through the building ties these functions together in a highly legible, simple geometry. The primary reading room consists of a double-height volume with excellent access to natural light, with reading areas positioned along the glazed northern façade, protected by high-level, directional roof louvers.

The lightweight steel and timber-trabeated roof structures are complemented by the heavy rammed earth walls that form the enclosure and connect the building with the earth it sits on.

Through the rammed earth, we are seeking a direct transformation of the ground of the site into built form, in a sense wrapping the earth of the site around the lightweight verandah like pavilions that open out to this extended horizontal landscape.

Within the shade of these louvered verandahs, community activities such as markets and music functions occur, as well as the natural spill of activity from within the library.

In addition to the core library services, the project includes an integrated local art gallery, café, childcare centre, computer training centre and meeting and function spaces.

The library is a key public building for Craigieburn, and will continue to bring people together and act as a focal point for the community in a warm, friendly and sustainable environment.

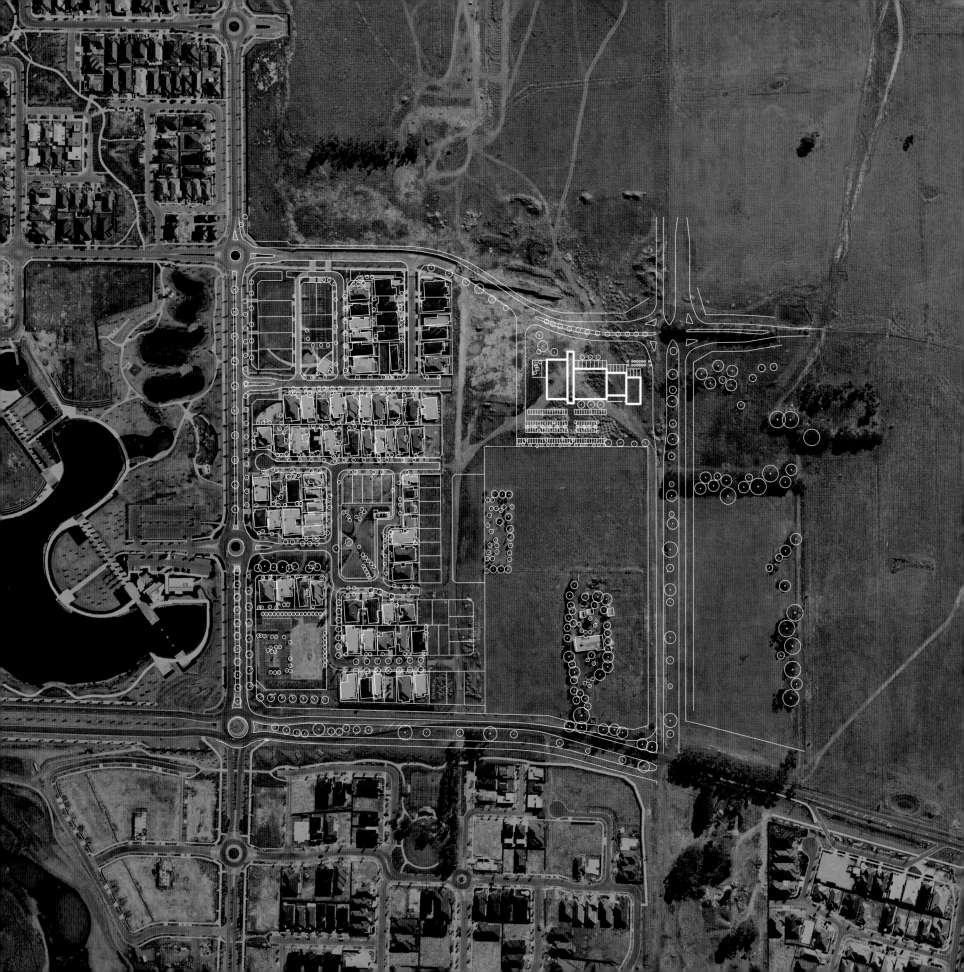

1 Louvred shade frame and rammed earth walls from locally sourced materials, are the primary forms of the building.

A Community and library volumes are joined through a central "arcade" that connects and defines a landscaped entry courtyard with the carpark.

B Library spaces are defined as a series of three volumes, or rooms, of varying scale, from the double-storey reading room to the low-scaled children's wing, each with a north facing verandah giving deep shade.

C The rooms are formed through U-shaped rammed earth walls connected through an east–west spine and open to the north via separate verandahs.

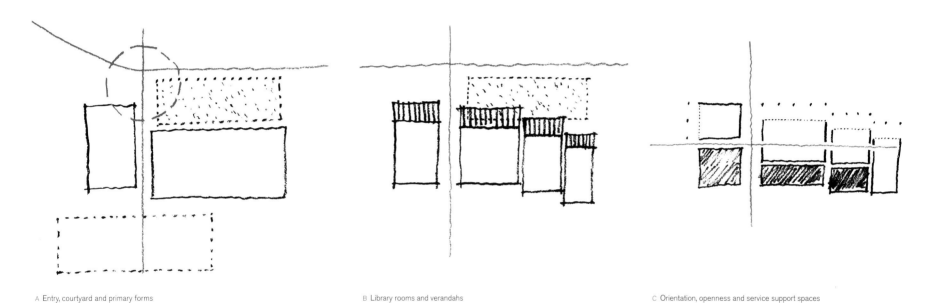

A Entry, courtyard and primary forms

B Library rooms and verandahs

C Orientation, openness and service support spaces

1 Entry foyer
2 Reception
3 Café
4 Reading space
5 General library
  collections
6 IT hub
7 Study zone
8 Children's collection
9 Staff work area
10 Gallery
11 Childcare facility
12 Mobile library parking
13 Meeting room
14 Breakout space
15 Staff kitchen
16 Function hall/
  multi-purpose room
17 Plant room

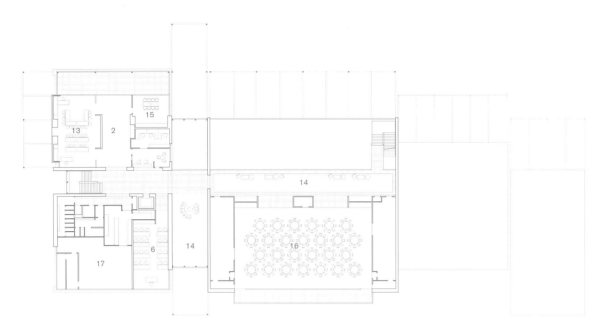

Plan: Upper level

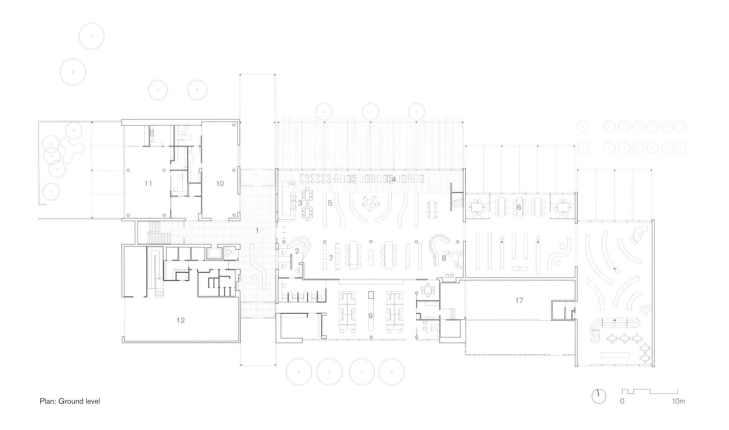

Plan: Ground level

0   10m

1 The rammed earth walls
and verandah spaces are
deeply shaded by profiled
aerofoil aluminium louvres
supported on fine steel
frames.

1 The primary reading room consists of a double-height volume with extensive natural lighting through a louvred skylight that extends the external louvred verandah within.
2 The hoop pine timber ceiling panels and rammed earth walls define a series of glazed quiet rooms that open towards the view.
3 The main entry and associated roof canopy viewed from the main verandah space of the courtyard.

1 The northern courtyard spaces shaded by the series of louvred verandah structures that diminish in scale towards the children's scale volume beyond.
2 Rammed earth walls which shade the pattern of louvres from the verandah.
3 The extended timber entrance canopy.

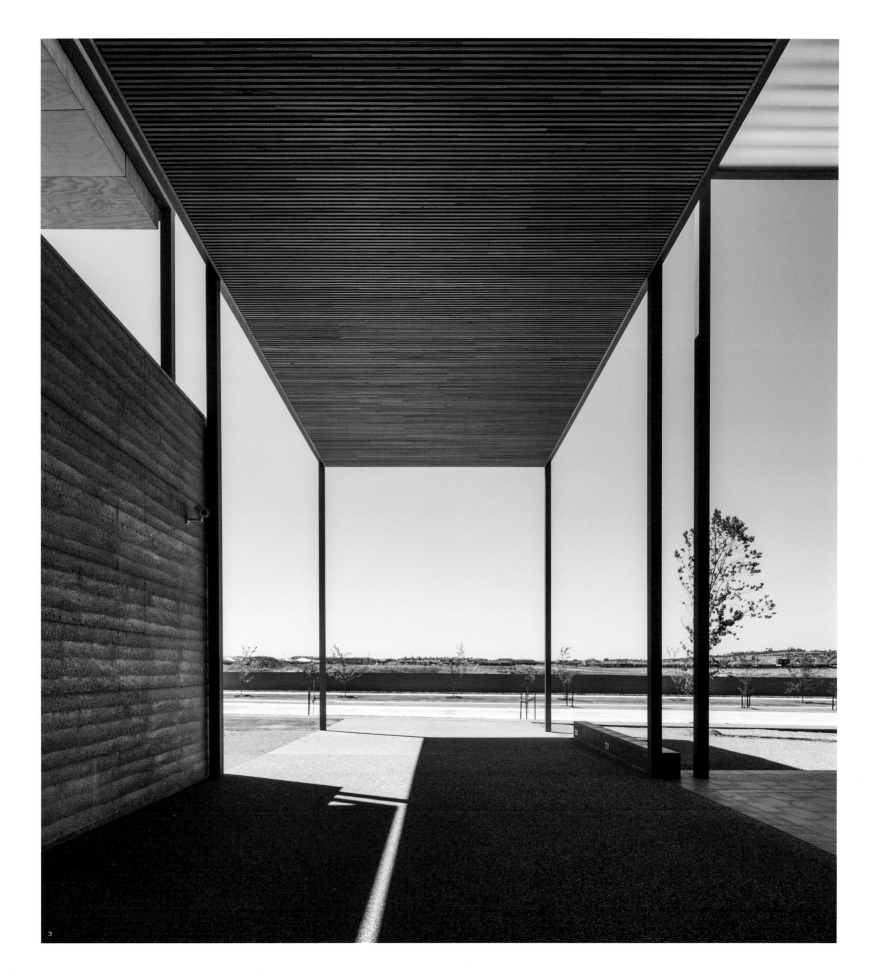

3

Façade detail, Sydney Law School, University of Sydney

I think of school as an environment of spaces where it is good to learn. Schools began with a man under a tree who did not know he was a teacher discussing his realisation with a few who did not know they were students. The students reflected on what was exchanged and how good it was to be in the presence of this man. They aspired that their sons also listen to such a man. Soon spaces were erected and the first school became… The entire system of schools that followed from the beginning would not have been possible if the beginning were not in harmony with the nature of man. It can also be said that the existence will of school was there even before the circumstances of the man under a tree.

Louis Kahn
"Form and Design," *Architectural Design* April (London: Wiley, 1961)

Campus

279

265

271

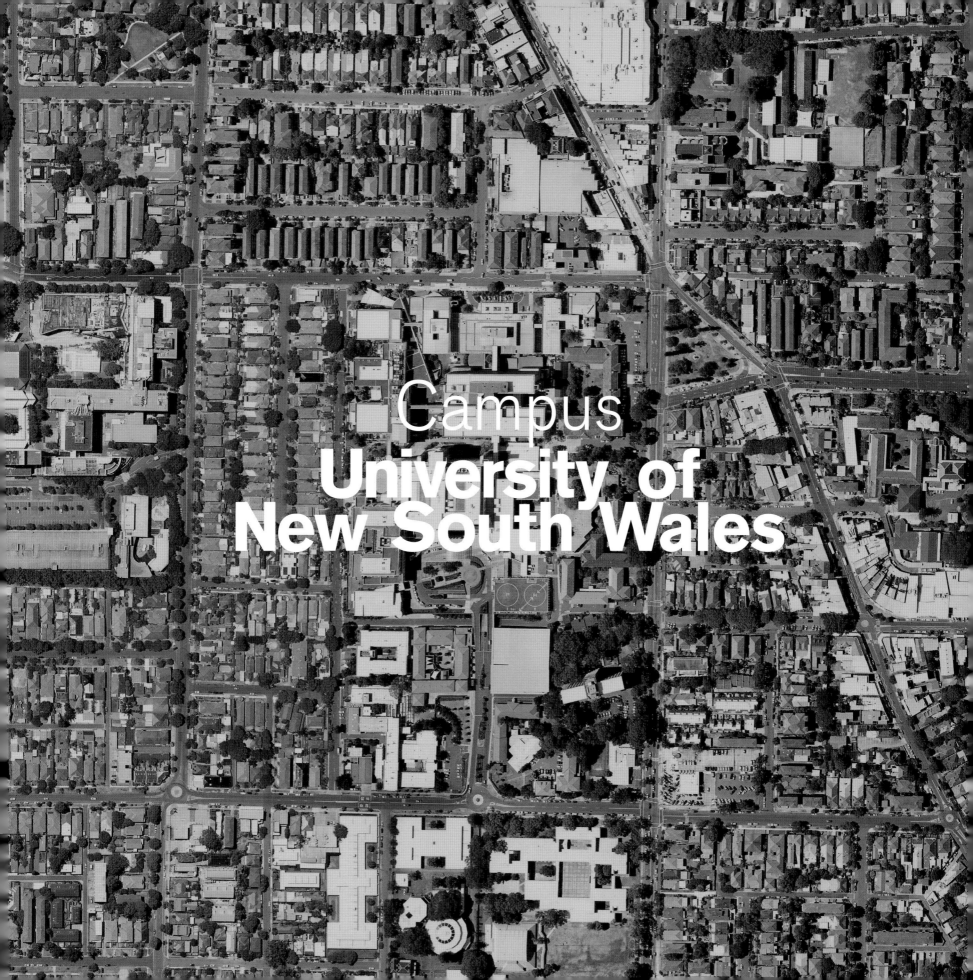

Campus
University of New South Wales

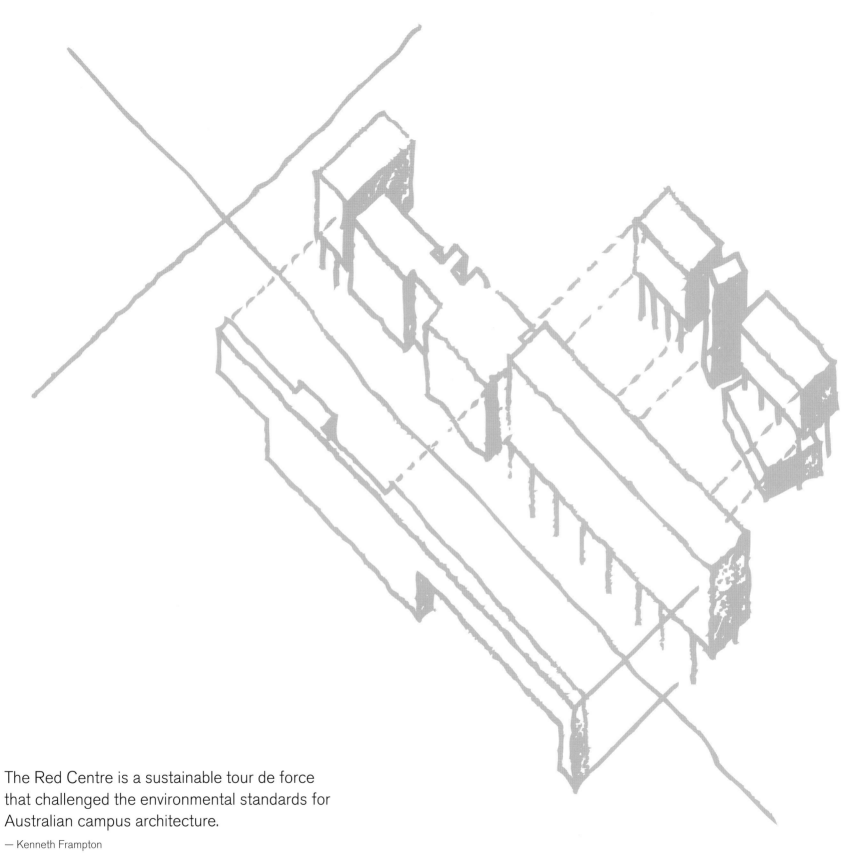

The Red Centre is a sustainable tour de force
that challenged the environmental standards for
Australian campus architecture.

— Kenneth Frampton

Red Centre

The University of New South Wales undertook an extensive building programme to transform a placeless 1960s campus of object buildings into interrelated courtyards and public places.

The site of this project is at the edge of a degraded linear landscaped mall. Here, an existing building is refurbished and two new buildings added: an international centre and a new school of architecture.

The sloping central mall was a lost opportunity, a potentially central axial space neglected and compromised by developments of the last thirty years. Our project uncovers this potential and transforms the mall into a unifying and identity-giving public space complemented by two significant public squares. The expression of separate buildings was rejected in favour of a continuous linear form defining the mall.

A planar wall of terracotta tile stretches across new and existing buildings, cut and folded to define the two public squares. This wall is the public face of the building. Minor openings for offices are suppressed to form continuous, linear coursing-like slots. Entry, exhibition and public spaces are given monumental expression through large openings and folded planes.

Behind this terracotta plane, the new building takes the form of two glass and metal volumes suspended on columns. The first volume sits opposite the main square and extends westward to reach down the mall and announce the presence of the square. The second volume located at the eastern end of the complex is turned through ninety degrees to define and characterise the second new square.

This composition of terracotta plane and recessed metal and glass volumes mediates the scale of the new building and complements the existing brick and curtain wall structures. To the south, the building takes a more fragmented form, responding to the courtyard, lane and service ways that provide only partial glimpses and lateral views.

Working closely with Arup, we developed a passive system of cooling, heating, ventilation and lighting. These passive environmental control systems are integral with the form, structure and representation of the building. For example, the independent terracotta plane that has such a significant urban and representational role is not merely a formal/symbolic strategy. The twin window design in a deep reveal was developed to simultaneously address environmental control and comfort. The twin openings provide even natural daylighting throughout the offices, with light penetrating deeply from the upper window and from the light shelf action of the reflective upper sill. The deeply set openings give appropriate sun shading and the twin opening design provides a carefully positioned window, able to be opened for views, with higher-level fixed glass for daylight, between which is an integrated bookshelf. Air can be drawn into the room through the open window or louvres integrated in the upper sill, which also serve as trickle vents.

These "breathing" façade systems are complemented by a ventilation system that draws air into the building through low-level vents and expels it through central air shafts connected to thermal flues. These flues are located on the north face of the building so the natural solar heating assists the drawing of cool air from low-level vents. Automatic dampers in the airshafts are adjusted according to the outside air temperature, so that air is drawn in to reduce temperature and cool the mass of the building for radiant cooling. In winter, the flow of air is reduced and the sunshades are adjusted for passive heating.

1 Exhibition space
2 Library
3 Campus security
4 Computer laboratories
5 Computer offices
6 Lobby
7 International student centre
8 Offices
9 Studio
10 Classroom
11 Workroom
12 Void
13 Studio mezzanine
14 Raked studio

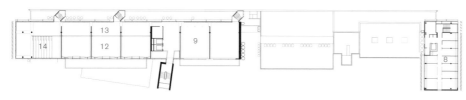

Level 6

Level 2 (typical)

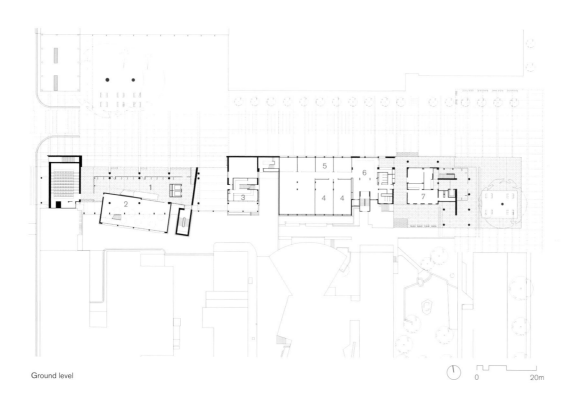

Ground level

0   20m

1 Campus mall, squares
and garden are formed and
figured through folds and
cut-outs in the planar
terracotta façade.

This is already the fjmt tectonic signature in that it combines
a basic structural form with precisely wrought metal and glass
elements, conceived and executed to the precise standards
of the international hi-tech architecture.
— Kenneth Frampton

John Niland
Scientia Building

Sited on a gentle hill at the end of the Mall, the John Niland Scientia Building is part of a major regeneration of the campus including the creation of the new University Square precinct, pedestrian mall, hard and soft landscaped terraces, lighting and reconfiguration of roads and access ways.

The centrepiece of the regeneration is Scientia. This ceremonial hall and multi-purpose function centre embodies the progressive spirit of the university, reflected by accessibility and openness to knowledge, and has been developed to make Scientia a gravitational centre, a place of gathering, and a ceremonial focus for the university and wider community.

The architectural expression of the building is separated into three parts of different formal and material character: the sandstone podium, metal boxes and timber foyer trees.

A sandstone podium anchors the building, absorbing the level change, and reinterpreting the natural sandstone of the hill on which the building stands. Woven through the stonework are precast concrete profiles that form continuous courses, with the presence of the sandstone granularly diminished to reveal the precast as louvres over openings, and terminating the podium in the form of balustrades. The podium is split at the line of the axial mall to create an open pedestrian passage through the building and into a new public square where the axial vista is finally terminated by a grove of poplars.

Two fine metal boxes enclosing Scientia's main rooms are raised on top of the podium either side of the central open passage. These volumes are clad in aluminium panels with continuous louvres to the east and west giving a translucency to the form, and filtering sunlight into the interiors. The interior of these volumes are lined with warm timber finishes of beech and silky oak panels, with the roof and ribbon-like ceiling of cast plaster supported by twelve columns of turned laminated Oregon.

Standing between the two volumes, in the central slot of the podium, is the timber tree-like structure of the foyer, which terminates the axial vista and mall and is an iconic image to represent the aspirations of the university community. These tall open forms raised to the sky form the central focus for the building, the axial mall and campus as a whole. The forms of these structures, in steel, glass, turned laminated Jarrah wood and metal louvres, give a gentle form of enclosure, and break the sunlight not unlike the shelter of a natural tree canopy.

In this way shelter, openness and transparency characterise the centre of Scientia and the centre of the university.

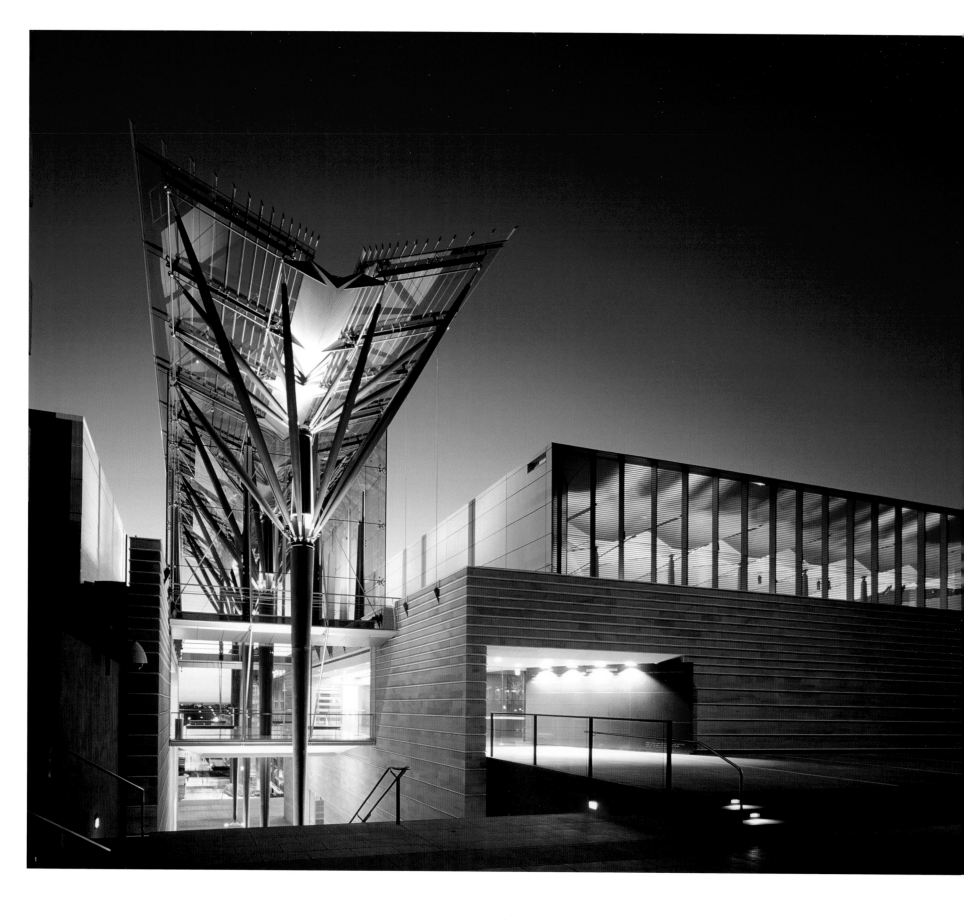

1 Ceremonial hall
2 Foyer
3 Cinema
4 Recital hall
5 Function room
6 Meeting room
7 Kitchen
8 Terrace

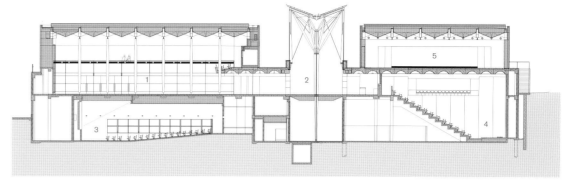

Section: North–south

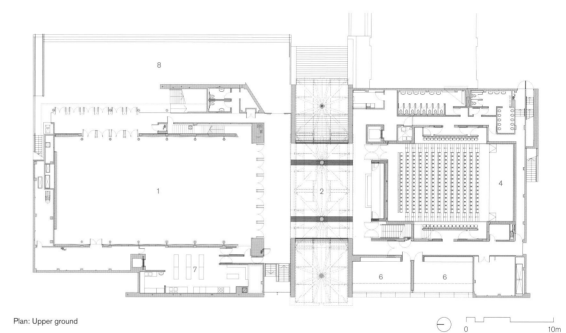

Plan: Upper ground

0   10m

1 Scientia arrival from the new square showing the central foyer structure and ceremonial hall.
2 Beneath the central tree-like structure, a light filled entrance welcomes visitors to the ceremonial hall.

275

1 Detail view of precast concrete louvres and sandstone podium elements adjacent to the glass, steel and timber foyer structure. 2 Ceremonial hall with profiled acoustic ceiling raised on tapered Oregon timber columns. 3 The warm interior of the hall is clad in beech and silky oak timber panels. 4 The central foyer structure of turned, laminated Jarrah struts and cruciform steel is an innovative system of frameless glass louvres, automated blinds and dampers, providing mixed mode environmental control.

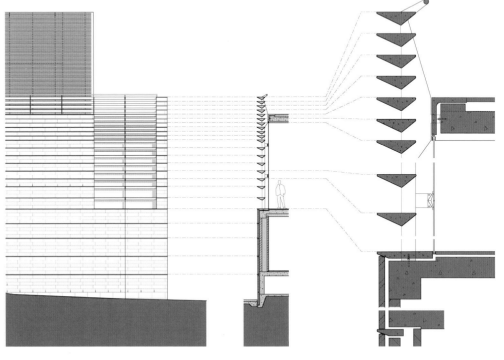

Detail: Elevation   Detail: Section

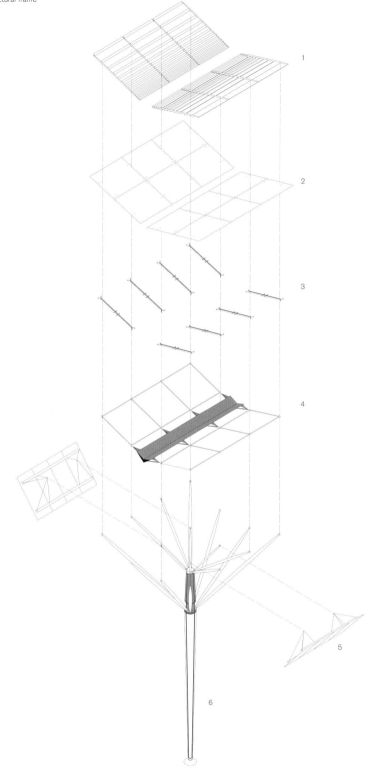

1 Aluminium louvres
2 Frameless glazing
3 Steel outrigger
4 Steel gutter profile and
   support frame
5 Frameless glass baffles
6 Composite steel/timber
   structural frame

Tyree Energy Technologies Building

Situated on the gateway site of the University of New South Wales main campus, at the junction of the Mall and Anzac Parade, is the Tyree Energy Technologies Building.

The site is of considerable strategic importance, as it occurs at the nexus of what can be considered as three interconnected "urban zones." Each of these zones has a particular landscape and built character that overlap and intersect with the building form, responding by differentiating form, scale, and detail complexity. Each of the building's façades are different and are characterised by a contextual design response.

Interwoven with the existing eucalypts, a series of form fragments open along the Anzac Parade frontage in a distinctive gesture of openness and welcome. These forms create an urban transition, or symbiotic weave, from the street-aligned blocks to the south to the verdant campus landscape to the north. A sensitive approach to the Mall, designed by Professor Spooner, was required for this frontage to enhance the character of this significant landscape—integral to the identity of the university—so by creating a continuous raised platform with north-facing seating steps, it transitions and visually extends the ground plane of the Mall into the building.

Overhead, a dramatic profiled roof is scaled to float above the canopy with a horizontal datum based on the mature height of the fig and cottonwood trees along the Mall. To the south, a series of articulated rectilinear forms reflecting the internal laboratory modules are set back to extend the street vista of Day Avenue into the site. The eastern laboratory module is turned to acknowledge the orientation of the Village Green.

Three key principles drive the interior design and spaces: interaction, transparency, and flexibility. Occupant interaction is encouraged by providing generous building circulation paths, social hubs, meeting rooms, oversized stairs, bridges and interconnecting labs. Functions of the building are opened or closed through varying levels of transparency, in both the façade and interior design. Laboratory spaces are conceived as flexible modules to be either separate, connected or combined as required, enabling the university to adjust spaces over time.

We applied an interdisciplinary, collaborative and integrated approach to sustainability originating with our initial competition entry and continuing through documentation and construction to operation. The building was conceived with sustainability at the forefront, to facilitate the world-leading research by the occupants, an achievement recognised by the Green Building Council of Australia with a 6 Green Star certification (Education Design v1).

Our design concept seeks a balance and resolution of the various aspects of the brief combining functionality and flexibility in the creation of best-practice environments for teaching and learning, research and workplace, aligning with the iconic aspiration of the university's strategic vision for this important gateway site.

The expansive atria, overlapping spaces, and opening of vistas to the landscape and campus beyond maximise circulation and the visibility of occupants. A sympathetic synthesis of architecture and landscape is achieved through a rich interweave of built form and landscape, modulating space and light.

1 The Tyree Energy Technologies Building relates to the Mall and Village Green. The Red Centre and Scientia are visible in the foreground.

A Synthesis, opening and embracing

B Anzac Parade zone: openess, engaging and fragmentary

C Spooner's Walk, module, spacing and canopy

D Mall zone: address, activation and continuity

E South zone: Day Avenue, New College and Village Green

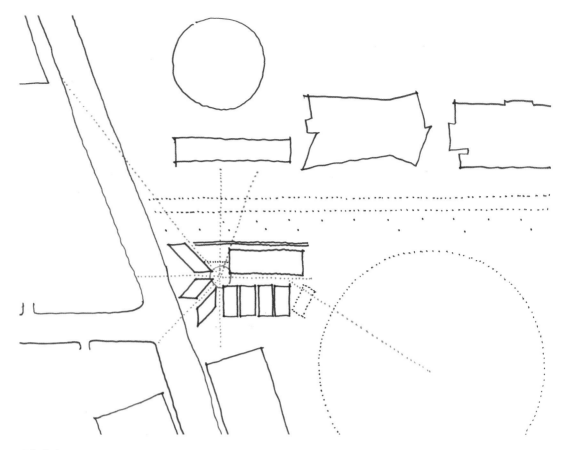

A Synthesis

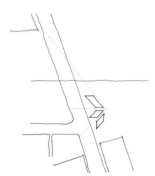

B Anzac Parade zone

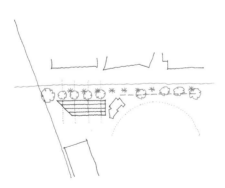

C Spooner's Walk

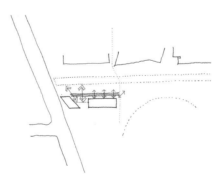

D Mall zone

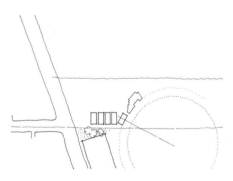

E South zone

1 Workplace
2 Write-up
3 Laboratories
4 Support laboratories
5 Collaboration space
6 Main atrium
7 Entry atrium

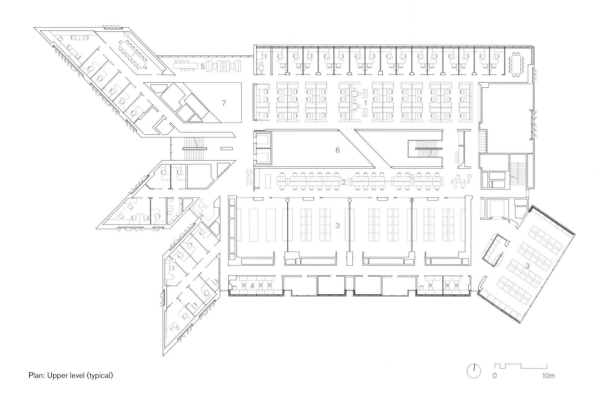

Plan: Upper level (typical)

0   10m

1 A raised plinth with continuous seating steps and profiled roof raised on slender columns combine with the canopy of existing trees to form a protected space of dappled light addressing the Mall.

1 Carefully scaled and modulated to float just above the mature canopy of the great trees, the curved roof integrates transparent photovoltaic panels. **2** The high performance curtain wall façade system is composed of non-reflective porcelain tiles and louvres angled to provide passive sun shading. **3** A junction of the profiled steel columns and the curved roof canopy. **4** A portal cube in precast concrete clearly defines the main entry and leads directly into the exhibition space and entry foyer.

1 The light-filled entry atrium and collaboration hubs overlooking the tree canopy on the Mall. 2 View of the main atrium from the student learning spaces on the lower ground floor. 3 The main atrium facilitates occupant interconnection and interaction fostering collaboration between different research groups.

1 Workplace
2 Write-up
3 Laboratory
4 Support laboratory
5 Main atrium
6 Café/collaboration space
7 Horseshoe theatre
8 Seminar room

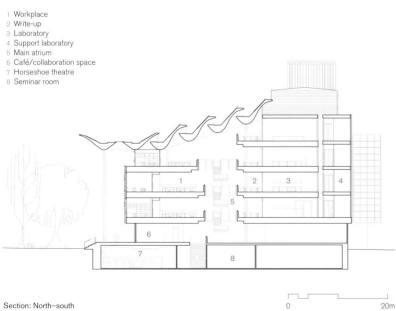

Section: North–south

0   20m

1 The distinct roof profile "floats" above the building volume, drawing indirect natural light into the centre of the research facility and orientates the integrated photovoltaic panels to the north. 2 The roof profile coalesces with the tree canopy.

295

Campus
Edith Cowan University

This project at Joondalup demonstrates two key aspects
of the work of fjmt: topographic placemaking and a sustainable
approach to local climatic conditions.

— Kenneth Frampton

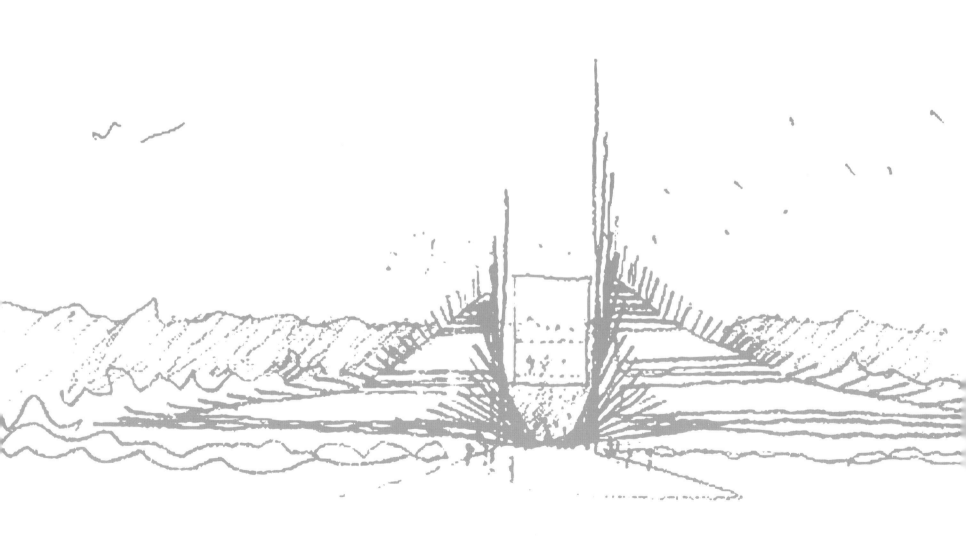

Chancellery & Business School

fjmt / HASSELL

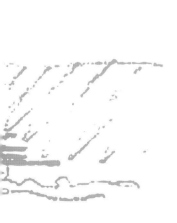

The new buildings are sited on a gentle rise, set amongst bushland and eucalypts. On one side are the broad lanes of Grand Drive leading into Joondalup city, and on the other a central pathway that leads down to a modest lake and peaceful green lawns. The forms, materials and character of the new buildings have been drawn directly from this landscape.

The Chancellery is made like two giant plants, their branches fanning out and rising up from the ground to almost touch at the centre. These two rising forms frame a vista down to the lake and open wide toward Grand Drive in a gesture of welcoming and invitation to the city. This curving form is assembled from Jarrah struts that begin almost parallel with the ground and gradually fold up and out, framing a new ceremonial open space and reaching up towards the sky.

The Jarrah screen provides shelter, shade and structural support to the assembly of work areas, courtyards, cafe and gallery spaces that step up from one to three levels. Within the interstitial space between the timber screen and the main enclosure, the circulation is concentrated. Stairways and lifts occurring in this shaded zone open to the view, creating informal meeting places and drawing occupants to the exterior as they move between the floors and wings of the building.

Positioned on either side of the central space, within the sheltering screen, are located the Council Chamber and the executive offices of the Vice Chancellor, held in visible democratic balance either side of the vista and connecting bridge.

In counterpoint with the Chancellery is the linear structure that accommodates the School of Business teaching and offices spaces. In another interpretation of the landscape, the ground plane has been extended and bent up into a gentle slope that looks back to the rising forms of the Chancellery. This form is made from the material of the earth: clay brick and concrete packed together to create an enclosing, bowl-like open space with seating for events or informal meeting and gathering. Intersecting this artificial landscape slope are metal enclosures accommodating the academic offices. These orthogonal forms look back towards the Chancellery and city beyond through a metal veil of automatic louvres that shield the sun.

The organic forms of the architecture have been developed to appear to rise almost "naturally" out of the landscape itself and to represent and embody the values and aspirations of the university. Equally important is the transformation of this site into an urban focus and catalyst for a dense future campus that defines a series of symbolic, open, public spaces, of democratic nature.

A Triangular Chancellery
  profiles and folded
  groundplane of the
  Business School
  related to the existing
  landscape and campus.
B The generating circular
  geometries and
  projected tangential
  posts around a
  central axis.

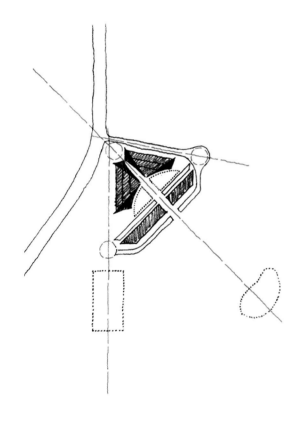

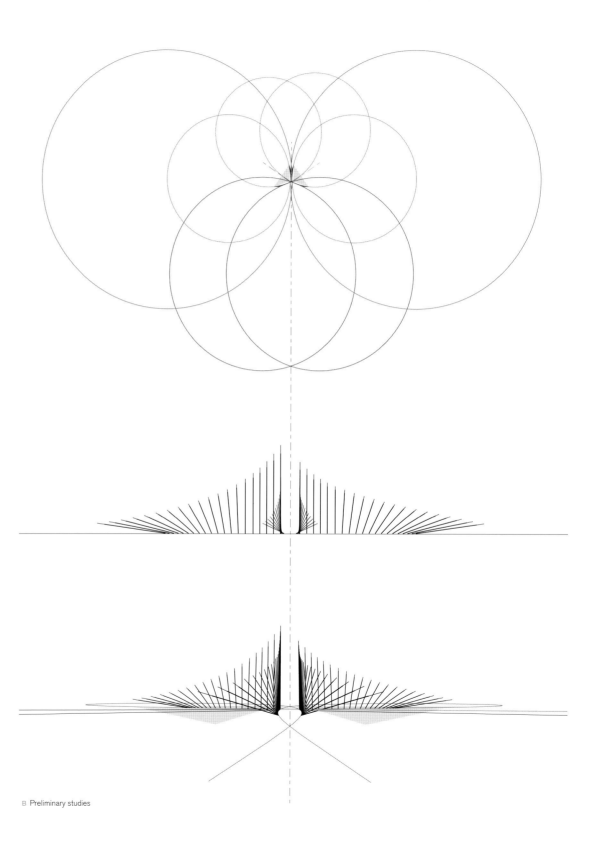

A Site study sketch

B Preliminary studies

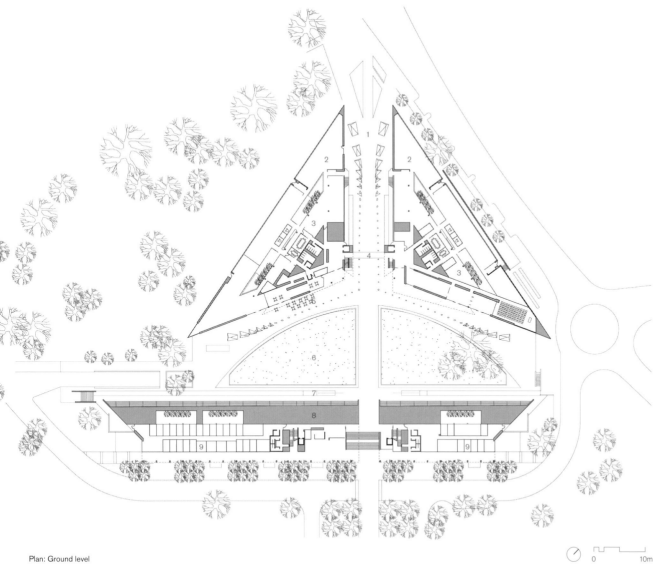

1 Entry plaza
2 Open plan administration offices
3 Meeting rooms
4 Bridge
5 Quadrangle colonnade and café
6 Campus Green
7 Seating steps
8 Services void
9 Academic offices

1 Central campus entry and axis framed by the winds of the new Chancellery wings. 2 The Jarrah posts and shade screens visible above the adjacent bushland landscape. 3 Aerial view of Chancellery wings and Business School form around the new crescent campus green and central axis.

Plan: Ground level

0   10m

1 The stepped profile and curved timber screen of the Chancellery. 2 The stepped amphitheatre profile and integrated louvred oculus of the Business School. 3, 4, 5, 6 Deep and extensive shading is provided by the Jarrah screen both to the glazing of the building volumes and the edges of the public space.

1 Stainless steel end-grain protection
2 Bolt and ferrule fixing with turned Jarrah spacer
3 Paired laminated Jarrah profiles
4 Universal steel column
5 Steel support with bolt and ferrule fixings
6 Tubular steel horizontal connector
7 Reinforced concrete footing
8 Steel outrigger connection to primary structure
9 Recycled Jarrah batten screen

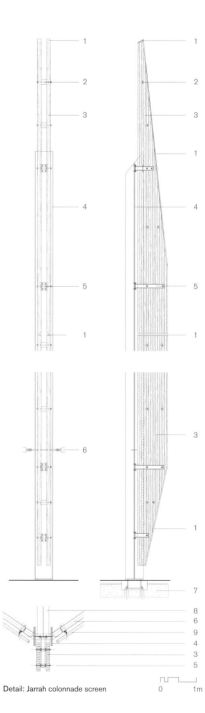

Detail: Jarrah colonnade screen   0   1m

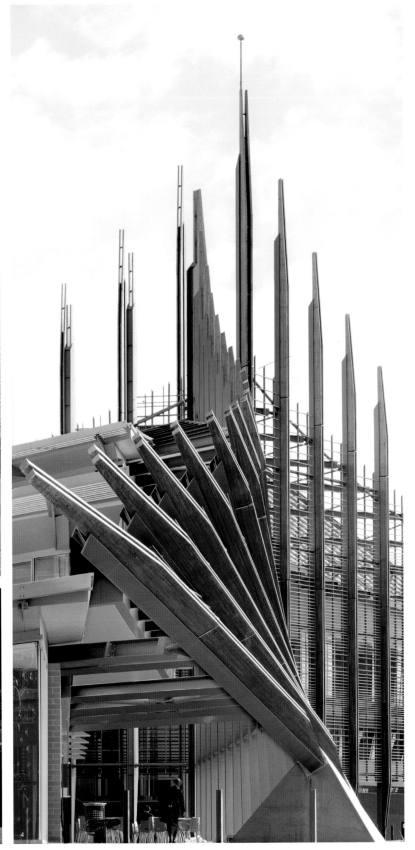

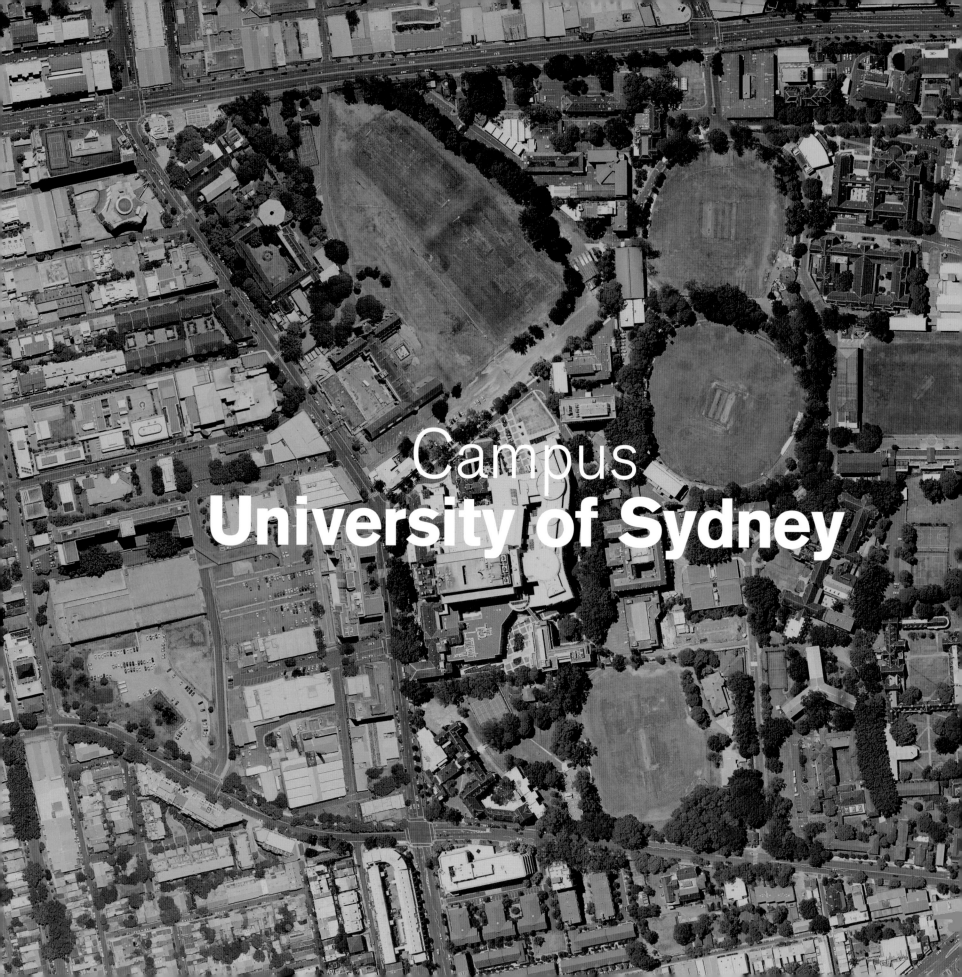

Campus
University of Sydney

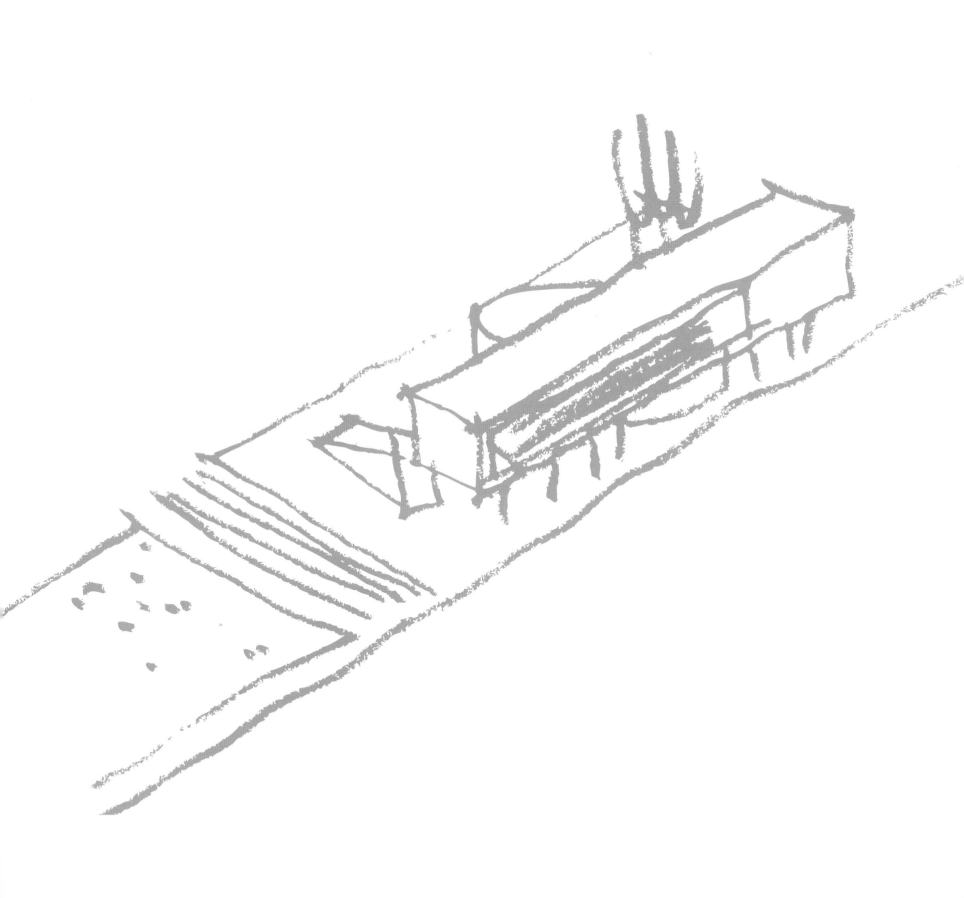

Eastern Avenue Auditorium

This project for a new central lecture and seminar facility aims to transform a degraded area of the campus into an integrated sequence of built form and open space. Courtyard, forecourt and garden are created through the careful placement of seemingly autonomous architectural forms.

The project comprises two essential architectural elements: the ground plane or podium, and the raised metal volume. The form, detail and materials elaborate and explore the different nature of these two elements. Between the platform and raised volume is a sequence of public spaces: foyer, courtyards and gardens that are defined and interconnected through pure geometric forms placed on the podium, triangular stair, cylindrical lift shaft, pyramidal skylight and circular auditorium.

The sculptural form of the triangular stair, the broad steps of the platform addressing a lawn, and the opening and balcony within the raised metal volume are intended as a stage and set elements for the theatre and ceremony of campus life.

The lower level connects directly into the teaching facilities of the existing Carslaw Building while the top of the podium establishes a level platform aligning with Eastern Avenue—a central "street" of the campus.

The metal rectangular volume is raised on a grid of columns above the brick podium and set parallel to Eastern Avenue to strengthen and reinforce the definition of this important campus street.

The sequence of circulation has been developed to relate the occupant moving through the building to significant campus vistas and landscape. The "window/eye" of the central stair is positioned to align with the western passage to the ovals, while the end stair orientates over Victoria Park toward the city.

1 A triangular stair, independent of the suspended metal volume, frames a vista towards the city and creates a pairing with the circular form of the auditorium.

1 Auditorium
2 Foyer
3 Seminar room
4 Lift
5 Lecture theatre
6 Garden
7 Public square

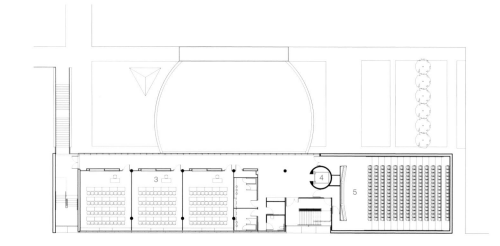

Plan: Upper level

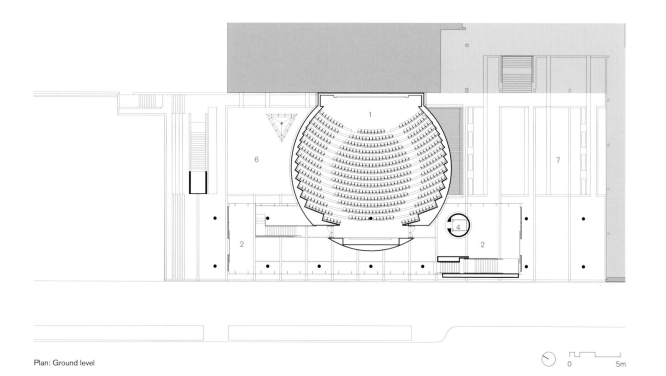

Plan: Ground level

0   5m

Although this is only a four-storey infill structure on a very restricted urban site with a considerable slope from one end to the next, it has been treated as a gateway building serving both to represent the existing engineering campus and to link it back into the community.

— Kenneth Frampton

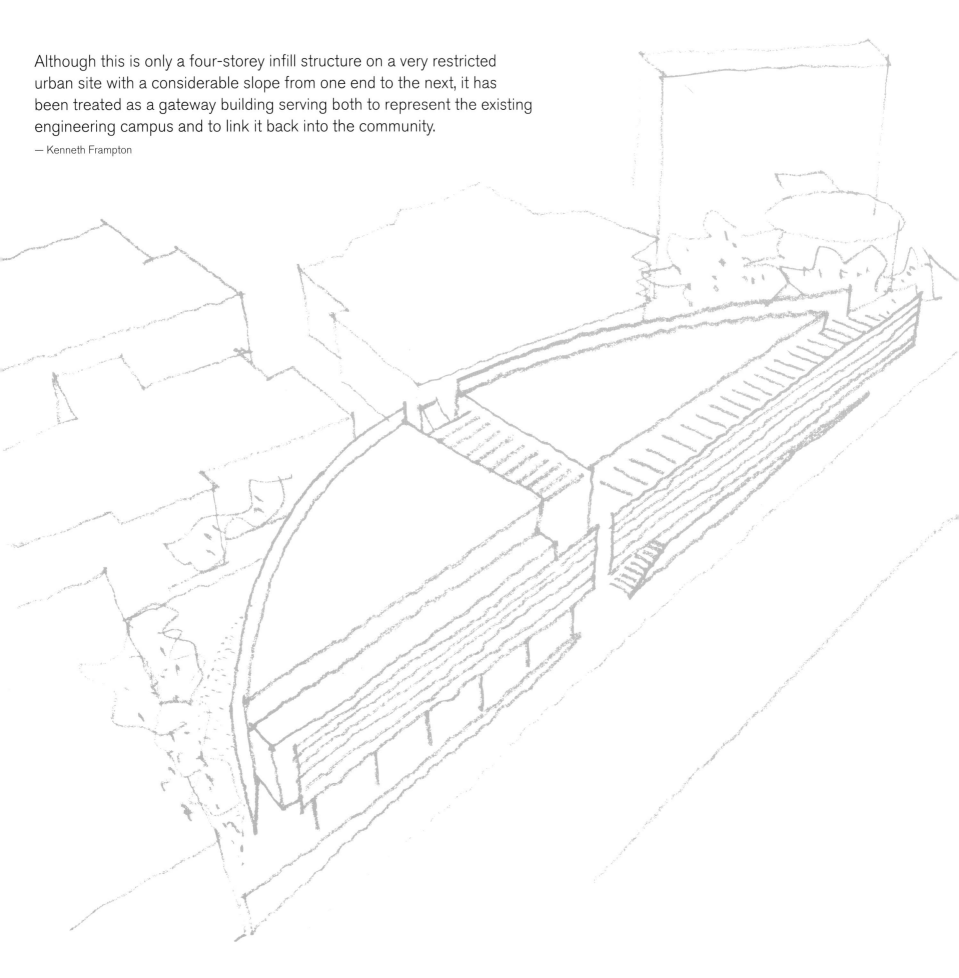

School of Information Technologies

The School of Information Technologies building creates a new campus gateway, transforming a vacant site adjacent to one of the city's major road junctions.

The overall form of the building has been determined to foster links with the Engineering Precinct, Seymour Centre theatre and wider community. The architecture presents a layered glazed environmental screen façade to Cleveland Street, forming a buffer between the building and the traffic noise and associated pollution of Cleveland Street. The screen provides acoustic attenuation to allow appropriate indoor workplace conditions, whilst presenting a contemporary image of transparency and interaction. This façade is discontinued at the Engineering Walk axis to visually connect the precinct with the neighbouring community, reinterpret the former configuration and extension of Rose Street, and announce the location of the main arrival/ entry lobby of the building. The screen extends past the building to the west to embrace the Seymour Centre forecourt.

To the south, the building has a curved stainless steel façade incorporating a unique perforated stainless screen to adjust the proportions of the building and provide assistance in the protection against unwanted glare. This site-specific approach creates the opportunity to provide generous landscape zones for passive recreation and "extend" the usage of the building to the adjoining campus areas.

The building is configured as two wings surrounding a central atrium and interconnecting stair. The main glazed entry foyer is centred within the atrium, allowing the extension of Engineering Walk into the school and the visual connection through to Cleveland Street. Vertical transport links are located within the entry foyer, facilitating ease of connections to the upper levels and interconnection of the main public or "front of house" facilities of the school. Each level of the building is provided with a "bridge" connection linking the eastern and western sections of the development across the Engineering Walk axis. Social hubs and meeting rooms are located within this naturally ventilated support zone to promote knowledge transfer through informal interaction and meeting.

At the lower levels, the building is provided with predominantly collaborative and specialist facilities including the school's specialist research laboratories, boardroom, common room and presentation suite. These facilities have been configured around generous wintergarden and exhibition spaces to both foster interaction within the school, and to embrace the wider community.

1 Workspace
2 Office
3 Meeting room
4 Teaching
5 Circulation spine
  and social hub
6 Wintergarden
  (enclosed)
7 Wintergarden (open)
8 Engineering Walk
9 Seymour Centre
10 Cleveland Street

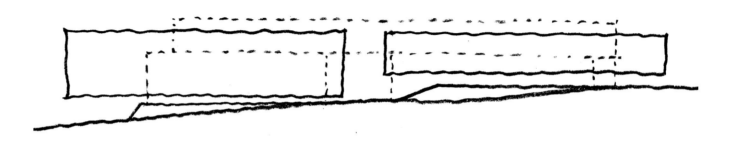

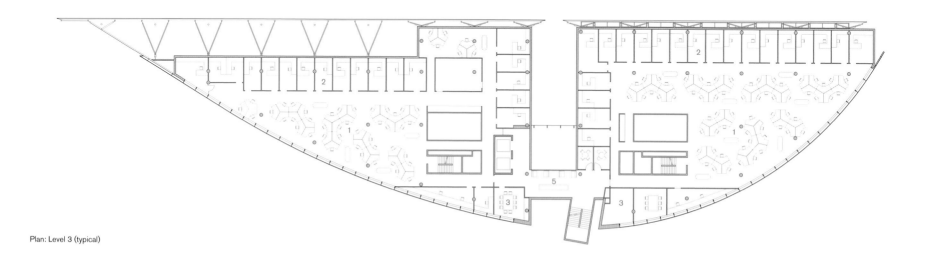

Plan: Level 3 (typical)

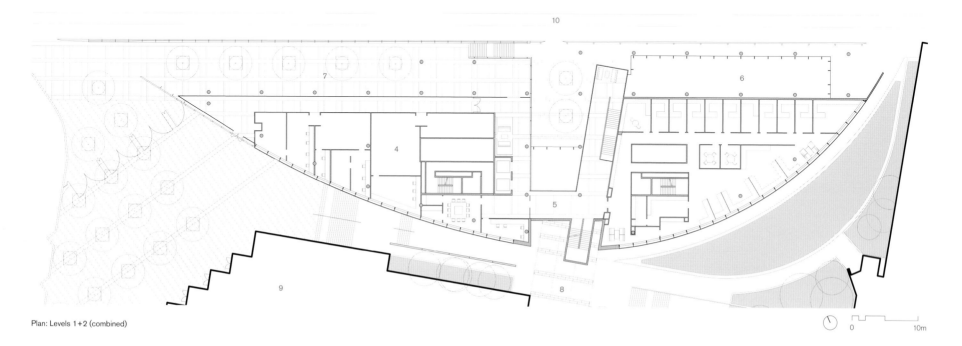

Plan: Levels 1+2 (combined)

0   10m

1, 2, 3 Concept model.

A Preliminary sketch studies of glazed street screen and stainless steel using form interpretation.

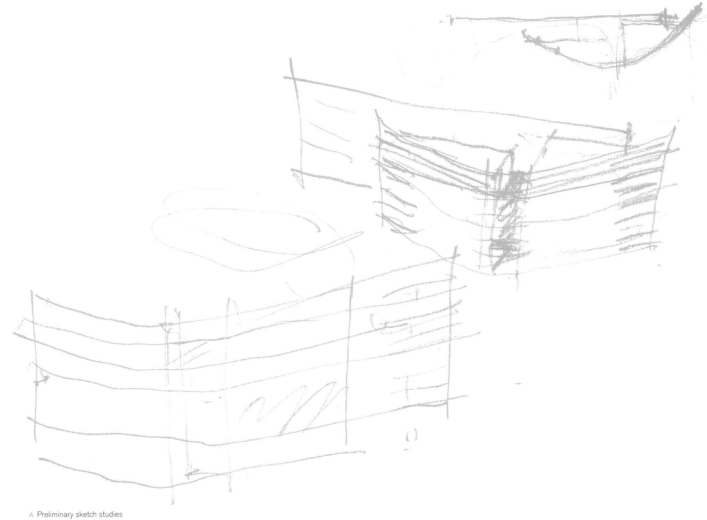

A Preliminary sketch studies

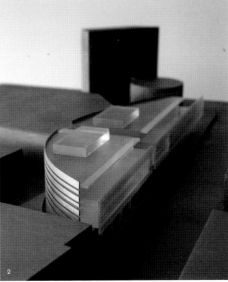

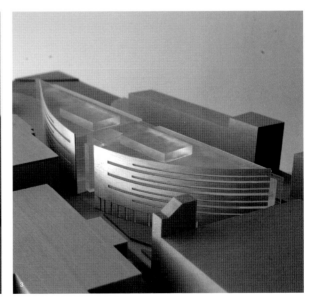

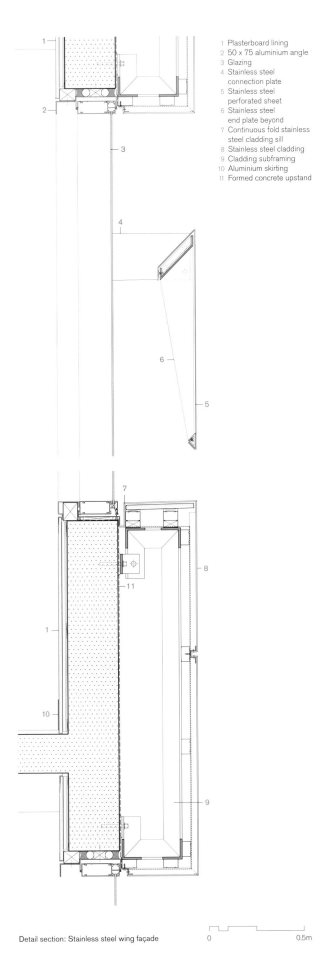

1 Plasterboard lining
2 50 x 75 aluminium angle
3 Glazing
4 Stainless steel
   connection plate
5 Stainless steel
   perforated sheet
6 Stainless steel
   end plate beyond
7 Continuous fold stainless
   steel cladding sill
8 Stainless steel cladding
9 Cladding subframing
10 Aluminium skirting
11 Formed concrete upstand

Detail section: Stainless steel wing façade

0   0.5m

A primary feature of fjmt's subtle reorganization of the campus
is the four-storey, somewhat Aaltoesque mass of the faculty office
building mediating between the original Gothic Revival fabric and
the picturesque expanse of Victoria Park to the east.

— Kenneth Frampton

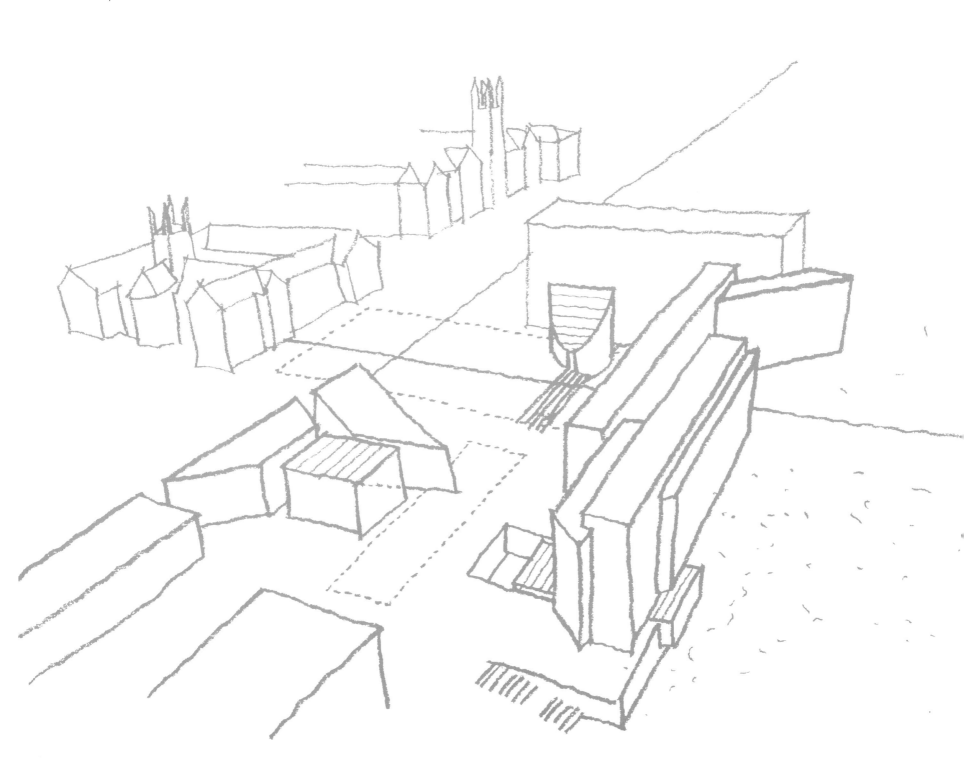

Sydney Law School

We interpreted this project as an opportunity to redefine and reinterpret the architectural dialectic between city and campus: to extend the public domain and create a new opening of the university to the community, parkland and city beyond, with the study of law balanced carefully at this new threshold.

We began by dividing the project's complex and extensive programme into podium and superstructures. This allowed us to create a new, open-space sequence of lawns, terraces and plazas adjoining Eastern Avenue, the primary public artery of the campus.

Below these open spaces and within the solid podium, we positioned the library and teaching spaces accessed from stepped terraces and naturally lit from above through skylights and clerestories. Suspended above this public platform are a series of slender superstructures that split and splinter the remaining programme fragments. These fragments then coalesce at specific moments to define and frame new open spaces.

The movement of the splintered form fragments are frozen or locked into position by three glass and metal elements, and finally through a historic urban axis.

A cubic glass atrium locks the fragments of the teaching form into a triangular spatial and urban alignment at the moment of primary vertical circulation.

A sculptural curvilinear "light-tower" of stainless steel penetrates the primary platform delineating this open space, and creating an architectural "figure" against the silent backdrop of the existing Fisher Library stack as it announces the presences of the new Law Library below and draws in and reflects natural daylight.

A louvered metal box extends the public circulation within the podium, reaching out towards the park in the form of a student lounge, a quiet suspended space over the green landscape, freezing the movement in a modest rectilinear moment.

The final locking of the splintered form fragments is through the historic axis of the campus envisioned by Leslie Wilkinson, that runs from deep within the campus through built form and open space, and through this project is extended out and released into the park and city to create a broad opening of the campus.

It is at this moment—on this axis where the wide public steps fold the ground of the podium to meet the park—that the splintered forms of the new law school are connected by a thin glass bridge, or "window": a place for informal meeting of students and teachers, suspended at this threshold of city and campus. It is therefore an openness and transparency that marks this new entry to the university, with the splintered form fragments above, extending wide like an open door or hand that gestures invitation.

The materials of the splintered forms that define this edge and opening are layers of glass and timber louvres, suspended on fine stainless steel rods. These splinters possess a kinetic grain that changes with the position of the sun and preferences of those behind the timber screens. The ventilated double-skin system of enclosure draws in and controls natural air circulating through and around the interior, tempering the environment to cool and heat as necessary. The varying grain of the timber screens are overlaid with reflections of the park landscape and neo-gothic sandstone façades: a distilled reflection of the form, its means and its intent.

1 View from the Anderson Stuart Building (Old Medical School) along the line of Lesley Wilkinson's campus axis.
2 Concept model.

A A new landscaped square connects and opens the campus to Victoria Park and the city. From this threshold the pathways and vista connect the campus through the park to the city and Darlington campus.

B The Eastern Avenue boulevard is further defined by a new built form extending to the new square, which in turn is defined by the Anderson Stuart Building, Fisher Library stack and new academic workplace built form.

C The "layered" academic workplace volume is lifted above the groundplane and, at the Anderson Stuart axis, the northern volume section is splayed back to create an "open door," orientating directly towards the city and creating a welcoming and inviting gateway from the park.

D Gathered within the central open space are the school's primary elements or "symbolic rooms" that characterise this as a place of legal teaching, research, learning and debate: the Law Library, Moot Court and teaching spaces.

E The orthogonal geometry of the adjacent built form and open spaces extends like a "tartan" over the site, positioning new landscape and forms to created an integrated and "woven" network of teaching facilities, circulation and open spaces.

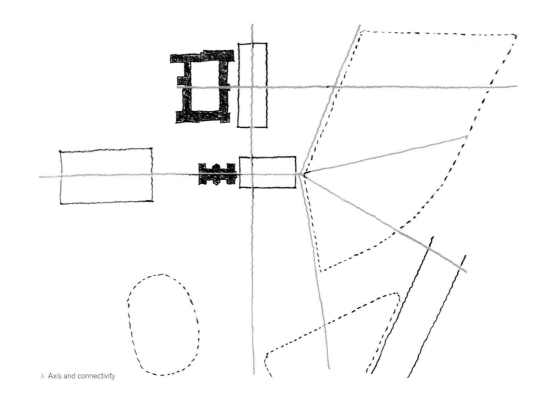

A Axis and connectivity

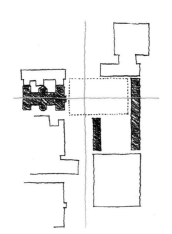

B Forecourt

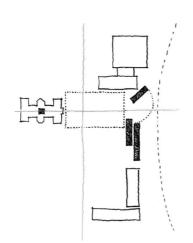

C Gateway

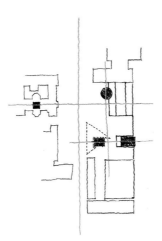

D Primary elements

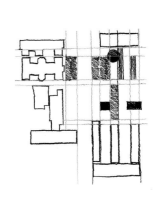

E Connection and geometry

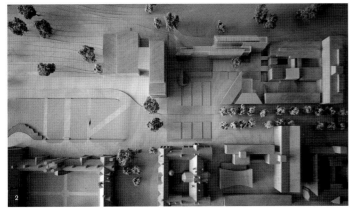

1, 3 A sculptural, stainless steel curvilinear light tower creates an architectural "figure" announcing the presence of the new Law Library below. **2** The open spaces and central campus spine defined by the new building are the focus of events and festivals.

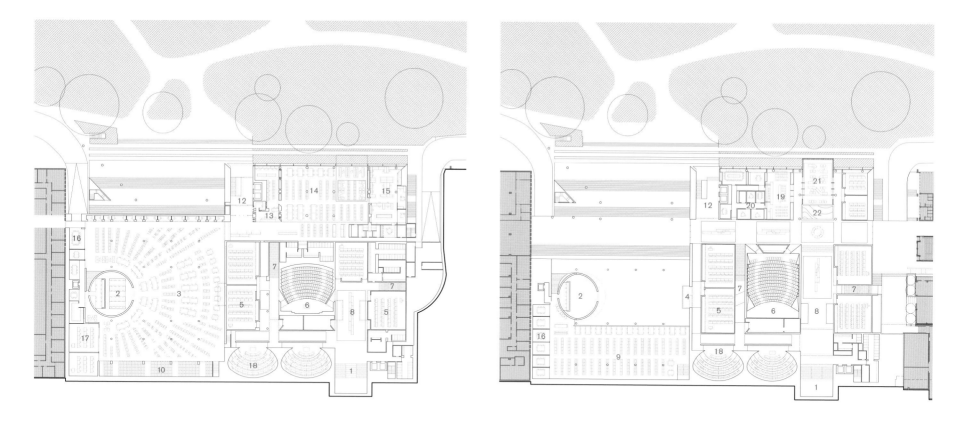

Plan: Level 0 (Law Library)

Plan: Level 1

1 Atrium lobby
2 Light tower reading room
3 Library
4 Gallery
5 Seminar room
6 Auditorium
7 Skylight stair
8 Concourse
9 Library stack
10 Library compactus
11 Social hub
12 Lobby
13 Library information desk
14 Open reserve
15 Staff area
16 Group study room
17 Computer teaching rooms
18 Lecture theatre
19 Moot Court
20 Moot Court mediation rooms
21 Lounge
22 Reflection pool/water court
23 Restaurant
24 Academic office
25 Meeting room
26 Common room
27 Board room
28 Forecourt/public square

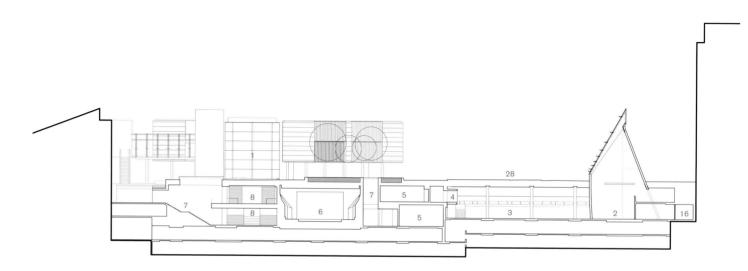

Section: South-north through auditorium, library and light tower

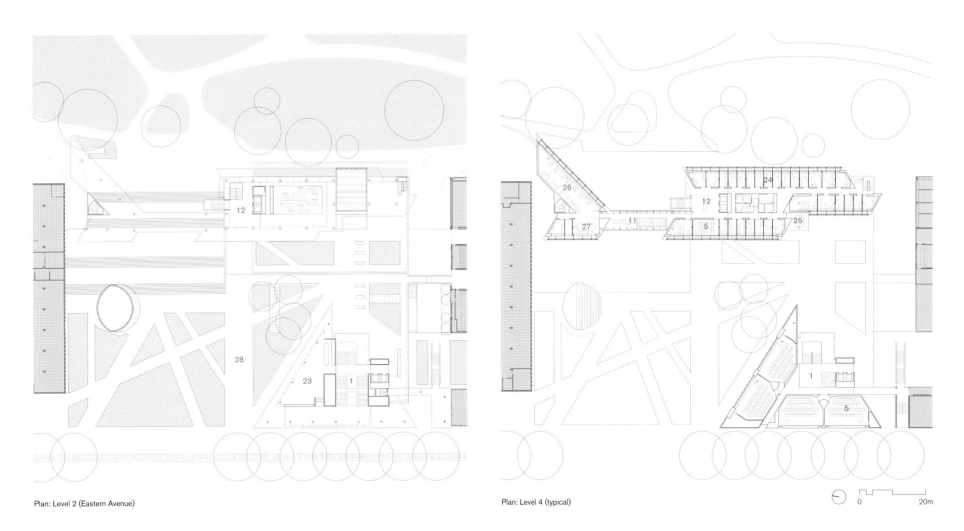

Plan: Level 2 (Eastern Avenue)

Plan: Level 4 (typical)

0   20m

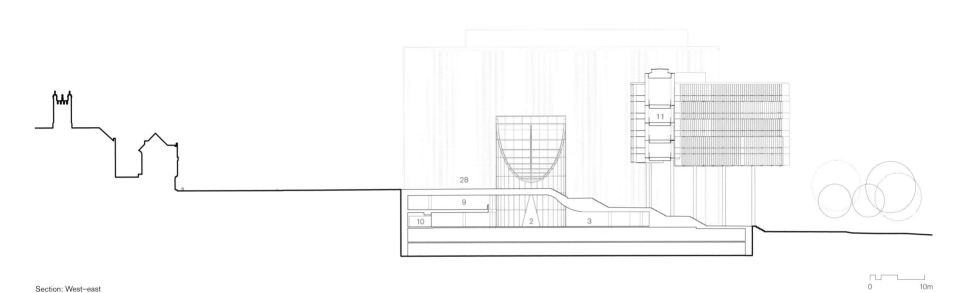

Section: West–east

0   10m

A Topographical study

1 The glass and steel connection makes visible the topographical position of the university on a gentle, contemplative rise above the city. **2** The bridge, suspended at the edge between campus and city, is an informal meeting space for students and teachers.

A Study sketch of "town and gown," campus and city topographical relationship.

1 Polished concrete topping
2 Zinc
3 Stanchion
4 Handrail
5 Structural steel diagonal
6 Façade
7 Cross beam beyond
8 Cast in structural steel
9 Cast in conduit
10 Structural steel
11 Mechanical services
12 Down pipe
13 Ventilation cowl beyond
14 Metal diffuser/walkway
15 Concrete slab edge
16 Cast in beam behind wall cladding
17 Structural steel plate extended
   from slab edge beam
18 Structural steel profiled fixing plate
19 Structural steel column
20 Structural steel profiled outrigger
21 Coupler and turnbuckle
22 Structural steel rod

1 Detail view of the glazed social hub bridge that connects the two wings of the academic workplace building.

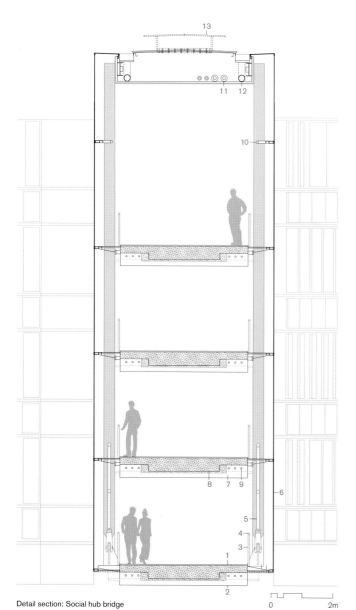

Detail section: Social hub bridge

0   2m

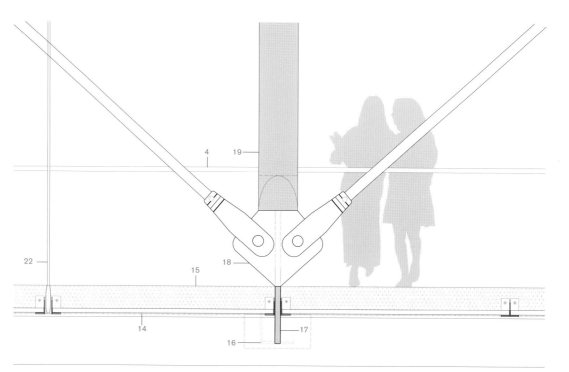

Detail section: Hanging column

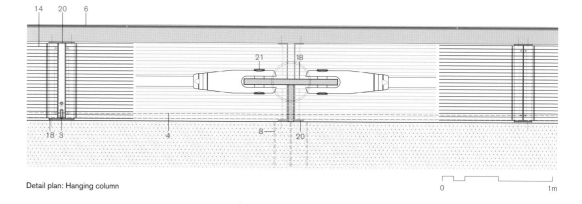

Detail plan: Hanging column

0   1m

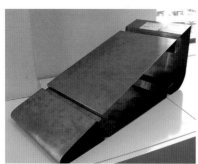

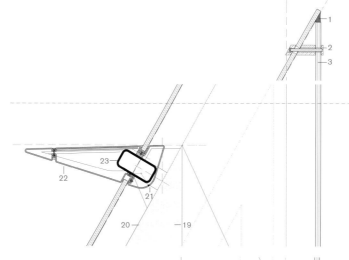

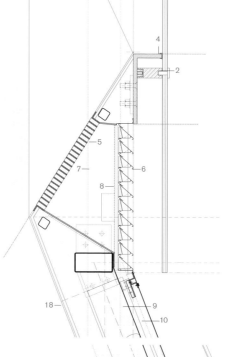

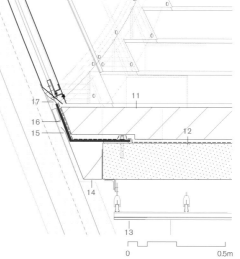

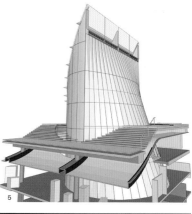

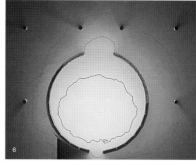

Detail section: Law Library light tower

0   0.5m

1 Silicone joint
2 Stainless steel plate
3 Glazing
4 Gasket
5 Air conditioning grille
6 Louvre bank
7 Blades between louvres
   supporting angle and
   vertical glazing
8 Bird mesh
   behind louvres
9 Zincalume sheet
10 Vertical support
   at panel joint
11 Stair tread
12 Concrete stair
13 Plasterboard
   painted black
14 Failsafe secondary
   gutter fixed to slab
15 Waterproof membrane
   carried up steel tread
16 Curved steel tread
   fixed to slab
17 Flexible membrane
   sealed to gutter
18 Curved plasterboard on
   curved furring channels
19 Flat plate connector
20 Blade truss
21 Tapered cruciform
   bracket to blade truss
22 Aluminium
   composite panel
23 Rectangular
   hollow section

1 Light tower façade prototype, steel framework and construction. **2** Stair connecting library level bends around the profile of the light tower. **3,4** A quiet and contemplative reading area within the Law Library light tower. **5** Light tower study model. **6** Natural daylight modelling.

1, 2, 3 Detail views of the automated profiled plywood louvre panels within the ventilated cavity system.
4 Detail view of double skin timber louvred façade with the light tower reflected.

1 SS cast arm glass support
2 SS patch plate
3 Toughened laminated glass
4 Louvre SS fixing bracket
5 SS main casting arm
6 SS casting connection rod
7 Timber louvre blade
8 Transom extrusion
9 Wiring recess

Detail plan: Double skin façade system

0   1m

Detail section: Cast steel support and plywood louvre

0   0.2m

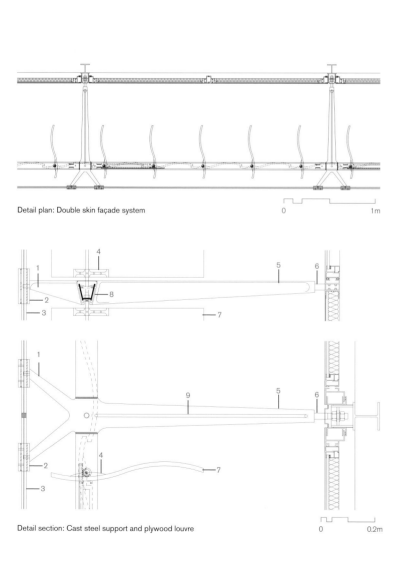

1 The reflection pool and student lounge adjoining the Moot Court. 2 View from the rear of the main auditorium with timber acoustic ceiling and side wall profile. 3 View illustrating the stepped sectional podium with linear glass and timber superstructure raised on columns.

Façade detail, Tyree Energy Technologies Building, University of New South Wales

Theory

Practice, Theory and Intuition

Richard Francis-Jones

Presented at Tectonic Form and Critical Culture, RAIA NSW Chapter Conference, Sydney, NSW, June 19, 2004

Practice

Contemporary architectural practice is far removed from the world of theory. In many ways it is an antithetical world, of high-pressure material action and reaction rather than cerebral reflection. The practitioner inhabits the trenches; the muddy defensive lines which we dig in the field of the instrumental property development and construction industry.

What the architect desperately needs within this environment is time, but of course this is what the industry has sought to remove—speed is its paradigm. Ironically the building processes themselves have changed relatively little: they are not significantly quicker, but the speed and volume of information surrounding the projects have exploded. Projects are now developed within a sea of information. But speed frequently wastes that which we hold most precious and that which it was supposed to overcome—time. We rush more and more hectically, transmit information ever more quickly and in greater volume but paradoxically have less and less time.

Within this world of practice, how does the architect launch the architectural project and thoughtfully respond to contemporary theoretical issues?

Intuition

It is perhaps through the avoidance of thought, through thoughtless action. The drawing of the first line across the site intersects the site with the programme, simultaneously exploring, discovering, and uncovering the project that is in some ways already there.

Thought and theory are ironically sometimes an impediment to understanding; at least the understanding that comes directly through action. Certainly they are impediments to intuition, and intuition is perhaps the primary means through which the architect engages, via the architectural project, with the pressing cultural and theoretical issues of our time.

Intuition is an existential quality: it is beyond the rational. It is rooted in our connection to the world we inhabit; it is our feeling rather than our knowledge. It is a manifestation of the interconnectedness of all things. Remarkably, it is the means for a holistic response to the vastly complex nature of our human condition. It is a response that comes less from us than through us.

But this first intuitive line drawn across the site, this formal concept, must be transformed, constructed, and assembled from materials to become architecture, and this will require direct engagement with the market and industry, with all its limitations, and possibilities.

Engagement

The architect must take this precious intuitive insight and jump into the fast and dangerous flow of the development and construction industry. This is a difficult swim and it is important to know the waters, the rips and the undertow.

The natural flow or outcome of the development and construction industry is not architecture at all, but building, understood as an optimised investment object, minimising cost, utilising standardised conventional techniques and presenting the most market-driven image with the least means and least substance. This is its natural course.

The planning and regulatory environment attempts to mediate this instrumental flow through protection of the public realm, environment and amenity: however, this is necessarily a defensive action and will therefore generally be inherently conservative.

These are the waters into which the architect jumps or is thrown. To assist the near-drowning figure, we will throw them 'architecture' and say "hang onto this, don't let go or you are lost". However, within these waters, the 'architecture' we are saying to hold onto is very heavy, like a lead weight. It does not help at all, but indeed, without it we are lost.

The only way to survive is to find shallower, safer waters in the form of sheltered supportive commissions or to understand the ebb and flow, the tide and character such that we can move with it, while still clinging to our weight, and in doing so perhaps make small changes to the direction of the current.

Theory

The architect gets tired in these waters; our first intuition is behind us now and it can be difficult to know where you are heading, where the shore is. Only when we stop for a moment and step out of the tide that we are trying to swim with or against, will we be able to look back at what it is we are doing, reflect on its nature. And this reflection is vital to understand what it is we do, the values, ethics and meaning behind the work, and how it affects the public good. We need a platform to rest on for a moment.

This is the space of theory; this is the space for which the architect yearns, a temporary rest on a platform. It may still bob around with the current and is not always so comfortable and in the end will though us back in, but without it, without this respite and reflection, we may let go of our heavy load and be lost. This platform is the meeting place between the academy and the profession, and at this moment, at this conference we are in this space, on this platform together. Soon we will be washed off again, but hopefully we will be slightly better swimmers.

Architecture and the Culture of Globalisation

Richard Francis-Jones

Presented at Critical Visions CV08, RAIA National Conference, Sydney, NSW, April 10, 2008

The intensity of contemporary global architectural production is extreme and without precedent.

The seemingly endless formal inventiveness and expressive possibilities of architecture are reaching new dimensions, together with the technology, will, and capital to realise these spectacular explorations, particularly in the fast-growing or oil-rich centres of the globe.

And yet these exciting expressions of apparent optimism and faith in economic growth are taking place at a time of distressing social inequality, cultural conflict and impending environmental crisis.

This is, indeed, an extraordinary moment in the history of architecture. Over the last decades we have witnessed growth and intense industry production across the globe at hard-to-imagine levels. Now, for the first time, more than half of the earth's population lives in cities. The number of city-dwellers is expected to top five billion before 2030, and remarkably China is building a city the size of Brisbane every month.[1,2]

It is hardly surprising then that global architectural practice/culture has become a reality. But what is its nature, and what shared values and social aspirations does it reflect?

During this period, economic growth has been extreme and this vast wealth and prosperity seems reflected in the extraordinary formal expressionism that is coming to identify this architectural moment.

What new, inventive, twisted and distorted form will rise high into the clear skies above Dubai, or into the amber fog over Shanghai, or for that matter, given the equalising nature of globalised development, into the overcast skies above St Petersburg or La Defence?

When we momentarily lift our heads from the multiple forms of global interconnected media washing over us, it does feel a little like we are bathing in a pool of unparalleled excess and formal architectural indulgence—reflecting perhaps an almost religious faith in economic growth and enamour with technology.

Within this culture of globalisation, architecture is exported and imported often as primarily a designer brand to give identity and market value. But what is the nature of the culture behind the commercial imperatives that drive this will to difference and identity?

Most disturbingly, at the same time as we seem to experiment and indulge in this free, inventive and exciting architectural expressionism, all around us is burning.

As Ian McEwen observed, "The sheer pressure of our numbers, the abundance of our inventions, the blind forces of our desires and needs, appear unstoppable and are generating a heat—the hot breath of our civilisation—whose effects we are now beginning to comprehend…"[3]

We are beginning to burn.

Almost every day we read new and more disturbing data on the effects of climate change and the inevitable consequences of our twentieth century complacency.

Our ice is melting; it may already be too late to save the Arctic sea ice and the Greenland ice sheet. By some estimates there will not be any sea ice in the summer months within 25 years from now. Only a few weeks ago the Wilkins Ice Shelf in Antarctica began to collapse and while the winter will seem to hold it for now it is expected to disappear early 2009.[4]

The reduced rainfall in the Amazonian rainforest threatens to claim large areas that will be unable to re-establish themselves. The El Niño climate system will become much more intense with profound effect on weather from Africa to North America.

To avoid an increase in global temperature of more than two Celsius degrees would require rich countries to cut emissions by at least 80 per cent by 2050, with a cut of 30 per cent by 2020. Emissions from developing countries would need to peak around 2020, with cuts of 20 per cent by 2050. This is a truly daunting task.

The United Nations 2007-08 Annual Human Development Report suggests the international community will need to invest two thirds on what is currently spent globally on arms to prevent this temperature rise of two Celcius.[5]

According to the Intergovernmental Panel on Climate Change the world will have to end its high output of carbon emissions within seven years and become mostly free of carbon-emitting technologies in about four decades to avoid killing as many as a quarter of the planets species from global warming.[6]

Another aspect of this disturbing backdrop to our formal architectural propositions is that despite the great wealth and economic growth of recent decades there has been significant increases in social and economic inequity.

More tragic is that the effects of climate change will only reinforce this inequity, as it is the poorer countries that are most vulnerable, although the least responsible. One person in 19 living in the world's poorest countries is at risk from climate dangers compared with one in 1,500 in the rich West.[7]

And yet it is the West that is primarily responsible for this mess: Texas has higher carbon emissions than the whole of sub-Saharan Africa; the average air conditioning unit in Florida emits more carbon dioxide in a year than a person in Afghanistan or Cambodia does in their lifetime; and the average dishwasher emits as much carbon dioxide in a year as three Ethiopians do.

If we consider equality of aspiration to the Western way of life, and turn this the other way a little, imagine for a moment that car ownership in China was equal to the per-capital rate of, say, Japan. There would be 575 million cars in China. This is only 70 million short of the total number of cars in the world today. It certainly does not make the carbon-dioxide reduction targets look any easier.[8]

This great period of economic growth and wealth creation, of progress and development, has not only failed in relation to climate and what it should have delivered in terms of social equity, it has put generous amounts of petrol on the fire.

According to Professor Rod Smith in a recent lecture at the Royal Academy of Engineering, a growth rate of three per cent means economic activity doubles in 23 years, he demonstrates that each successive doubling period consumes as much resources as all the previous doubling

periods combined. Put another way: if our economy grows at three per cent between now and 2040, we will consume in that period economic resources equivalent to all those consumed to date.[9]

This is the scale of the challenge we confront.

There is no doubt about the benefits of economic growth. Although the spoils may not be equitably distributed, growth has brought massive improvements in human welfare, housing, nutrition, medicine and sanitation.

But at what point should it stop?

It is somewhat ironic that it was a former governor of the US Federal Reserve, Henry Wallich who, in defence of our current inequitable economic model, observed, "Growth is a substitute for equality of income. So long as there is growth there is hope, and that makes large income differences tolerable."[10]

Growth is like a false promise of something better that allows an unequal, unjust, and unsustainable economic structure to lead us to our demise.

However, there are the signs of change, with the governor of our own Reserve Bank explained the sacrifices we will need to start making, "One of the things the community will have to accept is that there is a reduction in living standards insofar as our purchasing power over energy-intensive things is concerned."[11]

And perhaps there is a ghost in this economic machine. A financial system based on only free-market principles actually destabilises the health and stability of the capitalism that is its heart.

The current US Bank lead financial crisis will be according to Alan Greenspan be "the most wrenching since the end of the second world war."[12] The US economy is going to be largely trashed through the irresponsibly and greed of its bankers. How big is this, how big is the gap between the debt and the actual, estimate seem to vary between $2–3 trillion, how many banks will go bust? The global economy may wobble. Growth may curtail, slow; the resources consumption doubling delayed, irrespective of our own action or non-action.

All the predictions and disturbing data on climate change are regularly in the newspapers, and, if we can avoid the possible fatigue all this doom and gloom can induce and realise the scale of what we are up against, perhaps we can change.

However, the respected English scientist, James Lovelock– who, in 1962, warned that the greatest problem humanity would face in 2000 would be the environment–believes it is now just too late.

In his latest book The Revenge of Gaia he predicts that by 2020 extreme weather will be the norm, causing global devastation; that by 2040 much of Europe will be desert and parts of London underwater. Our only chance, according to Lovelock, is nuclear power and technology, but our greatest challenge will be food production. Maybe we can synthesise food, maybe, but he thinks not quickly enough and expects about 80 per cent of the world's population to be wiped out by 2100.[13]

So there is something disturbing, although undeniably poetic, in the beautiful, sparkling, attention-seeking architectural forms that rise fast out of the irrigated affluence of the Arabian Desert, all paid for, no doubt, with the oil that is fuelling our global demise.

But it is also this same drive to invent, innovate and create that can possibly shift paradigms and through some kind of lateral move enable us to step around this gaping void at our feet.

It is not just our consumption of resources that grows exponentially.

The pace of advances in technology means that the rate of progress will be 30 times faster in the next half century, opening up the prospects of innovation across all fields.

A think tank of 18 esteemed scientists convened by the US National Academy of Engineering is confident the sun is the tantalising source of all our energy needs: "We only need to capture one part in 10,000. of the sunlight that falls on the Earth to meet 100 per cent of our energy needs." They believe this will become feasible with nano-engineered solar panels and nano-engineered fuel cells.[14]

Already, mass-produced, wafer-thin solar cells printed on aluminium film are rolling off the production line in California by the Nanosolar company. They aim to produce the panels for 99 cents a watt, which is comparable to the price of electricity generated from coal (currently solar is three times as expensive). There is also our own Sliver solar technology, produced by the Australian National University, that is almost on the commercial market. An important advantage with solar is that the energy plants can also be deployed very quickly when compared with coal and nuclear.

The potential of nano-technology is far reaching and offers as significant a transformation as the Industrial Revolution. For example, carbon nanotubes, one hundred times stronger than steel and eight times lighter and capable of being woven into sheets and mixed with composites, alone are likely to revolutionise our construction industry.

Artificial intelligence will also provide enormous future possibilities as "once non-biological intelligence matches the range and subtlety of human intelligence, it will necessarily soar past it because of the continuing acceleration of information-based technologies, as well as the ability of machines to instantly share there knowledge."[15]

It may well be that it is this spirit of global technological embrace, invention and creativity that lies within the exciting formal free expressionism and digital investigations of our contemporary architecture.

However the group of scientists in this think tank also point out that while there may be technological solutions none of the challenges can be met without the economic and political will.

The great challenges of climate change, mass urbanisation and the related social and economic inequity that form a back drop to the architecture of our time are shared, and global in nature. They will require a global multilateral response despite the religious, economic, social and cultural conflicts that hinder such cooperation.

It may be the strength of our emerging global culture that could assist in overcoming the great divides that prevent a unified and essential response to the great challenges that confront us. A global culture of shared values and aspirations possibly united and induced through, as history has illustrated, a great external and mutual threat.

Are we witnessing the beginnings of a new global culture independent of the nation state and the international corporation; a horizontal culture interconnected in social depth through media and free access information technology?

If so, what are the values and aspirations of this nascent globalised culture? And what form could it take beyond a self-referential formalism?

Is a hybridised, plural and specific global culture possible, one that embodies and represents a deeper architecture instead of the mere importation of designer curiosities?

What is the form of a sustainable architecture beyond some accounting of 'green' points? What is the form of an architecture of equity? And when are we going beyond the superficial allure of form and technology to deep and substantial investigations of our field?

At this time of great challenge and opportunity within our increasingly globalised culture, what critical visions can we offer?

1 Thoraya Ahmed Obaid, *State of World Population 2007*, (New York: United Nations Population Fund, 2007).

2 John Cheong Seong Lee, *Will China Fail? The Limits and Contradictions of Market Socialism*, (Sydney: Centre for Independent Studies, 2007).

3 Ian McEwen, "Save the Boot Room" in *Global Sustainability: A Nobel Cause*, ed. Hans Joachim Schellnhuber, (Cambridge University Press: Cambridge, 2010), xviii.

4 Claire Truscott, "Giant Antarctic Ice Shelf Breaks into the Sea," *The Gaurdian*, March 28, 2008.

5 Kevin Watkins, *Human Development Report 2007/08*, (New York: United Nations Development Programme, 2008), 15.

6 R.K Pachauri and A. Reisinger, eds., *Climate Change 2007: Synthesis Report. Contribution of Working Groups I, II and III to the Fourth Assessment Report of the Intergovernmental Panel on Climate Change* (IPCC: Geneva, 2007).

7 Kevin Watkins, *Human Development Report*, 76.

8 "World Development Indicators 2008, "Motor vehicles (per 1,000 people)", The World Bank

9 Roderick Smith, "Carpe Diem: the Dangers of Risk Aversion" 2007 (paper presented at Lloyd's Register Educational Trust Lecture, London, May 29, 2007).

10 Henry C Wallich, "Zero Growth," *Newsweek*, January 24, 1972.

11 Jessica Irvine, "Get Used to Being Greener, Poorer," *Sydney Morning Herald*, April 5, 2008.

12 Alan Greenspan, "We Will Never Have a Perfect Model of Risk," *Financial Times*, March 16, 2008.

13 James Lovelock, *The Revenge of Gaia* (New York: Basic Books, 2007).

14 Carter Phipps, "Envisioning the Future," *EnlightenNext*, June (2009).

15 Ray Kurzweil, *The Singularity Is Near* question and answer supplement, (New York: Viking, 2005).

Architecture Not Language– A Note on Representation

Richard Francis-Jones

Published in *UME* 3 (Melbourne: UME, 1997): 50–51

Issues of representation or meaning in architecture seem to bring such insecurity to architects, theorists and critics alike, that we immediately set off in desperate searches of other fields for credible explanations that can in some way be applied to architecture. This tendency to explain architecture with reference to other arts has been evident since the beginning of the modern period. But in more recent times references— particularly to literary theory—have become normative. Architectural theorists, critics and commentators seem to prefer excursions into literary theory for borrowed insight, rather than genuine investigation into the nature of our art.

Among architects themselves, there is a certain feeling of inadequacy, an embarrassment about our craft to the extent that we envy so-called purer arts that do not suffer the pollution of function or the limitations of construction. This art envy is evident in the projection of architecture as sculpture in the work of such architects as Zaha Hadid and Frank Gehry, and in the proliferation of overworked graphic simulations so prevalent in our numerous publications.

Not that we should be hermetically sealed within architecture: clearly this would be a contradiction of the collective and social nature of our work. But it is necessary to take great care with references and searches outside architecture. There is danger in turning to other arts to seek models and rules, as in this way architecture can be reduced to mere translation, with its subtlety, specificity and complexity consequently obscured.

This is particularly the case in discussion and investigation of the issue of architectural representation, where the turn to literary analogy is most common. Architecture is often discussed in terms of syntax, text, palimpsest, etc., and it is suggested that architecture is a language, or perhaps many languages, as the term "language" in architecture now appears to be synonymous with style. But architecture is not a language. It does not communicate like language. It is not spoken, written or read. It is built, crafted, assembled and inhabited. It is a social and collective endeavour.

This misunderstanding of the representational nature of architecture, so prevalent in contemporary debate, can possibly be traced back to the birth of modernity and the fundamental split, or fracture, in architecture that followed: a fracture that began to separate the surface from construction, intellect from craft, image from the reality of making, and theory from practice.

Perhaps the first signs of this fracture can be located in the work of Leon Battista Alberti (1404–72). Alberti did not rise through the guilds or trades; his interest in architecture was primarily intellectual. His famous treatise on architecture contains no illustrations; architecture was to be thought, idealised and theorised. Alberti placed great emphasis on the idealised representational role of the façade, most clearly illustrated in the Palazzo Rucellai (1446–51) in Florence, where an idealised conception is applied over the actual reality of its assembly and construction. The stone construction of the façade economically conforms to the restriction of the block size and coursing but is completely masked through the application of an independent veneer that geometrically idealises and represents. With the Palazzo Rucellai, the fracture of modern dualism has been made and the space opens between the surface and construction, between the intellectual architect who reads and the master craftsperson who makes, between the idealised image and the reality of its making.

Despite many attempts to repair this fracture in architecture— such as the eighteenth-century Enlightenment search for absolutes and origins within a structural logic[1]—the space of modern dualism continued to open, to the extent that in the nineteenth century architecture was reduced to the conception of a series of ready-made representations of moral and historic ideals: a value-free eclecticism, a veneer of good manners drawn over an instrumental rationality.

But at the beginning of the twentieth century, modern architecture made a heroic attempt to bridge this increasing gap or representational void, through the tearing away of the idealised façade and outright rejection of stylistic and metaphorical devices of tradition. Modern architecture was not viewed as neutral constructions on whose surfaces representation is displayed, but as an autonomous, internal and abstract search for meaning behind reality. Abstract modernism turned inwards, separating from the world of myth and tradition in an autonomous search for truth and Utopia. This search of seemingly absolute formalism was intimately and ideologically connected with the new technology and actual productive forces of society. Although built largely with traditional materials and techniques, modern architecture projected an idealised representation of technology and myth of the new Utopia.[2]

However, after World War II, when the building technologies proposed by modern architecture began to succeed in the realm of production, idealised and rhetorical representations faded. The forms of Modern architecture, seemingly out of ideological necessity, became perfectly transparent to function, pure instruments of the production process. Architecture was reduced to serviced, sealed containers, glazed within the ubiquitous structural frame, barely registering either use or location. This bankruptcy of architectural representation left a void in modern architecture, an absence of content raised to a poetic silence in Mies van der Rohe's Seagram building in New York of 1958.

The "almost nothing" has become a "big glass"… reflecting images of the urban chaos that surrounds the timeless Miesian purity… It accepts [the shift and flux of the phenomena], absorbs them to themselves in a perverse multi-duplication, like a Pop Art sculpture that obliges the American metropolis to look at itself reflected… in the neutral mirror that breaks the city web. In this, architecture arrives at the ultimate limits of its own possibilities. Like the last notes sounded by the Doctor Faustus of Thomas Mann, alienation, having become absolute, testifies uniquely to its own presence, separating itself from the world to declare the world's incurable malady.[3]

After the Seagram building there were some attempts to breath life into this silent emptiness—for example, in the rhetorical worship of structure and desperate display of services in works by high tech architects: artificial life-support systems strapped to neutral constructions in the hope that some sign of meaning would emerge.

However, the bridge of the modern project that offered some hope of restoring the fracture in architecture seemed too difficult to cross. The modern project was abandoned and the separation that brought this crisis of representation was embraced. The multiple languages of post-modernism filled the silence and covered the modern emptiness. Architecture returned to the convenience of a separation

most clearly expressed in Robert Venturi's concept of the 'decorated shed': idealised, clever and witty representations were applied to neutral constructions—a system admirably suited to contemporary production methods and speculative development. This is the period of multiple architectural languages, over-intellectualism and extensive borrowing from literary theory: loud, scenographic representations of little or no tangible meaning or significance, completely separated from the craft of architecture.

Furthermore, the predominance of the photographic image over the built reality, and the publication over the work, in contemporary architectural culture increases this separation of surface from construction, image from reality, theory from practice.

Our contemporary pluralism of architectural languages seems a little like the ill-fated Tower of Babel. The project of architecture collapses and disappears beneath the multiple languages that merely talk architecture.

It is therefore necessary to understand architectural representation beyond this intellectual separation. Architecture is not really like language; it is not read like text. It is at once more direct and ambiguous: it is an art that we inhabit. Architecture's representational force derives from the way it frames and orients us in relation to the world. It is perhaps most accurately understood as the proposition of alternative realities within reality, worlds within the world.[4]

In architecture, representations of reality are explored and postulated through the formal relations of the building and the reality of its making—not merely through the surface application of an idealised image but through the spatial organisation, formal order, structure, construction and specific relation with the site and interpretation of the programme.

Thus, the representational nature, or meaning, in architecture does not depend on its stability, function or the efficiency of the means of its production, but on the way in which all of these have been limited and subordinated or transformed by purely formal requirements. Purpose is therefore not a restrictive condition that compromises our art, but an integral element of specific representation.

1 Eighteenth-century neo-classicism, in its rejection of the surface emphasis of the Rococo, developed a series of diverse attempts to bridge the gap of modern dualism. These investigations ranged from Jacques-Francois Blondel's (1705–74) proposition of Caractere as the expressive function of a building, and Abbe Marc-Antoine Laugier's (1713–60) proposition of the primitive hut as the origin of all possible forms of architecture (together with his emphasis on structural logic and a new concept of functional ism that was more systematically developed by Carlo Ladoli), to Giovanni Battista Piranesi's (1720–78) pursuit of the sublime, and the visionary searches for meaning of Etienne-Louis Boullee and Claude-Nicolas Ledoux.

2 The restricted role of the new technology in the social and cultural project of modernism is examined in an essay by Alan Colquhoun, "Symbolic and Literal Aspects of Technology," *Architectural Design*, November (London: Wiley, 1962): 508–09.

3 Manfredo Tafuri and Francesco Dal Co, *Modern Architecture* (Milan: Electra Editrice, 1976), 314.

4 This understanding of (classical) architecture as a temenos, "as a world within the world," is examined and analysed by Alexander Tzonis and Liane Lefraivre in *Classical Architecture: the Poetics of Order*, (Cambridge: MIT Press, 1986).

Architectural representations should not simply present a record or expression of reality, but should provide critical frames within which to understand our human condition. The presence of conflict in our society should be acknowledged, together with the need for social criticism and social engagement of architecture as a critical activity. We shall therefore be made aware of the conditions of our lives through the construction of alternative realities within which things are reset in a slightly different order.

Architectural representation becomes the making of critical frames in which to understand reality, a formal means of cognitive effect, with an ethical and social purpose.

This is far removed from individual acts of personal expression or the generation of recognisable personal styles. Critical representations are not simplistic statements of the world's contradictions and conflict, nor false reassurances of our well being. Social contradictions should not merely be stated, but should be critically examined and resolutions sought.

Finally, it is important to emphasise architectural representation not as a separate intellectual act of idealism but as relative and specific investigations. Meaning in architecture does not come from the work's detachment from the world, but from the way it frames and transforms as an extension of its site and ethical interpretation of its social purpose.

Zeitgeist, Nostalgia and the Search for Authenticity

Richard Francis-Jones

Presented at NZIA Professional Development Day, Wellington, May 25, 2007
Published in "Time Regained," *ArchitectureNZ* 4 (Auckland: AGM, 2007): 26–30

The Mint project in Macquarie Street, Sydney, is neither a project of restoration or reversion to an idealised past nor a frozen notion of a perfect architectural moment. There is no blind reinstatement of the past, and no nostalgia. Or, is there? What is this romance with the ruin? Why not tidy it up, clean up those edges and remove the scars and wounds? And what of the Zeitgeist? Are these new, refined modern interventions the culture of our time? What of a vision for the future?

The Zeitgeist and nostalgia are about time: two opposite poles, perhaps, of an attitude to time, but in fact closer together than first appears. The Zeitgeist (so frequently the catch-cry of the avant-garde) and nostalgia (so beloved of conservatives) are both a resistance to time—to the flowing, equalising continuous motion of moments and events that is time. One wants to forget, fight and resist the pull of the past, thinking that it itself will never become past. The other wants desperately to remember what is already lost, longs for the security of the past, for what is known.

The shining flight of the Zeitgeist and the grounded melancholy of nostalgia. So-called architectural heritage so often struggles under the weight of nostalgia; it turns its back, hoping it can forever resist time. Go back and restore what has been compromised or damaged. Seek comfort and meaning in our history. But I want to discuss in more detail the language of its disaffected twin, the Zeitgeist, the avant-garde, and also the contemporary context that has given rise to these quarrelling siblings. Appropriation, sampling, infection, parasitic morphing and palimpsest: what do we mean by these terms in an architectural context?

Are they a repackaging of terms such as quotation, reference, interpretation—20 year-old terms recycled and updated from 1980s postmodernism? Or is this the language of the avant-garde, the critical edge of our culture, adopting the partial strategy of 'infecting' the conservative, obese body of our moribund society? Inviting us to scratch that itch and spread the virus, only to find that it is deadly, kills the host or, better, transforms it like some Hegelian anti-thesis into a purer new form. The heroic task of the avant-garde then seems complete—only once more to be morphed into a new parasite, creating innovative infection, immune to the new cultural antibiotic, immune to our defences.

Is there a meaningful difference between these two possibilities? Is there really a political dimension to what is behind these terms, beyond that of the conservative maintenance and updating of syntax that is essential to our free market consumer culture and political slumber? Recently I was reading the novel *Cosmopolis* by the American author Don DeLillo. The protagonist, Eric Packer, is a young multi-billionaire. Almost the entire novel is set within his stretch limo, which cruises through Manhattan as his money moves around the world at unimaginable speeds, and the Yen stays high, losing him millions each minute. As the car moves into Times Square Eric and his "chief of theory", Vija Kinski (yes, he has a theory advisor), are caught in a violent anti-globalisation protest.[1]

The only people undisturbed by the protest are those queuing for cheap tickets, consumers steadfast to the end. On the TV screens in his bullet-proof limo Eric watches the protest raging outside; it makes more sense on TV The protestors are rocking the car and urinating on it. Tear gas wafts through the air as police in riot gear and protestors clash. At this moment his theorist explains that the protesters and their violence are desirable; they are an integral and necessary part of the system they wish to destroy. The protestors are market-produced, they energise and perpetuate a total system; their actions fundamentally change nothing. In the riot, DeLillo writes, there was "a shadow of transaction" between protestors and the body politic. Violent protest is characterised as "a form of systemic hygiene". The market is, without doubt, the greatest appropriator, absorbing all into a single valuation system. What is our human relationship to this market? Where are we? What space do we occupy?

Well, alienation no longer seems to bother us; we accept and indulge in our isolation and separateness. We are suspended within disconnected, universalising zones of consumption and mobility, freed from the weight of content and meaning. We sate ourselves with appearances, efficiency, image and interest rates. Only the most extreme acts of transgression, of human violence and environmental vandalism, will momentarily disturb us from our abstract flotation. We are imbued with the ideology of globalisation, to the extent that we are primarily shareholders or subjects of the free market, rather than citizens of the state.

Information overwhelms us, but we understand less and less. Information, the ultimate commodity, moves between us at incredible speeds. The velocity at which information travels is now over 500,000 times the rate at which people and goods move, but we are still frustrated. We want it faster. Speed and Efficiency are our masters; we're all living longer but we have less and less time. We must change, keep changing, and be faster. Speed and information are our obsessions, yet speed frequently wastes that which we hold most precious, and that which it was supposed to overcome: time.

This is our postmodern world, dominated by the angel of speed, and the ideologies of efficiency and the free market, it is a world of consumerist obsession, wherein our needs are so completely transformed and distorted through ideology and advertising that we only need what is current, follow the dictators of fashion and measure the success of Christmas through consumer spending.

But back to DeLillo's novel for a moment. The violent confrontation between the protestors and the police is interrupted by an extreme action, the kind of transgression I was referring to earlier, that stops everything for a brief moment. Everything except, of course, the media news crews. Cameras quickly refocus from the police special forces and protestors to this new spectacle. A man has sat down with his legs crossed on the footpath, covered himself in gasoline and set himself alight. His glasses melt into his face, his flesh turns black and bubbles and all is momentarily frozen in horror. Our multi-billionaire sees all this live through the limo's windows and also, in more real from, on the multiple flat screens inside. He turns to his theory chief for an interpretation, only to be told that even this extreme act is lacking, is not original—it's "appropriation". Remember those Vietnamese monks?

Of course appropriation is all about context. Take the burning man off a Manhattan street, place him in Baghdad or the West Bank, and we would barely bat an eyelid. It probably wouldn't even make the news. In 2001, 3,000 people died in Lower Manhattan in a single day but on that same day, the United Nations reports that approximately 30,000 children under the age of five suffered preventable deaths from causes such as malnutrition, starvation and lack of basic health care.[2] Appropriation is about context. Does this change the content, the meaning?

Duchamp's tired, old, appropriated toilet in the gallery certainly scandalises no one anymore, nor for that matter does a cow cut in half or a shark's head. How about a dead foetus in a gallery? Is it a problem? Is it even interesting? What happens to these objects? These ready-mades? Do they infect and transform the space of the gallery, or are they transformed by the host, rarefied and commodified? Bits of dead animals, stamped with the signature of the artist: valued investments absorbed and transformed by the market, pulling in the crowds, getting in the papers, part of what makes it all go around.

What happens when art objects are removed from these rarefying enclosures? Every summer in Sydney sculpture is arranged, often precariously, at the edge of the sea between Bondi and Bronte. One such object was a broad overlapping bowl of water placed on a rock overlooking the ocean. The surface of this captured water reflected the sky and the clouds, measuring the passing of time. The work, in a sense, was made of the very site in which it was displayed—immune to the gradual rise in interest rates, or the persistently high levels of the yen or, for that matter, the name of the artist and the notes in the catalogue.

The main gathering room of our project at the Mint could be anywhere; it is entirely autonomous. It is suspended on columns, over the archaeology of the very machinery for the production of money. The wave shape of the ceiling above—is it a device to orientate the room, a metaphor of shelter and sky, a random gesture, or the sign of the press of the books and artefacts stored in the repository above? The louvres, opening panels and sliding glass could open out to the a view of the harbour (after all, it is Sydney), or native bushland, but in fact opens to the courtyard honouring the rear—much altered and almost accidental—façade of the Mint offices.

The proportions, plan, section and volume of this timber box could have resulted from a clear analysis of the brief and the requirements for an auditorium, but the brief was, in fact, for a larger flexible black-box, raked auditorium. The actual constructed proportions match exactly those of the adjacent superintendent's pavilion—it is its antithesis, its matching opposite, its sister. Is this room autonomous, or entirely dependent? Is this an intervention, an adaptation, an infection, or the result of our interrogation of the site? If appropriation is all about context, what is ours? What is our contemporary architectural landscape?

Certainly it is intimately linked to the processes and ideology of globalisation. The symbolism and metaphorical allusions of the late 20th century seems to have been, on the one hand, abandoned and, on the other, formally updated with a revised digital shape making. The seeming abandonment of representation is manifested in an endless series of neutral expressionless boxes, layered in varying transparent surfaces to give an illusion of visual depth, together a seemingly conscious lack of substance. The almost uniform anonymity and homogeneity that results is rarely raised to the poetic. Is this work a deliberate 'transparent' presentation of our condition as it is, void of any rhetoric of history, place or ideology, a critical poetic of absence and alienation stripped of any pretence of meaning? Or is it merely a thoughtless and pragmatic reflection of our consumerism and a market-driven globalisation: an architecture reduced to an obsessive fetish of the surface.

These anonymous silent enclosures being reproduced around the globe are juxtaposed with the apparently free expressionism of digitally manipulated sculptural surfaces and forms. Then there are also the morphed digital images, fractured and random, that we could somehow easily imagine sliding from our flat screen 3D software, and wrapping the shopping centre or the service station or the car park and airport. These are ideal programmes to receive such artistically loaded forms. They are desperate for an update; it is essential to the nature and the continued commercial health of these places of consumption. A slick and even challenging new packaging, the cooler the better.

Both tendencies have in common a focus on the surface and a reductionist or complacent attitude to the poetic of architectural assembly and construction, as well as a seeming indifference to the specifics of place. Hence, we see both side by side in publications. The context of this work is a world now characterised by non-place, pseudo-public realms and consumption disguised as community and individual expression. It may be that the expanding horizon of our knowledge and extension of our possibilities though the electronic media make the world, in a sense, more accessible, more familiar, but at the same time this extended territory is less and less meaningful.

All the more, we experience a zone or space where we interface or intersect in some fleeting social simulation at speed, rather than experience of a place as somewhere to be in and meet. Airports, shopping malls, hotels and other transit zones are non-places, of consumption and mobility, encouraging thoughtless, constant action, and offering no moment nor place to stay. We have an overwhelming amount of information, space, stimulation, simulation and individualisation, but so little sense of being, community or place, and so little time.

How does architecture escape this seemingly endless cycle of market-driven flux and meaningless inventive repackaging? How can the work avoid reduction to consumer artefact, either in the form of decorated speculative investment such as icon apartments, or constant new suburban images for the wealthy, or the spectacular object to brand a new institution, corporation or city—Disney or Bilbao?

First, is it a problem at all? What are we really so worried about? Just join the party, get into the language, stick to the surface, and if you have a occasional feeling of anxiety of disconnection or isolation, try watching TV or even try buying something you don't need, or focus on the problem of interest rates… All this works, we know that for sure. But to actually resist the market appropriation, the mere packaging and repackaging and consumer updating of syntax, we can only have partial strategies. Perhaps integral to such a partial strategy is the concept of place. Remember that one of the most commonly asked questions to those we meet for the first time is, Where are you from? The place where we live is among our most defining features. Yes, we build these towns and cities filled with the buzz of human inhabitation, but equally the place makes us, builds our character, determines us at the same time as we continue to build and transform the place. There's a symbiotic mutual transformation—or infection, if you prefer.

The character of the natural and built landscape actually does hold great significance for us. It figures our settlements and ceremonies. Places assume a sacred nature though our relationship with them. We build not only in relations to water supply, shelter and other pragmatic benefits of landform but in relation to more spiritual forces that the landscape holds for humanity. Uluru is the most significant cultural and spiritual place in Australia, and this has nothing to do with the intervention of humanity, indigenous or European

1 Don DeLillo, *Cosmopolis* (London: Picador Pan Macmillan, 2004).

2 Carol Bellamy, *The State of the World's Children 2001* (New York: UNICEF, 2001).

settlement, nothing to do with shelter, access to fresh water or other pragmatic issues of comfort and economy. Its presence moves us, connects us with the world, and allows us to somehow experience something outside ourselves, a profound interconnection.

But most places acquire meaning and cultural significance through human use, ceremony and transformation. Places assume a sacred nature though our relationship with them. This is perhaps what we should mean when we talk of heritage, the transforming of a site into a place of meaning: the creation of a deep interconnection that extends beyond a single generation. Not age as such, nor the profile of a cornice, but the embodiment of our values and ceremonies that connect us to place. Our attention could, and should, be focused on a deeper understanding of the place in which we build. Our work can become a transformation of the site, of the place; it can uncover a potential, an energy already inherently within the very fabric of the site: the dirt, the breeze and landscape of the place. The work may be considered as a kind of meditation on place.

But how is such a meditation on the site possible within the circumstances of contemporary practice? We all know that the natural flow or outcome of the development and construction industry is not architecture at all, but building, understood as an optimised investment object, minimising cost, utilising standardised conventional techniques and presenting the most market driven image with the least means and least substance. This is the industry's natural course. How can the architect even think within this noise of production and pressures, of the development and building industry, fashion, talks and publications? Let alone respond authentically and actually read or meditate on the site.

It is perhaps though the avoidance of thought, through thought-less action. The drawing of the first line across the site intersects the site with the programme simultaneously exploring, discovering, and uncovering the project that is in some ways is already there. Thought and theory are ironically sometimes an impediment to understanding, at least to an understanding that comes directly through action. Certainly they are impediments to intuition, and intuition is perhaps the

primary means through which the architect engages, via the architectural project, with the pressing cultural and theoretical issues of our time. Intuition is in some respects the opposite of thought; it goes around the cognitive limitations of thought. It is through intuition that the limitations of time can be overcome, as intuition requires no time, it is immediate. Time and thinking may in fact block this creative insight.

Intuition is an existential quality; it is beyond the rational. It is rooted in our connection to the world we inhabit; it is our feeling rather than our knowledge. It is a manifestation of the interconnectedness of all things. Remarkably, it is the means for a holistic response to the vastly complex nature of our human condition. And it is a response less from us than through us. Surprising and radical possibilities emerge. Perhaps, even the possibility to open a space for us to pause, to escape momentarily the speed, flux and superficiality of our lives.

I take a seat on the bus. I am late. I am behind in my work. My family needs more time from me. I am surrounded by blank, tired faces and advertising. The seat is uncomfortable. I am struggling under the burden of everyday existence. I place headphones in my ears and the sounds of Phillip Glass or Mahler fills my head. Or I begin to read the words of David Malouf or Milan Kundera. Slowly a space opens for me to climb into. Freed from the environment of the bus, the uncomfortable seat, the crowd. The dreadful limits of my own existence are overcome in some way, for a moment. The interconnectedness of the world is revealed in some form. As I get of the bus I begin to see things differently; although I am still late, I am no longer rushing. I see the sky rather than the advertising. I feel the wind. I see in faces lives being lived. But only for a moment. The world will soon again close in.

Architecture can also create these moments, through the way it frames and orientates us in relation to the world. This is perhaps most accurately understood as the proposition of alternative realities within reality, worlds within the world. We are made aware of the conditions of our lives through the construction of alternative realities within which things are reset in a slightly different order. Finally, our art is the making of these critical frames through which we attempt to reconcile our place in the world on an emotional and spiritual level.

The [Im]Possibility of Slowness

A note on globalisation, ideology and speed in contemporary architecture

Richard Francis-Jones

Published in *UME* 13 (Melbourne: UME, 1999): 10–13

May I lead you to the shores of a mountain lake? The sky is blue, the water green and everything is profoundly peaceful. Mountains and clouds are reflected in the lake, and so are houses, farmyards, courtyards and chapels. They do not seem man-made, but more like the product of God's workshop, like the mountains and trees , the clouds and the blue sky. And everything breathes beauty and tranquillity.

Ah, what is that? A false note in this harmony. Like an unwelcome scream. In the centre, beneath the peasants' homes which were created not by them, but by God, stands a villa: Is it the product of a good or a bad architect? I do not know, I only know that peace, tranquillity and beauty are no more. Why does the architect both good and bad violate the lake…[1]

— Adolf Loos

Trivial

Quentin Tarantino, the writer and director of two brilliant films, *Reservoir Dogs* and *Pulp Fiction*, is rightly acclaimed as one of the most promising filmmakers of our time. Tarantino has detected that speech at speed becomes abstract, a kind of self-referential game. He presents our conversation as a language game centred around consumerist trivia and product obsession and illustrates our exceptional ability to say nothing in this game, at voluble length.

Interlaced within these flat, continuous and humorous language games, and seemingly almost more trivial than the content of our conversations, are acts of extreme violence, which disturbingly somehow also seem funny.

This distinctive mix of immediacy, consumerist obsession and extreme violence skilfully woven by Tarantino is a defining product of the *fin de siécle*. His work may indeed represent the final stage of postmodernism, where an art work is emptied of all content, stripped of politics, metaphysics, and moral and ethical interest. Tarantino mirrors the conditions and values of postmodern existence: a contemporary life disconnected from the concreteness of existence, where we can be more interested in the price of consumables than in the question of being.

More

The cultural context of our contemporary postmodern crises is evident in the emphasis on the signifier over the signified, on language over being. We have rejected the Utopian meta-theories of modernism, with its logocentric domination of metaphysics, as oppressive ideology, and we seem to have overcome modernity's existential crisis through simple acquiescence in our alienation. Ironically, we have done this at the same time as recuperating the imagery of modernism.

Alienation no longer bothers us: we accept and indulge in our isolation and separateness. We are suspended within disconnected, universalising zones of consumption and mobility, freed from the weight of content and meaning, absorbing ourselves with appearances, efficiency, image and interest rates. Only the most extreme acts of transgression, of human violence and environmental vandalism, momentarily disturb us in our abstract flotation.

We are imbued with the ideology of globalisation, inflation and technology to the extent that we are primarily shareholders or subjects of the free market, rather than citizens of the state. Information overwhelms us, yet we understand less and less. Information has become the ultimate commodity. It travels now at over 500,000 times the velocity at which people and goods move, but we are still frustrated: we want it faster.

Internet

For a price all can now have their say in the ultimate abstract realm of communication, the Internet, a worldwide structure of communication connecting (and isolating) everyone—as does the world market—into an identical system. And yet this vast network leaves virtually no physical traces. While the Internet provides everyone with an opportunity to speak, is this freedom of speech, democracy, or merely a Babel-fest where everyone can equally have their say and be ignored?

Speed

Speed and information are our obsessions, and hardly anyone actually makes anything anymore. While architects deal in information and don't actually make anything either, our entire purpose and meaning depend on fabricating/building. What is the impact of the angel of speed?

Building processes themselves have changed relatively little: they are not significantly quicker, but the speed and volume of information surrounding architectural projects have exploded. Buildings are now developed within a sea of information: more and more and more information is required to construct a building, and despite the apparent speed at which it travels, the sheer volume of information now more than consumes anytime saved. Submissions, responses, quality assurance, just-in-time management: more information engulfs our projects, but to what end? Is the work better or even quicker, or is it more compromised, more wasteful?

Speed frequently squanders what we hold most precious and what it is intended to overcome—time. We rush ever more hectically, transmit information ever more quickly and in greater volume, but paradoxically we also have less and less time. Any time that may be saved is to be quickly invested in the consumption of new goods or indeed in the production or processing of more information. Speed, Change and Efficiency are now values in themselves: ends rather than means.

Our postmodern world is a world of consumerist obsession where needs are so completely transformed and distorted by ideology and advertising, and through technology, that we only want what is current, follow the dictates of fashion, and measure the success of Christmas through consumer spending.

Quentin Tarantino perfectly expresses this all, demonstrating that what is of interest to us is not any loss of being but the quality of the coffee or the speed and efficiency with which we can clean out the car.

So what is the place of architecture and culture, if it is not wholly integrated into this market system of consumerist products?

Postmodernisms

The architectural landscape of the contemporary postmodern condition seems to be emerging from a period of heterogeneity. Within the last ten years there is evidence that the emphasis of contemporary work has moved from context, history, identity, art envy and directions in French philosophy towards a greater homogeneity and universality that may be related to the processes of globalisation. Central to this development in contemporary architecture is an apparent return to Modernism, or perhaps a neo-modernism, universal to the extent that it may need to be considered as a new cultural dominant.

Within this pervasive cultural dominant there remain residual and varied directions or styles, all granted a certain equivalence and each servicing particular market demands.

Still commercially popular is historical postmodernism, either in the form of a kind of neo-metropolis in the city, or the falsely reassuring images common to residential suburbs. There are various forms of deconstructivist postmodernism, with their destabilising images now assuming a high-art market value. deconstructivist postmodernism may reflect more accurately our present condition; but while historical postmodernism, with its comforting and familiar images, may be falsely reassuring, we have to consider that the destabilising images of deconstructivism are no longer received, nor intended, as critical. Much of this work has failed to move beyond literal architectural interpretations of complex constructs borrowed from contemporary philosophy, so frequently presented as literal formal fragments, oblique angles or folds. In this guise, the ultimate form of expression is the exhibition, the conference paper, the printed or electronic image. Even more than historical postmodernism, which retained a populist ideal, deconstructivist postmodernism is projected as high art for the elite.

Recently it has been suggested, primarily by Charles Jencks, that a new form of postmodernism derived from developments of nonlinearity in mathematics and science is the correct avant garde. This is an architecture inspired by nonlinear dynamical systems and chaos theory, so-called new science (although not so new). Eisenman, Libeskind, Cehry, and Ashton Raggatt McDougall are all apparently exponents of this New Science-Postmodernism.[2]

Despite the apparent variety in direction, these postmodernisms focus primarily on the signifier, on the immediacy of experience: there is a neutral attitude towards content. With very few exceptions, architecture is projected as image, surface effects drawn over neutral constructions, with the various directions and styles competing for consumption in the market modernism?

But what of the seeming return to modernism or neo-modernism—or perhaps both within this pluralist postmodernism? Is there really a return to the modern project of human emancipation and liberation, and what possible relevance can it have to postmodern existence? Or is this return to modernity better understood as merely the predictable swing of the pendulum of fashion: a retro-modernism exploiting ironic nostalgia for a century almost past? Or an updating of syntax relative to market opportunity, acknowledging the reduction of architecture to commodity, style, or designer-product: more form than content? Is this return to modernity simply reflective of a general exhaustion with the endless images of a postmodernism that now seems fleeting, more difficult and weaker than we first imagined? In other words, have we just given up and gone back to what we know, what we know failed, but what we know nevertheless?

Contradiction

In any event, what of the irony of a return to modernity: how can it be possible, when returning contradicts the essence of modernity? modernity by its nature is directed towards the future. It overtakes the present. The avant garde is by definition forward and must not risk turning from the future to look back on the wreckage. Is not a return to modernity a contradiction in terms?

Contemporary international modernism is, without doubt, a reaction against the various incantations of postmodernism; but also it seems linked to the processes and ideology of globalisation and the associated homogeneity. Much of this work is characterised by fully-glazed, expressionless building forms, neutral boxes projecting an insubstantial transparency and a conscious lack of substance. Rendered to the level of the poetic though careful detailing, these works frequently project a deliberate homogeneity and anonymity. Symbolism and metaphorical allusion, so fundamental to postmodernism, are foregone in lieu of a fetish of surface and material. It may be that market forces, globalisation and consumerism are now

being expressed without the rhetoric of place, history or radical protest, and without any false pretence of meaning; and this may represent a first step towards a more authentic and critical contemporary architecture, or merely a simple acquiescence.

The context of the neo-modern is a contemporary world characterised by non-place, pseudo-public realms and consumption disguised as community or individual expression. Perhaps the expanding horizon of information and knowledge, and the extension of possibilities though the electronic media, make the world, in a sense, more accessible, more familiar; but at the same time, this extended territory is less and less meaningful. More and more often we experience a zone or space where we interface in some fleeting social simulation, at speed, rather than experience a place in which it is simply possible to be and to meet. Airports, shopping malls, hotels and other transit zones are non-places of consumption and mobility, encouraging thoughtless, constant action and offering no moment or place to stay. Even our image-conscious apartment/retail complexes are more investment locations, designer products, and frames in which to be seen rather than places to actually be.

We have an overwhelming amount of information, space, stimulation, simulation, individualisation, and speed, but so little sense of being, community or place, and so little time.

Ideology and the Seagram Building

Of all the arts, architecture has the most direct and unmediated relationship with the economy and society itself. While Western society has experienced many changes and transformations since the Industrial Revolution, the basic organising and overriding principle of social and economic life has remained the capitalist production of profit. The attraction of capitalism is not difficult to understand: the private accumulation of wealth and individualism are powerful influences, and capitalist modernisation has achieved real and positive gains for society. This includes reduction of nature-imposed necessities, contact between different societies through the formation of the world market, and new cultural possibilities brought about by the stimulation of new wants and needs, and perhaps most important, the possibility of wealth and access to technology.

However, all this has been achieved at considerable cost to humanity—in the forms of violence, oppression, and the destruction of traditions—as the valuation of all activity has been reduced to the calculation of profit. All fixed, fast-frozen relations, with their train of ancient and venerable prejudices and opinions, are swept away, all new-formed ones become antiquated before they can ossify. All that is solid melts into air, all that is holy is profaned.[3]

The massive upheavals, social violence and conflicts of capitalism were mediated through the operation of ideology—ideology understood as a distortion of reality, or justifying mask to specific interests, or perhaps best as Hal Foster suggests, the limitation of thought in such a way that social conflicts and historical contradictions are magically resolved. The bourgeois revolutionary slogan liberty, equality and fraternity ,for instance, or the scientific positive secularism of the nineteenth century, are examples of ideology, as is our more recent corporatist ideology of the market place, with its miraculous cure-all, world trade.Think of the unquestioning, almost religious zeal with which we pursue privatisation and globalisation. "Debt as the devil" and "Kill inflation" are the catch-cries of this line of socioeconomic myth-making that glorifies the service economy and legitimises financial speculation. The consequences of such ideology are an oppressive conformity and passivity: it is the market that makes the decisions. At its command we are prepared to disassemble, cut and restructure our social systems. If the will of the market requires us to abandon a town or abandon a community, so be it.

However, a quite separate reconciliation of the human conflicts within capitalism is attempted by culture. Throughout the late nineteenth century and early twentieth century, culture's attempts to reconcile the irreconcilable frequently either confronted or tried to compensate the modern alienated condition.

As Franca Moretti remarks: "While capitalist society is unthinkable without the scientific and technical progress reflected in the separation of intellect and morality, it is equally unthinkable without the incessant attempt to annul that separation and remedy it, an attempt to which the extraordinary and apparently inexplicable proliferation of aesthetic activities that distinguishes capitalism bears witness."[4]

During the modernist period, the critical reconciliation offered by art and architecture maintained its separation from the instrumental operation of ideology only through turning inwards and exploring increased abstraction in an attempt to get behind the surface and the immediate to reveal essential meaning.

However, as art and architecture became increasingly withdrawn, capitalism—through the development of the mass media, advertising and technology—began to penetrate previously uncommodified areas, to the extent that in late-twentieth-century advanced capitalism, culture is no longer a separate reconciliatory and, possibly, critical force, but is fully integrated in the operation of capital. Culture is commodified and extended through the mass media and advertising to penetrate our unconscious. Such a complete infestation of commodiflcation may even allow the disappearance of ideology, as Jameson observes: "The practices of consumption and consumerism themselves become enough to reproduce and legitimise the system, no matter what 'ideology' you happen to be committed to. No abstract ideas, beliefs, ideologies, or philosophical systems, but rather immanent practices of daily life may now occupy the functional position of 'ideology' within a purified Advanced Capitalism."[5]

The point at which Modern abstraction, and the ability of architecture and culture to be a reconciliatory force independent of capitalist ideology, reached its limit can be precisely located with the construction of the Seagram Building on Park Avenue, New York, in 1958.

As revealed by Manfredo Tafuri:

The "almost nothing" became a "big glass"…reflecting images of the urban chaos that surrounds the timeless Miesian purity…It accepts [the shift and flux of phenomena], absorbs them to themselves in a perverse multi-duplication, like a Pop Art sculpture arrives at the ultimate limits of its own possibilities. Like the last notes sounded by the Doctor Faustus of Thomas Mann, alienation, having become absolute, testifies uniquely to its own presence, separating itself from the world to declare the world's incurable malady.[6]

What does this mean for our contemporary so-called return to modernity? How do the minimalist images of our postmodern neo-modernism relate to the confrontation of Mies van der Rohe's sublime declaration of our poverty?

Paradigm

One of the great paradigms of modernity that changed dimension around this decisive moment is speed. For modernity at the beginning of the century, speed was like the machine: a symbol, an expression of progress and confidence in the future. Slipstreams, aerodynamic forms, buildings firmly in the ground yet given the visual potential to accelerate. An aesthetic of speed projected an image or poetic vision of a reality not yet present, a poetic anticipation of the effect of modernisation and technology.

But speed lost its poetic relevance as high-speed trains, cars, rockets and aeroplanes brought with them pollution, environmental damage, energy crises, urban degradation, gridlock, etc. The speed of people and machines that was the obsession and symbol of Modernity gave way, as did modernism itself, to the speed of information in our present postmodern age.

But what is the speed of architecture? Is it not generally stationary and seeking some kind of permanence? Or is architecture—reduced to the surface skin of a neutral construction to be updated with fashion—travelling at a market-driven speed, where occasionally, if neglected long enough, it will become fashionable again as the latest retro-style? Or can such a reduction of architecture to a consumerable be resisted?

And what, if there was a modernist poetic aesthetic of speed, could possibly be a poetic aesthetic of slowness?

If speed rarely saves time, why do we thirst for speed and treat slowness with contempt? Milan Kundera gives us a possible explanation: "The man hunched over his motorcycle can focus only on the present instant of his flight; he is caught in a fragment of time cut off from both the past and the future; he is wrenched from the continuity of time; he is outside time; in other words he is in a state of ecstasy. In that state he is unaware of his age, his wife, his children, his worries, and so he has no fear, because the source of fear is in the future, and a person freed of the future has nothing to fear.

Speed is the form of ecstasy the technical revolution has bestowed on man. As opposed to a motorcyclist, the runner is always present in his body, forever required to think about his blisters, his exhaustion; when he runs he feels his weight, his age, more conscious than ever of himself and of his time of life. This all changes when man delegates the faculty of speed to a machine: from then on, his own body is outside the process, and he gives over to a speed that is non-corporeal, non-material, pure speed, speed itself, ecstasy speed.

And later: "There is a secret bond between slowness and memory, between speed and forgetting. Consider this utterly commonplace situation: a man is walking down the street. At a certain moment, he tries to recall something, but the recollection escapes him. Automatically, he slows down. Meanwhile, a person who wants to forget a disagreeable incident he has just lived through starts unconsciously to speed up his pace, as if he were trying to distance himself from a thing still too close to him in time.

In existential mathematics, that experience takes the form of two basic equations: the degree of slowness is directly proportional to the intensity of memory; the degree of speed is directly proportional to the intensity of forgetting.[7]

A profound fear and need to forget explain our obsession with speed. We rush to forget our loss of being, to forget our lost sense of dwelling, to forget our homelessness and our alienation. We speed because we have nowhere to stop.

Homelessness

Non-dwelling is now the essential characteristic of contemporary life. The home and dwelling are past, are no longer possible. Developing from this, only a contemporary architecture that reflects the impossibility of dwelling can succeed in obtaining a form of authenticity. A silent architecture such as that of Mies van der Rohe may escape ideology and mystification though a supreme indifference to dwelling, a poetic testament to its absence.

The Farnsworth house in Illinois constructed in 1950, before the Seagram Building, is a clear acknowledgement of our non-dwelling. Here, liberated humanity is suspended

1 Adolf Loos, *Architecture* (1910).

2 Charles Jencks, "Nonlinear Architecture: New Science = New Architecture?" in *Architectural Design* 67/9 (London: Wiley, 1997).

3 Karl Marx, *Communist Manifesto* (1848).

4 Franco Moretti, *Signs Taken for Wonders* (London: Verso, 2005), 30.

5 Frederic Jameson, "Architecture and the Critique of Ideology" in *Architecture Criticism Ideology*, ed. Joan Ockman (Princeton: Princeton University Press, 1985), 77.

6 Manfredo Tafuri and Francesco Dal Co, *Modern Architecture* (Milan: Electa Editrice, 1976), 314.

7 Milan Kundera, *Slowness* (London: Faber & Faber, 1996).

from the world in which it can no longer dwell. The sparse and purified platforms permit no masks of comforting self-deception but instead confront us with the reality of our estrangement, while the natural world is preserved only through emphatic separation from our corrupting presence.

This may be a negative artwork or a negative place to begin, but it is, importantly, an authentic revelation of our impoverishment: we cannot dwell, we can only stay somewhere and confirm and confront our homelessness. If there is the opportunity for an authentic reexamination of the modern project within the contemporary conditions of post-modernity, then the basic objective of modernity—that of human emancipation—must be re-evaluated, and the questioned asked: how is such a project now relevant and possible?

The place of architecture in such a revised project must not only begin from an acknowledgement of our homelessness, our alienation, but also develop from an understanding of architecture's susceptibility to commodiflcation and ideological influence, reject the mere updating of syntax, and acknowledge the depth of architecture's representative nature beyond surface effects and image.

Reconciliation

Through architecture as the creation of critical frames through which to understand and interpret the world, we must somehow resolve our place in it. We can begin from the negative, from confirmation of our homelessness and alienation. Yet architecture is fundamentally an attempt to reconcile our human presence in the world: surely this is its project.

Like Mies's Farnsworth house, the houses of Glenn Murcutt hovering over their bushland sites develop a similar acknowledgement of our estrangement: we are suspended and separated from a world we can only corrupt Yet there is another dimension to the form, space and fabric of Murcutt's buildings, a kind of poetic longing to be part of, to belong. Empathy is sought with the land and with the trees, and separation itself is empathetic. It seems to me that in Murcutt's work there is at once a representation

and acknowledgement of our homelesness as well as an expression of our deep desire to once again know what it is to dwell. We are suspended because we wish so much to be brought to ground without destroying it with our touch.

Jørn Utzon's first house in Porto Petro, Majorca, seems to go one step further. Remarkably, Utzon creates a place for us to stay. Here it seems it may actually be possible for us to momentarily belong, momentarily stop. This work does not violate its site: it is of the rock. It has a primordial quality yet lies within the project of Modernity, it is at once ancient and modern.

It is interesting that both Murcutt and Utzon practised outside the norm. They both occupied the margin. I could not describe either of them as efficient. They were outside the market, they resisted commercial reality and were stung by it. They were also slow.

The ideology of our time, with its emphasis on efficiency, change, speed and the free market, in many ways establishes the antithesis of the necessary conditions for making architecture. Architecture is not efficiency; in fact it is often the way in which efficiency is subordinated to other values that distinguishes architecture.

Architecture is not mere change: architecture is more about transformation and permanence; it is most often about uncovering what it is in humanity that does not change.

Architecture cannot be the servant of the free market. Architecture should not be reduced to a market-dependent consumerable, as at this point it becomes merely decorated building within the flux of fashion.

Architecture does not move at speed, as any of us know who have tried to make architecture.

Architecture is slow.

Finally, an authentic contemporary architecture should not only attempt to somehow begin to reconcile humanity's place in the world but also be directed towards rejuvenating and repoliticising our desiccated public realm. We should pursue an architecture appropriate to citizens rather than consumers.

Search for the Universal

Richard Francis-Jones

Presented at On Monumentality: Place, Representation & The Public Realm, RAIA NSW Chapter Conference, Sydney, NSW, October 11–12, 2002
Published in "Search for the Universal," *On Monumentality* (Sydney: RAIA, 2002): 8

At the close of World War II Louis Kahn, in an essay entitled 'Monumentality', attempted to map out the direction for twentieth century architecture. He wrote enthusiastically of the possibilities provided by new technology and new science, "of living in an unbalanced state of relativity." Kahn was excited at the new structural possibilities, the new social programs, and the new monumentality of continuous structures. Much as we are today excited by globalisation, fragmentation, and computer aided design and manufacturing.[1]

But in this excitement and simplification he pointed out the enigmatic nature of monumentality, suggesting that it cannot be intentionally created and that it is more about content than form: "Neither the finest material nor the most advanced technology need enter a work of monumental character for the same reason that the finest ink was not required to draw up the Magna Carta." The character and content Kahn referred to has both a spiritual and social dimension and it is perhaps not so much what is changing in humanity as what is unchanging that is the subject of monumentality.

Of course, temporal human values, deeds, and the glorification of individuals will continue to be the subject of architecture attempting to represent and monumentalise. But if we untangle the showy images, the branding and the attention seeking, we realise that the quality that remains, that continues to have meaning for us, has nothing to do with the individual, with the ego of the patron or the architect.

Monumentality is concerned not with the private interest but with what is shared—the public interest, the willing sacrifice of the interests of the individual for the collective. These are the values and content to be embodied and represented in our public institutions, in a monumental architecture. But equally, it is concerned with what is outside any temporal human institution and seeks a spiritual connection to something absolutely fundamental to our humanity, something eternal.

When we look out at the horizon over the ocean it has a calming, meditative effect; we are placed in relation to the world in a way that is at once overwhelming, emphasising our insignificance in relation to the vastness of the ocean, or the stars. But at the same time we are comforted, we are pleased to be such a small part, our egos recede and we feel momentarily connected.

Uluru, the greatest monument in Australia, communicates this sense of the eternal, of the universal, in a way that moves all of us, allowing us to experience something outside ourselves, a profound interconnection.

Architecture can also have this effect. This is monumentality in architecture. It has little to do with the size or even the purpose of the building. It is the ability to lift us beyond our short and very limited existence. Although this architecture may decay and fall into the ground, it creates relations and provokes emotions that touch some deep part of all of us.

At about the same time as Louis Khan was writing his essay, Arthur Stace was writing one word in chalk all over Sydney: "Eternity". His fragile words washed away and rewritten again and again are etched in the memory of Sydneysiders. This word, in Copperplate script, in that hand, although so intangible, became monumental. It is also the word that more than any other explains monumentality.

The spiritual element of monumentality is our desire to reach towards to the eternal, to something beyond our limits, our brief moment. The social element of monumentality is our desire to connect to the other(s), to move beyond isolated self-interest to shared representations and values.

Both desires are an effort to move outside ourselves, to overcome in some way the tyranny of the ego, towards something greater than our individual being.

1 Louis Kahn, "Monumentality," in *New Architecture and City Planning*, ed. Paul Zucker (New York: Philosophical Library, 1944), 577–88.

Labyrinth of Images

Richard Francis-Jones

Published in "Labyrinth of Images," *Architecture Australia* March (Melbourne: Architecture Media, 1993): 71–3

Contemporary practice shrinks the role of the architect from that of an active agent in the construction of community and its structures to that of an exterior designer or interior specialist.[1]

— Diane Ghirardo

Contemporary architectural practice is in a state of pluralism. postmodernism, deconstructivism, neo-modernism and regionalism all have currency. This heterogeneity is not the critical cultural endeavour of an un-coerced society but, as critic Hal Foster explains, a "cultural dominant", a conception which allows the coexistence of a range of different features.[2]

In a pluralist state, criticism tends to be dispersed and rendered impotent. Equivalence is granted to various directions and "difference" becomes desirable to market operation. The supreme commodity value in architecture— style—is revised and we are given the freedom to choose. Pluralism presents the illusion of change and the illusion of democracy while furthering the capitalist need to innovate and yet change nothing—a role previously reserved for fashion.

An important characteristic of the various directions within our pluralist condition is the neutral attitude to content. Attention is focused almost exclusively on the signifier and on the immediacy of experience: surface effects drawn over a neutral construction. Architecture is projected primarily as image and presented for consumption, with the various styles competing in the market.

Commodification

Commodification is the process whereby the social relations behind the production of a commodity, together with its 'use value,' are eroded and masked by the abstraction of the market as 'exchange value' becomes primary. Social labour is similarly separated from its product to become a mere factor in production, and accordingly is treated in instrumental terms. Commodification provides a universal basis for linking everyone into an identical system of market valuation. The human conflicts produced by such abstract valuation are significant, but were mediated through the operation of

ideology—understood as a distortion of reality, or justifying mask for specific interests. Importantly, art and architecture offered an alternative, critical, reconciliation.

However in our contemporary advanced consumer society, art and architecture no longer are a separate, reconciliatory and possibly critical force but are fully integrated with the instrumental operation of capital. Such complete infestation of commodifcation allows the disappearance of ideology, as consumption itself becomes enough to reproduce and legitimise the system. Symptomatic is the way we measure Christmas in terms of consumption and refer to our citizens as mere "consumers."

History

History is being reduced to available and immediate images for consumption while the social reality of historical events and their pressure on the present recedes. Mass media in the form of publications, advertising, television and video ensure our historical isolation through the reduction of world history to multiple images on television, nostalgia films and museum culture.

Architecture has also contributed to this distortion of history. Postmodernism effectively erased historical content, reducing the past to a vast collection of value-free images for 'double-coding' and assembly over neutral constructions: Western classicism for the classicists, art deco/*Metropolis* for the slick corporate practices, early Le Corbusier for the neo-modernists and Russian constructivism for the deconstructivists. All sources are devoid of social content.

Mesmerised and distracted by these images while our sense of real history recedes, we become incapable of forming critical representations of our present experience.

Postmodern Architecture

As we know from the innumerable architectural publications with which we are bombarded, the historical postmodernism of Michael Graves and the like reacts against Modernism's abstraction. It seeks a return to history and the humanist tradition through the development of narrative ornament and figure. Deconstructivist postmodernism on the other hand assumes an anti-humanist decentering of humanity and is against the return to representation. Deconstructivist postmodernism may be a more accurate position-paper on our present condition, but while historical postmodernism's comforting historical images may be falsely reassuring we have to bear in mind that the destabilising images of deconstructivism are no longer received, nor I suspect intended, as critical. Both postmodernisms focus exclusively on the signifier, and the immediacy of experience, having little or no interest in content. Both project architecture primarily as image: image drawn over social instrumentality.

While historical postmodernism is well established in Australia, particularly in large commercial practices, deconstructivism is confined to the architectural schools and the planimetric shifts of contemporary practitioners. In Australia there also is a certain attraction and market for regionalism but where this work is image-based and, for example, aestheticises the landscape, it also reduces architecture to image.

Postmodern Theory

Contemporary cultural theory, as offered by Michel Foucault, Jean-Françoise Lyotard and Jacques Derrida, attempts a critique of the dominating operation of Western ideology, but rejects any totalising and Utopian alternative, such as that offered by Karl Marx, as reductive and necessarily containing repressive ideology. So-called "postmodern thinkers" condemn broad interpretive analysis, doubt the existence of universal or elemental truths, and above all seek to avoid forms of political oppression legitimised by resort to "reason." The focus and context of postmodern thought is the plural and the specific, the fragmentary and the chaotic.

Foucault's analysis of the micro-politics of power in different interstitial localities—prisons, asylums, hospitals— reveals the operation of power built up independently of any systematic strategy of class domination. Utopian schemes cannot explain what happens at each locale nor escape what Foucault describes as "the power-knowledge relation" in non-repressive ways.

Lyotard also believes knowledge to be the principal source of power. But for him the operation of power and repression lies in the multiple "language games" of different social groups within contemporary society. Lyotard accepts the flexibility and contradictions of these heterogeneous language games in the interest of openness but is concerned that only selective games give rise to institutions—universities, legal systems etc.—that control knowledge. His heterogeneous acceptance attempts to open the entry for excluded sections of society such as women, gays and other minorities.

Derrida believes the logocentric philosophical tradition, with its domination of metaphysics and strong assertions about truth, is more accurately understood as ideology. As Derrida wishes to avoid exposing one source of suppression only to replace it with another, his own deconstructive terms (deconstruction, difference, trace, etc.) are subject to analysis and are posited as "undecideables" with no claim to single meaning. Meaning is constantly deferred.

Postmodern theory, in its determination to avoid promoting alternative sources of domination, adopts the strategy of dispersal, embraces fragmentation and pluralism, minimising the authority of any single group. However, this occurs at the expense of some coherence and may diffuse resistance to more central forms of social manipulation and coercion. Neo-Marxist critics such as Frederic Jameson and Alex Callinicos are critical of postmodern culture and suspect that such fragmentary strategies may unintentionally align with the forces of commodification in a "plurified" capitalism.

Postmodern theory, however, is by nature difficult to collect and generalise. The revelations offered by such disciplined and specific investigation are valuable in exposing the repressive operation of ideology and are important in the development of a more liberated and complete social body.

The Modern Project

The Enlightenment project of human emancipation through rational social organisation turned, as we know, full circle. The oppression of myth, religion and superstition were lifted—only to be replaced by the "rational," instrumental operation of capital, consumerism and the illusion of democracy.

In architecture, the naive pursuit of purified expression and social content appropriate to a "liberated" society was defeated by this same "rationality." Modern totalising Utopias promising liberation contained their own alternative, repressive ideology.

We therefore find ourselves isolated as "modern individuals," politically marginalised and distracted from the impoverishment of our experience by a continuous chain of production and consumption. It is doubtful that we have enough confidence or energy to rescue this blighted "modern project" of liberation.

Homelessness

In "Building Dwelling Thinking," Martin Heidegger uses the example of a farmhouse in Germany's Black Forest to explain a deep and complete form of "dwelling." Dwelling, for Heidegger, requires building and artefacts to articulate and support an integrated and harmonious human presence. It is a world of traditional, cultural and spiritual connections to place. However our contemporary condition makes this poetic form of dwelling an impossibility for all but perhaps those, as yet "unliberated" indigenous people.[3]

The myths and rituals from which we have been "liberated" cannot be recovered. Nor can we be compensated by the superficial decoration of our buildings with empty symbols and motifs. Such desperate strategies only confirm our impoverishment, as does the invention of "contemporary myths" in the work of American practitioners such as John Hedjuk.

We cannot overcome our modernity. We can, however, acknowledge our homelessness.

Silence

The "silence" in the work of Mies van der Rohe is such an acknowledgment. A silence perhaps at its most compelling in the Farnsworth house, Illinois. Here, liberated humanity is suspended from the world in which it can no longer dwell. The sparse and purified platform permits no masks of comforting self deception but instead confronts us with the reality of

our estrangement, while the natural world is only preserved through emphatic separation from our corrupting presence. The work is at once beautiful, true and terrifying.

It is only from such silent revelation of our impoverishment that an authentic contemporary architecture is possible. These silent and rigorous assertions of our homelessness, most powerful in the work of Mies van der Rohe, are also characteristics of Louis Kahn's and more recently Tadao Ando's architecture.

Tectonics

If contemporary architecture is to affirm and move beyond such melancholic silence, a means of expression capable of resisting commodification is vital. Such inherently resistant expression is, in fact, the basic medium of architecture— tectonics. Architecture as craft—not architecture as sculpture, text, double-coding or package marketing. A re-grounding of architecture within tectonics is now essential.

It is important to understand tectonics as not merely a reference to the structure and construction of a building, but as the medium with which we work. Tectonic expression necessarily is a selective and formally controlled process perhaps better explained as the "poetics of construction." Poetry, understood as the formal construction of alternative realities within reality. Constructs, which through their resolution, have the capacity to comment on and critically reveal the nature of the human condition.

Tectonic expression cannot be easily reduced to image and is inherently resistant to commodification through the clear assertion of reality. It is the antithesis of Robert Venturi's "decorated shed," which aligned architecture with commercial building and marketing techniques, to become merely decorated building.

The nature of tectonic expression in architecture is well illustrated in the work of Louis Kahn. The library designed by Kahn at Exeter, New Hampshire is not merely the articulate expression of construction and structure, and the adoration of the joint, but a critical expression of the program and nature of our social institutions in the structure and construction of the work. The works of Jørn Utzon serve as equally clear examples of tectonic expression, in particular the church built at Bagsværd, Denmark. Clearly these are not buildings of surface effects or mere images, but complete works of architecture in depth through the plans, sections, structure, construction and materials.

Content

An authentic contemporary architecture through the construction of alternative realities will comment on and reveal the nature of our human condition. The specific function of each architectural project focuses such intentions. Institutions, commercial enterprises and 'community' all are accommodated, formed, embodied and represented in building. It is in the critical interpretation of these functions that it may be helpful to draw on the work of contemporary thinkers such as Foucault and Lyotard.

However amongst the most important objectives for contemporary architecture is the need to repoliticise our desiccated public sphere of communication. The "political" public realm must be affirmed as an alternative to the isolation and indifference of the suburbs. Architecture and public places need to be appropriate for citizens rather than consumers.

Site

Architecture by nature is site-specific. However, it is important to understand this specificity at a deeper level than the mere aestheticisation of the Australian landscape or the application of various sun-shading devices over an otherwise neutral construction.

The locations for architecture have a social as well as a physical aspect. Places are not only urban or 'natural' landscapes, but are marked by human inhabitation embodying social memory and aspiration. Sites are already rich in cultural expression—not only that of relocated western culture but also the deep indigenous culture of this land. In the meeting of these cultures, it is difficult to avoid the destruction or the reduction of indigenous culture to commodity status. It may not be possible to move beyond an acknowledgment of indigenous culture that will inevitably affirm the depth of our own homelessness.

An architecture of its site will reveal what is already present—that is, it will manifest the social and physical character of a specific site.

The work of art is the material's highest form of existence once it has been removed from its natural surroundings. All other forms describe the material's gradual devaluation, ending in its complete violation in the production of objects for daily use and in today's common architecture. The process of architectural design interests us as an instrument for the perception of and engagement with reality. This is where we search for the ethical and political contents of our work.[4]

— Jacques Herzog

1 Diane Ghirado, "Past or Postmodern in Architctural Fashion," *Telos* 62 (Candor: Telos Press, 1984):190.

2 Hal Foster, "Re:Post," in *Art After Modernism: Rethinking Representation*, ed. Brian Wallis (New York: The New Museum of Contemporary Art, 1984).

3 Marin Heidegger, "Building Dwelling Thinking" in *Poetry, Language, Thought* (New York: Perennial Classics, 2001).

4 Jacques Herzog, "La Geometria oculta de la Naturalesa. The Hidden Geometry of Nature," in *Quaderns d'Arquitectura i Urbanisme*, 181/182 (Barcelona: Association of Architects of Catalonia, 1989): 96–109.

Social-hub bridge, Sydney Law School

Architecture of Learning

Jeff Morehen

I never teach my pupils. I only attempt to provide the conditions in which they can learn.

— Albert Einstein

The university campus provides a rich backdrop for learning, meeting, thinking and social interaction. Although this has always been the tradition of our institutions, today the need to move beyond structured and formal teacher-led and directed education is of increased importance. It is, however, often not reflected in the design of spaces that are provided to facilitate new processes of learning.

Contemporary learning reflects a departure from the pedagogy of the past. Today's students have attitudes, expectations, constraints and methodologies of studying that differ from the previous generation.

An understanding of the shifts that are taking place in education is therefore essential in providing learning facilities. New emerging technology, generational change, commercial pressures, globalisation and the expectations of society are all combining to require a re-think of traditional teaching and operational paradigms.

The embrace of technology and the increasing mobility and connectivity of society, both physical and virtual, requires new models and spatial experiences to facilitate learning. Modern pedagogy is increasingly focused upon collaborative learning by doing rather than learning by listening. This is an important shift of emphasis and one that has a direct impact on the architecture of learning. Traditional physical settings that typically characterise the design of teaching spaces, lecture theatres and classrooms constrain new and innovative approaches to learning, communication and knowledge exchange.

Historically, the lecture theatre or classroom has been the forum for structured learning and direction, and the primary focus for university attendance. New learning technologies and approaches have emerged that create opportunities to complement traditional forms of teaching. This, however, creates challenges for universities and educational institutions, as they increasingly seek to adopt such new approaches and create new and more effective collaborative pedagogical environments of innovation and excellence.

It is clear that the design of learning environments plays a major role in the effectiveness of learning and impacts cognitive and behavioural responses. The contemporary university must challenge convention, and provide flexible spaces that accommodate diverse experiences, recognising that people learn in different ways.

Teaching and learning facilities need to embrace key issues of flexibility, comfort, stimulation, technology, interaction and engagement.

It is important to recognise that learning does not only happen in the classroom or lecture theatre, at prescribed times, delivered through a lecturer who provides a transfer of information through structured, instruction-driven learning; it is also a highly social experience of knowledge exchange gained via peer participation, chance encounter, spontaneous meeting or informal interaction. In many respects, this is increasingly becoming the primary benefit of attending a university rather than study in isolation.

In recognition of the importance of multidisciplinary interaction, knowledge exchange, and the campus experience, the design of educational buildings has evolved. Accordingly, today's learning must combine traditional "talk and chalk" approaches with an additional focus on active, participatory, social learning in environments that overcomes the constraints of the traditional classroom and lecture theatre. A wide array of technology-enabled spaces and experiences is required in order to balance the formal with the informal, the traditional with the contemporary.

The proportions, furniture arrangements and selections, technology, acoustics and environmental conditions of the contemporary learning spaces including lecture theatre, seminar and classroom space, for instance, require careful consideration to facilitate a range of teaching methodologies and learning experiences.

Traditional layouts of auditoria and lecture theatres have rarely provided for social engagement and are not conducive to group discussion. The design of the contemporary lecture theatre should no longer be singularly focused with the lecturer as sole provider and source of information. The spatial proportions, furniture selection, and lighting approach must facilitate discussion, active participation and engagement within the audience. Considered spatial arrangements and proportions must enable interactivity, discussion and group work in lectures, thus engaging students and improving the learning experience.

Radial arrangements of comfortable seating in raked lecture theatres, for example, as well as horse-shoe tutorial/case-room configurations, where teaching "in the round" with the audience in close proximity to the speaker, create an intimate environment that encourages active participation and discussion.

Traditional design criteria, however, also continue to apply. The importance of sightlines remains fundamental, as is acoustics. Attention to these issues will ensure that the lecturer can achieve a comfortable conversational relationship with the audience rather than reliance on systems of voice augmentation.

Similarly, other teaching environments such as flat-floor classrooms must also depart from static, rectilinear, single orientated, uniformly lit arrangements, and provide learning within flexible and inspiring environments.

As technology is becoming increasingly integrated within the teaching and research experience, the built form must recognise the associated requirements to maximise its benefit. Colour and lighting are key issues of consideration for the design of technology-enabled spaces. Today's equipment, however, does not require such rigid blackout criteria as before, enabling spaces to incorporate natural light and view—the importance of which cannot be underestimated in controlling fatigue and concentration.

It is not only the formal teaching facilities however that must embrace the latest pedagogical approach. Wireless connectivity and virtual communications have liberated and extended the learning experience to complement the structured learning of primary teaching facilities. Electronically networked support areas offer flexibility to maximise learning, social interaction and the collegiate experience. The importance of support spaces for the primary

teaching/learning areas, including circulation systems, external landscaping, corridors, breakout, learning commons and group study areas, therefore cannot be underestimated.

Unlike commercial developments where traditional measures of efficiency are of prime importance, university buildings need to carefully consider a "duality of purpose" whereby circulation and support facilities contribute to informal teaching, and knowledge exchange. Accordingly, support areas must not only facilitate the changeover of a large number of students between lectures, but also be carefully proportioned to provide informal meeting space and breakout that will enhance interaction.

All facilities must offer a range of pedagogical possibilities to motivate students within healthy environments full of fresh air and natural light, which are a delight to inhabit. Clearly a one-size-fits-all approach is not the answer, nor is it one that is specific or single-purposed. Formal and informal spaces need to provide the backdrop for learning, enabling both educator and student to configure and tailor environments to suit specific need that may vary from week to week and continue to evolve over time.

To embrace connectivity and flexibility, it is of vital importance that the infrastructure is the most reliable and user friendly. Sophisticated technology that cannot be easily used or is unable to be readily adapted to meet the demands of tomorrow will result in unsuccessful buildings. It will inhibit the dissemination of knowledge and learning, with inefficiencies resulting from operational aspects related to the time required for set-up and preparation.

The continued advent and increased speeds of reliable wireless networking, however, will continue to liberate the physical restraints on computer-based teaching. Such potential is particularly attractive when combined with online teaching methods and portable technology that allows computer-based teaching to no longer be confined to purpose-built facilities. The design of spaces should emphasise the requirements of students and staff, rather than the needs of the equipment.

All campus areas should be considered as opportunities for learning and research. The modern educational institution must focus upon the process of learning throughout. It must combine the structured and unstructured, the formal and informal, the expected and unexpected, and the physical and virtual within an uplifting environment characterised by fresh air, comfort and natural light.

Today's learning environment is not a singular building but must be considered as a cohesive campus that provides a complementary and interrelated array of spaces, to facilitate learning and social experiences within an integrated learning environment. Flexible internal and exterior spaces, accommodating different approaches and function, facilitate the process of effective learning. In many ways this parallels the changes to the contemporary workplace and associated trends throughout industry and the wider community.

The function of educational facilities must therefore also extend beyond the constraints of envelope, and provide important enhancements to the public domain and campus life. Spaces between developments are of equal importance to the design of individual buildings.

A cohesive campus requires a sequence of hard and soft landscaping, to create informal complements to the primary teaching facilities. A technology-enabled and connected, integrated landscaped campus extends the learning experience fostering informal knowledge exchange, chance encounter and casual conversation, supported by the all-important provision of food and coffee that characterises contemporary student life.

Educational developments must provide important contributions to the wider campus experience projecting a new 'built pedagogy' that represents and underpins the vision and architectural embodiment of the educational philosophy of our institutions.

The architecture of learning therefore remains a significant issue demanding serious attention. The spaces created must seek to inspire all students to fulfill their potential in order to benefit the wider community.

Its importance to contemporary society cannot be underestimated.

Bridge detail, Tasmanian Museum & Art Gallery

Richard Francis-Jones	Melika Aljukic	Mary Dewar	Tina Jackson	Jordan Molnar	Zuzana Semelak
Jeff Morehen	Rana Amarindra	Cara Doherty	Jacob JeBailey	Sebastian Monroe	Laura Shapiro
Richard Thorp	Kalpana Amin	Karina Dorman	Hallum Jennings	Gareth Morgan	Daniel Sharp
	John-Paul Araujo	Fleur Downey	Mia Jeong	Jeffrey Morgan	Owen Sharp
	Robert Asher	Myles Drummond	Conrad Johnston	Rhiannon Morgan	Olivia Shih
Elizabeth Carpenter	Yeganeh Atri	Ben Duckworth	Christopher Jones	John Morris	Rhea Shortus
Geoff Croker	Adrian Baldari	Nikolce Dunoski	Alison Jones	Alexandra Mowday	Jason Sim
Richard Desgrand	Milica Barac	Noor El-Gewely	Aya Kalaw	Vikram Mukherjee	Heidi Sinclair
David Haseler	Alicia Basa	Nataly Ernst	Alex Kalliris	Christopher Mullaney	Scott Skipworth
Christine Kwong	Richard Beere	Daniel Evans	Petra Kandusova	Tony Musson	Ben Smith
Johnathan Redman	Amanda Beh	Sam Faigen	Arcadius Kaniewski	Tony Nam	Robertson Smith
Matthew Todd	Barbara Beier	Mathieu Faliu	Daniel Karamaneas	Antony Ng	Fawzi Soliman
	Hiren Bhatt	Kitty Fan	Karina Kerr	Melissa Ng	Gaia Starace
	Stephen Blanche	Natalie Fan	Joanne Kieltyka	Phillip Ng	Marie-France Stockdale
Annie Hensley	Tegn Bond	James Feghali	Miriam Kodeschova	Rosa Nuen	Tomoko Suga
Sean McPeake	Daniel Bourke	Emma Fenton	Sahar Koohi	Dustin Nyugen	Dita Svelte
Lance White	Mark Brandon	Isabella Fleck	Lubo Kulisev	Salleigh Olsen	Henry Szmelcer
Adrian Yap	Chaya Bratoeva	Chris Fletcher	Ronald Kumar	Kim Malcolm Ong	Koichi Takada
	Andre Braun	Damien Furey	Helen Kuo	Heidi Parker	James Thanudchang
	Christopher Bridge	Jze Gan	Roger Kuo	Stephen Pennock	Andrew Thomas
Simon Barr	Graham Brindle	Monica Gayed	Sandra Kuzman	Sean Pettet	Roger To
Janine Deshon	Ian Brumby	Christine Godschalx	David Lam	Phillip Pham	Samuel To
Lina Francis-Jones	Vanessa Bunbury	Kate Gooch	Caroline Lamb	Holly Picker	Katherine Tracey
Adam Guernier	Kathryn Bunn	Louise Goodman	Andrew Langford	Alex Pienaar	Richard Tripolone
James Perry	Vanessa Caldwell	Sam Guo	Lilian Lau	Kaylene Pitts	Caiyen Tse
	Damian Campanella	Philip Green	Liz Lau	Susanne Pollmann	Jerry Tseng
	Fiona Campbell	Jessica Haldane	Annis Lee	Nathan Porter	Josephine Turner
	Walter Carniato	Martin Hallen	Eric Lee	Trasey Poulellis	Laura Vallentine
	Cristian Castillo	Cassandra Halpin-Smyth	Simon Lee	Marcel Pradella	Shaila Van Raad
	Vincent Chen	Thomas Haltenhof	Andrew Leech	Kerri Pratt	Bodil Veibaek
	Alfred Cheng	Samantha Hands	Anne-Lise Li Sik	Stephen Pratt	Christian Voss
	Joey Cheng	Sara Hansen Earley	Jesse Lockhart-Krause	Stewart Price	Frank Wang
	Seng Lim Cheong	Tim Harper	Sandra Loschke	Adriano Pupilli	Kuang Hao Wang
	Quah Ji Chian	Margaret Hawke	Jason Luk	Kathryn Riccio	York Wang
	Birgit Chinnery	Adam Higginbotham	Bjoern Lueders	Basil Richardson	Lucy Warnock
	Kenneth Chou	Michelle Ho	Jonathan Lynn	Soo-Jin Rim	Catharina Weis
	Andrew Chung	Prudence Ho	Kirk Macdonnell	Patrick Roberts	Huw Wellard
	Jason Chung	Sam Hodgkinson	Patrick Maitland	Reine Roberts	Rebekah Whitney
	Anthony Clarke	Ian Hollen	Sheena Males-Duggan	Christopher Roberts-Brewer	Nicole Whittaker
	Hannah-Jean Cole	Thomas Holliday	Boris Manzewski	Jane Robinson	Karla Wilford
	Erin Colgrave	Gesa Hopkinson	Matthew Mar	Adele Rowland	Cherry Williamson
	Renee Cooper	Sophie Hoppe	Prayrika Mathur	Katherine Russell	Peter Wise
	Eleanor Cosgrove	Edward Hosken	Brooke Matthews	Peter Russell	Nicole Witney
	Christina Crowe	Paul Hrycko	Jodie Matthews	Natalie Sachdev	Julian Wong
	Kimberley D'Souza	Cecilia Huang	Alicia McCarthy	James Sandwith	Justin Wong
	Yohann Daruwala	Katty Huang	Irene McGee	Camille Sargent	Murray Wood
	Georgia Davidson	Kylie Joann Hughes	Nicholas McLeod	Yvonne Savvas	Beth Xotta-Dickson
	Peter Dawson	Francis Hur	Dodie McMenamin	Diana Scalici	Rosalind Yang
	Misha de Moyer	Matthias Irger	Ophelia McMillan	Daniel Schagemann	Noel Yaxley
	Paul De Sailly	Anya Isarotaikul	Fiona Miller	Bernd Schlinke	Ken Yeh
	Soenke Dethlefsen	Christelle Ithier	Igor Molitor	Kathleen Selle	Terence Yong

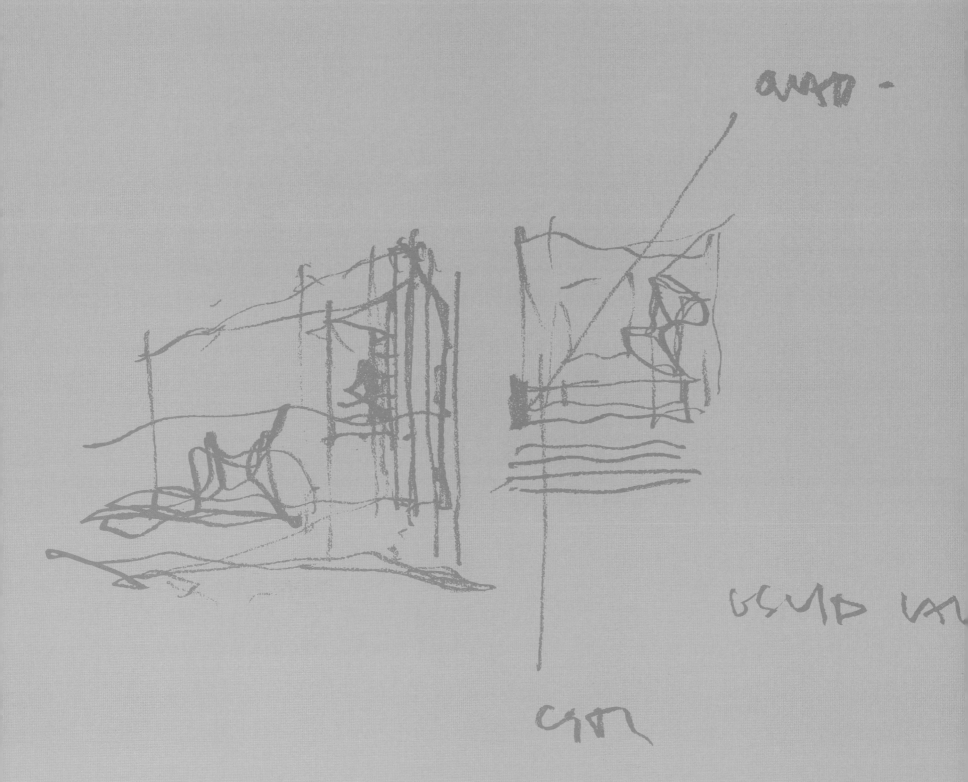

Studio

The process of making architecture is a weaving of overlaid networks made up of text, sketch, physical and digital model, discussion, collaboration, experience and precedent.

It is an evolution of concept that begins to find its own independent life and direction through testing, critique and prototype. It is a collaborative search that holds back over-determinism and wilfulness, creating a space for the concept to develop its own life, often with surprising results. But it is also a process that demands rigour, discipline and the avoidance of the peripheral distraction and inessential.

A search for anything worthwhile must also include a preparedness to return to the beginning, and the admission of failure. It is a search that can only approach its object; an investigation, an exploration, an attempt to find what is there already. It is not owned or authored and there is no method.

The multi-disciplinary fjmt design studio explores the evolution of architectural form by synthesising place and programme through an elaboration of the tectonic. The studio culture and collaborative methodology are central to the creative energy, innovation and rigour that underpin our work.

Credits

Auckland Art Gallery Toi o Tāmaki
Kitchener & Wellesley Streets
Auckland New Zealand
Completed: August 2011
Client: Regional Facilities Auckland

fjmt + Archimedia (architects in association)
FJMT: Richard Francis-Jones, Christine Kwong, Alexander Pienaar, Eric Lee, Martin Hallen, Brooke Matthews, Phillip Pham, Michelle Ho, Jeff Morehen, Richard Desgrand, Matthew Mar, Daniel Schagemann, Katty Huang, Zuzana Semelak, Matthew Todd. Archimedia: Lindsay Mackie, Neil Martin, Russell Pinel, David Pugh, Surya Fullerton, Hamish Cameron, Yogesh Dahya, James Raimon, Sakouna Traymany, Edwin Chen, Sen How Tan, Jaime Don, Shaun Wong, Damon Aspden

Heritage: Salmond Reed Architects, Quantity Surveyor: WT Partnership, Planning: Barker & Associates, Structural: Holmes Consulting Group, Acoustics: Marshall Day Acoustics, Fire: Holmes Fire & Safety, Services: Aecom, HVAC: Montgomery Watson Harza (MWH), Façade: Aurecon / Thermosash Commercial Ltd, Security: BCC, Landscape: Melean Absolum Limited, Lighting: Steensen Varming, Contractor: Hawkins Construction

Bayside Police Station
25 Abbott Street
Sandringham VIC Australia
Completed: April 2010
Client: Victoria Police

Francis-Jones Morehen Thorp
Richard Francis-Jones, Geoff Croker, Lance White, Phillip Ng, Christina Crowe, Peter Wise, Stephen Blanche, Amanda Beh, Nathan Porter, Andrew Thomas, Sean McPeake; Landscape: Matthew Todd, Richard Tripolone, Mark Brandon

Civil & Structural: Taylor Thomson Whitting, Stormwater: Taylor Thomson Whitting, Services: BRT Consulting, Acoustic: Watson Moss Growcott Associates, Building Surveyor: PLP Building Surveyors, Quantity Surveyor: Turner & Townsend Construction and Management Consultants, Access: Morris Goding, Environmental: Irwin Consult, Traffic: Arup, Planner: Davis Langdon, Geotechnical: Douglas Partners, Project Manager: Coffey Projects, Contractor: St Hilliers Contracting

Chancellery & Business School
Grand Boulevard & Kendrew Crescent
Joondalup WA Australia
Completed: January 2003
Client: Edith Cowan University

mgt + Spowers (fjmt / HASSELL)
fjmt: Richard Francis-Jones, David Haseler, Elizabeth Carpenter, Lance White, Justin Wong, Jason Wedesweiler, Olivia Shih, Johnathan Redman, Matthew Todd. HASSELL: Graham Bedford, Phil Skeels, Brenden Kelly, Jurg Hunziker, Phil Stejskal, John Crabtree, Joe Santoro, Tony Naso

Structural: Bruechle Gilchrist & Evans, Hydraulic: RC Oma Design Services, Mechanical: BCA Consultants, Electrical & Lift: Engineering Technology Consultants;, Wind: MEL Consultants; Fire: Arup Fire, Acoustics: Arup Acoustics, Environmental: Advanced Environmental Concepts, Building Surveyor: John Massey Group, Quantity Surveyor: Ralph Beattie Bosworth, Programmer: James Clark & Associates, Furniture: Duro Consultancy, Landscape: Tract (WA), Contractor: John Holland

The Concourse
409 Victoria Avenue
Chatswood NSW Australia
Completed: August 2011
Client: Willoughby City Council

Francis-Jones Morehen Thorp
Richard Francis-Jones, Jeff Morehen, Richard Thorp, Matthew Todd, Elizabeth Carpenter, Annie Hensley, Kathleen Selle, Basil Richardson, Andrew Chung, Karina Mason, Sahar Koohi, Jze Gan, Cecilia Huang, Jason Luk, Murray Wood, Catharina Weis; Landscape: Matthew Todd, Richard Tripolone, Mark Brandon

Structural & Civil: Taylor Thomson Whitting, Façade: Aurecon, Mechanical: WSP Lincolne Scott, Electrical: WSP Lincolne Scott, Lighting: Vision Design, Hydraulic/Fire Services: Warren Smith & Partners, Acoustic: Marshall Day Acoustics, Theatre: Marshall Day Entertech/RTMI, Fire: Arup, Sustainability: Built Ecology, Building Surveyor: The Hendry Group, Catering: The Mack Group, Vertical Transport: Transportation Design Consultants, Wind: Windtech, Quantity Surveyor: WT Partnership, Library Consultant: David Jones, Retail: Wilmot RPS (Previously Wilmot Murchie), Public Art: Pamille Berg Consulting, Artists: Warren Langley (Ingress); Wendy Mills (Visiting Enki), Feng Shui: Feng Shui Dragon Enterprises, Project Manager: Quadro Projects (design), Savills (delivery), Contractor: A.W. Edwards

Craigieburn Library
75-95 Central Park Avenue
Craigieburn VIC Australia
Completed: May 2012
Client: Hume City Council

Francis-Jones Morehen Thorp
Richard Francis-Jones, Geoff Croker, Lance White, Fleur Downey, Kitty Fan, Amanda Beh, Kim Ong, Stewart Price, Peter Wise, Edward Hoskins; Landscape: Matthew Todd, Richard Tripolone

Structural & Civil: Taylor Thomson Whitting, Mechanical & Environmental: Murchie Consulting, Building Surveyor: McKenzie Group, Rammed Earth: P.J.YTTRUP & Associates, Signage: Design by Pidgeon, Fire: JP Fire, Access: ONEGroup ID, Acoustic: Arup Acoustics, Kitchen: Cinni Little, Traffic: GTA Consultants, Quantity Surveyor: Aquenta Consulting, Project Manager: Hyder Consulting, Contractor: WATPAC Construction

Darling Quarter
Harbour Street
Sydney NSW Australia
Completed: September 2011
Client: Lend Lease Corporation and
Sydney Harbour Foreshore Authority

Francis-Jones Morehen Thorp
Richard Francis-Jones, Jeff Morehen, Johnathan Redman, Sean McPeake, Adam Guernier, Peter Russell, Sahar Koohi, Martin Hallen, Stephen Pratt, Soenke Dethlefsen, David Haseler, Annis Lee, Karina Kerr, Simon Lee, Samuel Faigen, Gareth Morgan, Ian Brumby, Joey Cheng, Prudence Ho

Landscape: Aspect Studios, Interiors: The E.G.O. Group, Davenport Campbell, Structural: Arup, ESD: Arup, Mechanical: Arup, Electrical: Aurecon, Hydraulic & fire services: Warren Smith & Partners, Quantity surveyor: Lend Lease, Fire: Defire, Developer, Builder, Project Manager: Lend Lease, Contractor: Lend Lease

Eastern Avenue Auditorium
F19 Eastern Avenue
Camperdown NSW Australia
Completed: February 2001
Client: The University of Sydney

Francis-Jones Morehen Thorp
Richard Francis-Jones, Johnathan Redman, Elizabeth Carpenter, Richard Thorp, David Haseler, Dua Cox

Structural & Civil: Taylor Thomson Whitting, Quantity Surveyor: Rider Hunt, Landscape: Tract Consulting, Mechanical/Electrical: Steensen Varming, Hydraulic: Warren Smith & Partners, Project Manager: Incoll Management, Contractor: Belmadar Constructions

John Niland Scientia Building
G19, University of New South Wales
Kensington NSW Australia
Completed: June 1999
Client: University of New South Wales

mgt Sydney (Francis-Jones Morehen Thorp)
Richard Francis-Jones, Jeff Morehen, Romaldo Giurgola, Richard Thorp, Angelo Korsanos, Conrad Johnston, Rhiannon Morgan, Jason Trisley, Douglas Brooks, Ninotschka Titchkosky

Structural: Taylor Thomson Whitting, Electrical: Barry Webb and Associates, Mechanical: Egis Consulting, Hydraulic: Harris Page and Associates, Acoustics: Ove Arup and Partners, Civil: Ove Arup and Partners; Cost: Project Cost Planning, Contractor: Lend Lease

Little Bay Apartments
1–9 & 2–8 Pine Avenue
Little Bay NSW Australia
Completed: November 2011
Client: Stockland

Francis-Jones Morehen Thorp
Richard Francis-Jones, Jeff Morehen, David Haseler, Annie Hensley, Simon Barr, Jodie Matthews, Katherine Tracey, Petra Kandusova, Chris Bridge, Andrew Chung, Igor Molitor, Janine Deshon, Natalie Fan, Owen Sharp, Lilian Lau

Structural: Aurecon, Electrical & Mechanical: George Floth Consulting, Hydraulic: LHO Group, Building Surveyor: AE&D, Environmental: Cundall Johnston & Partners, Planner: Helen Mulcahy Urban Design, Waste Management: JD MacDonald, Quantity Surveyor: WT Partnership, Traffic: Colston Budd Hunt & Kafes, Landscape: Oculus, Acoustic: Renzo Tonin & Associates, Access: Accessibility Solutions, Heritage: Tanner and Associates, Project Manager: SJA Project Management, Contractor: St Hilliers

Max Webber Library
Flushcombe Road & Alpha Street
Blacktown NSW Australia
Completed: October 2005
Client: Blacktown City Council

Francis-Jones Morehen Thorp
Richard Francis-Jones, Richard Thorp, Lance White, Aya Maceda, Janine Deshon, John Morris, Andrew Chung, Boris Manzewski, Matthew Mar, Olivia Shih, Nikolce Dunoski, Peter Wise

Structural & Civil: Taylor Thomson Whitting, Electrical, Mechanical, Services, Environmental & Lighting: Steensen Varming, Hydraulic: Warren Smith & Partners, Acoustic: Arup, Cost: Rider Hunt, Contractor: Adco Construction

The Mint
10 Macquarie Street
Sydney NSW Australia
Completed: October 2004
Client: Historic Houses Trust

Francis-Jones Morehen Thorp
Richard Francis Jones, Jeff Morehen, Elizabeth Carpenter, Matthew Mar, James Perry, John Morris, Janine Deshon, David Haseler, Cecilia Huang, Sheena Males Duggan, Vikram Mukherjee, Matthew Todd, Lance White, Stephen Pennock, Karl Bennett

Landscape: Francis-Jones Morehen Thorp, Heritage: Clive Lucas, Stapleton & Partners, Cost: Page Kirkland Partnership, Archaeology: Godden Mackay Logan, Structural: Taylor Thomson Whitting, Mechanical/Environmental: Steensen Varming, Electrical/Communications: Steensen Varming, Hydraulic: Warren Smith & Partners, Acoustic: Arup Acoustics, Building Surveyor: Trevor Howse & Associates, Fire: Trevor Howse & Associates, Surveyor: Drummond Parmenter, Access: Access Australia, Contractor: St Hilliers

Newcastle Museum
Workshop Way
Honeysuckle NSW Australia
Completed: June 2011
Client: Newcastle City Council

Francis-Jones Morehen Thorp
Richard Francis-Jones, Jeff Morehen, Elizabeth Carpenter, Janine Deshon, Mathieu Faliu, Daniel Karamaneas, Scott Skipworth, Simon Lee, Anne-Lise Li Sik, Tim Harper; Landscape: Matthew Todd, Richard Tripolone

Heritage: Clive Lucas Stapleton and Partners, Exhibition: Cunningham Martyn Design, Archaeology: C & MJ Doring, Structural & Civil: Taylor Thomson Whitting, Mechanical, Electrical & Environmental: Steensen Varming, Hydraulic and Fire Services: Warren Smith and Partners, Acoustic: Arup Acoustics, Fire: Arup Fire, Building Surveyor: Davis Langdon, Access: Accessibility Solutions, Traffic: Better Transport Futures, Contamination: RCA Australia, Geotechnical: Douglas Partners, Quantity Surveyor: Rider Levett Bucknall, Project Manager: Newcastle City Council; Contractor: ISIS Group Australia

Owen G. Glenn Business School
12 Grafton Road
Auckland New Zealand
Completed: September 2007
Client: University of Auckland

fjmt + Archimedia (architects in association)
FJMT: Richard Francis-Jones, Christine Kwong, Simon Barr, Owen Sharp, Richard Desgrand, Jeff Morehen, Andrew Chung. Archimedia: Neil Martin, Lindsay Mackie, Russell Pinel, Heidi Sinclair, Surya Fullerton, Yogesh Dahya, Sakouna Traymany, David Pugh

Civil & Structural: Beca, Fire: Beca, Façade: Connell Wagner, Services: Connell Wagner, Acoustic: Marshall Day, External Façade & Curtain Wall Glazing: Thermosash, Excavation & Piling: Vuksich & Borich Ltd, Project Manager: Beca, Contractor: Fletcher Construction Company

Red Centre
H13, University of New South Wales
Kensington NSW Australia
Completed: October 1998
Client: University of New South Wales

mgt Sydney (Francis-Jones Morehen Thorp)
Richard Francis-Jones Jeff Morehen Romaldo Giurgola Johnathan Redman Angelo Korsanos David Conley Rhiannon Morgan Elizabeth Carpenter Nicky Ross Jane Davie Burt Greer Ramin Jahromi

Structural & Services: Ove Arup & Partners, Cost: Project Cost Planning, Landscape: Tract Consultant, Building Surveyor: Trevor Howse & Associates, Contractor: Hansen Yuncken

St Barnabas Church
Mountain Street & Broadway
Ultimo NSW Australia
Completed: April 2012
Client: Anglican Property Trust, Diocese of Sydney

Francis-Jones Morehen Thorp
Richard Francis-Jones, Johnathan Redman, Annie Hensley, Susanne Pollmann, Lina Francis-Jones, Janine Deshon; Landscape: Matthew Todd, Zuzana Semelak

Structural & Façade Engineer: Taylor Thomson Whitting; Mechanical, Hydraulic, Electrical, Lift: Aecom (formerly Bassetts); Quantity Surveyor: Page Kirkland Group; Access: Accessibility Solutions; Building Surveyor: The Hendry Group; Fire: Arup Fire, Primary Certifying Authority: Davis Langdon, Traffic: MWT Transport Planning, Acoustic: Acoustic Studio, Wind: Windtech, Planner: JBA Urban Planning Consultants, Kitchen: Cini Little, Heritage: GBA Heritage, Project Manager: Winton Associates, Contractor: Buildcorp

School of Information Technologies
1 Cleveland Street
Darlington NSW Australia
Completed: September 2006
Client: University of Sydney

Francis-Jones Morehen Thorp
Richard Francis-Jones, Jeff Morehen, Janine Deshon, Kate Gooch, Vanessa Gribben, Roger Kuo, Aya Maceda, Brooke Matthews, Vikram Mukherjee, Philip Ng, James Perry, Alex Pienaar, Matthew Todd, Lance White

Structural & Civil: Taylor Thomson Whitting, Mechanical & Electrical: Lincolne Scott, Hydraulic: ThomsonKane, Environmental: Advanced Environmental Concepts, Acoustic: Arup Acoustics, Façade: Connell Mott MacDonald, Landscape: Francis-Jones Morehen Thorp, Cost: Davis Langdon Australia, Project Manager: Insight, Contractor: AW Edwards

Southbank Cultural Precinct
The Arts Centre
Soutbank VIC Australia
Masterplan completed: May 2008
Client: Arts Victoria, The Arts Centre Trust

Francis-Jones Morehen Thorp
Richard Francis-Jones, Geoff Croker, Jeff Morehen, Louise Goodman, Martin Hallen, Adam Guernier, Christina Crowe, Kerri Pratt, Matthew Todd, Zuzana Semelak, Phillip Ng, Melissa Ng, Jacob JeBailey

Landscape: Jeppe Aagaard Andersen + fjmt, Lighting: Rachel Burke + Electrolight, Building Services: Umow Lai & Associates, Environmental: Umow Lai Environment, Structural & Civil: Irwin Consult, Heritage: Lovell Chen, Traffic: GTA Consultants, Acoustics, Theatre Planning & Fire: ARUP, Building Surveyor: PLP, Access: Accessibility Solutions, Project Manager: Flagstaff, Arts Victoria

Surry Hills Library & Community Centre
405 Crown Street
Surry Hills NSW Australia
Completed: May 2009
Client: City of Sydney

Francis-Jones Morehen Thorp
Richard Francis-Jones, Simon Barr, Lance White, Alison Jones, Josephine Turner, Misha De Moyer, James Perry, Peter Wise, Mark Brandon, Matthew Todd
Landscape: Francis-Jones Morehen Thorp

Structural & Façade: Taylor Thomson Whitting, Engineer; Mechanical, Environmental, Electrical, Lifts, Lighting & Security: Steensen Varming, Civil & Hydraulic: Warren Smith & Partners, BUilding Surveyor: Davis Langdon, Acoustics: Acoustic Studio, Fire: Arup Fire, AV: Noisebox, Access: Accessibility Solutions, Design Manager: City Projects, Project Manager: City Projects, Contractor: WBHO Pro Build

Sydney Law School
Eastern Avenue
Camperdown NSW Australia
Completed: February 2009
Client: University of Sydney

Francis-Jones Morehen Thorp
Richard Francis-Jones, Jeff Morehen, Richard Thorp, Johnathan Redman, Lina Francis-Jones, Alison Jones, Richard Desgrand, Martin Hallen, Phillip Ng, Prudence Ho, Vikram Mukherjee, James Feghali, Karla Wilford, Nataly Ernst, Kate Gooch, Ian Brumby, Anthony Clarke, Pei Katty Huang, Conrad Johnston, David Lam, Jason Luk, Alexander Pienaar, Samuel To, James Sandwith, Daniel Schagemann, Christopher Bridge

Mechanical, Electrical, Communication, AV & Lift: Lincolne Scott, Structural: Taylor Thomson Whitting, Hydraulic & Fire Services: Warren Smith & Partners, Façade: Connell Wagner, Landscape: Jeppe Aagaard Andersen + Tinka Sack + Turf Design Studio, Fire & Acoustic: Arup, Quantity Surveyor & Code Compliance: Davis Langdon Australia, Access: Accessbility Solutions, Environmental: Advanced Environmental, Lighting: Vision Design, Traffic: Halcrow MWT, Geotechnical: Douglas Partners, Substation: DEP Consulting, Irrigation: Hydroplan, Wind: The University of Sydney Wind Engineering Services, Project Manager: Capital Insight, Contractor: Baulderstone

Tasmanian Museum & Art Gallery
Dunn Place
Hobart TAS Australia
Completed: March 2013 (Stage 1)
Client: Tasmanian Museum & Art Gallery

Francis-Jones Morehen Thorp
Richard Francis-Jones, Jeff Morehen, James Perry, Lilian Lau, Elizabeth Carpenter, Patrick Maitland, Annis Lee, Tony Musson, Phillip Pham; Landscape: Matthew Todd, Richard Tripolone, Zuzana Semelak

Structural, Civil & Traffic: Taylor Thomson Whitting; Mechanical, Electrical, Communications, Lighting, & Lift: Steensen Varming, Hydraulic & Fire Services: Warren Smith & Partners, Fire, BCA & Accessibility: Philip Chun, Acoustic: Acoustic Studio, Security: Business Risks International, Heritage: Design 5, Archaeology: Godden Mackay Logan, Indigenous: Groundworks, Environmental: Arup, Food Services: Historic Houses Trust & Cinni-Little, Project Manager: Root Projects Australia, Contractor: VOS Construction

Tyree Energy Technologies Building
H6, University of New South Wales
Kensington NSW Australia
Completed: February 2012
Client: University of New South Wales

Francis-Jones Morehen Thorp
Richard Francis-Jones, Jeff Morehen, Matthew Todd, Janine Deshon, Heidi Sinclair, Michelle Ho, Alison Jones, Martin Hallen, Laura Shapiro, Petra Kandusova, Cherry Williamson, Damian Campanella, Jodie Matthews, Sam Hodgkinson, Andrew Chung; Landscape: Matthew Todd, Richard Tripolone

Structural, Façade & Civil: Taylor Thomson Whitting, Mechanical & Specialty Gas: Steensen Varming; Electrical: Arup, Hydraulic & Fire Services: Warren Smith & Partners, Lighting: Arup, Fire: Arup, Acoustic: Acoustic Studio, Environmental: AECOM, Informatics: Wizard + Spinifex Group; BCA: City Plan Services, Access: Morris Goding, Lift: Arup, Wind: Windtech, Quantity Surveyor: Davis Langdon, Clean Room: AB Mandal, Project Manager: Capital Insight, Contractor: Brookfield Multiplex

Photographer credits

Atelier Illume—126, 130, 131

Stephen Barker—388

Brett Boardman—275, 276.3

Andrew Chung—IV, VI, 26, 27, 63, 85, 92.1.3, 139, 149, 197, 208.1, 209, 232, 235, 238, 240.1, 242.2, 244.2.4, 245, 258, 286.2.3, 290, 291, 314, 318, 319, 324, 325, 326, 327, 327.2, 333, 335.4, 336.3, 337, 338.2, 378, 379

Mathieu Faliu—41.1.2, 112.2, 113.3, 370, 378, 379

fjmt—26, 27, 60, 119.2.3.5, 136, 140, 141, 159, 162.2, 174, 202.1, 317, 334, 378, 379

Richard Glover—378

John Gollings—VIII, 2, 4, 6, 7, 8, 11, 15, 16, 17, 21, 22, 26, 27, 30, 46, 51, 52, 53, 54, 55, 56, 57.4.6, 66, 72, 73, 74, 75, 76, 77.3.4.5.6, 78, 79, 82, 87, 88, 89, 90, 91, 92.4, 93, 94, 104, 107, 108, 109, 110, 111, 112.1, 113.4, 146, 151, 152, 153, 156, 161, 162, 163, 164.1, 165, 167, 184, 187, 189, 190, 191, 194, 199, 200, 201, 202.2, 203, 204, 205, 206, 207, 208.2.3, 212, 214, 215, 216, 217, 220, 223.2, 225, 226, 227, 228, 229, 237, 240.2.3, 241, 242.1.2, 243, 244.1.3.5, 266, 269, 272, 274, 276.1.2, 277, 280, 285, 286.1, 287, 288, 289, 296, 300, 301, 302, 303, 322, 327.3, 330, 331, 335.2.3, 336.1.2, 338.1, 339, 340, 342, 383, 385, 386

Martin Hallen—334.1 (bottom right)

Annie Hensley—92.2, 166.1

Lend Lease—77.2

Luminova—13, 38, 41.1.3, 43

John McIver—162.2

John Marmaras—71

Trevor Mein—26, 178, 248, 251, 253, 254, 255, 256, 257

Phillip Ng—119.4, 378, 379

Sean Pettet—378, 379

Phillip Pham—164.2, 239, 374, 378, 379

Patrick Reynolds—Cover, II, 18, 26, 168, 169.3

Ethan Rohloff—84, 282

SKM—34, 48, 62, 68, 98, 100, 106, 114, 118, 122, 128, 132, 138, 142, 148, 158, 170, 186, 196, 222, 223, 234, 250, 262, 292, 298, 304, 308, 311

State Records NSW—40

Steensen Varming—12, 208.A

Martin van der Wal—57.5

Peter Wise—378, 379

Nursing and Medical Museum (Prince Henry Hospital Trained Nurses Association)—223.3

Awards

Auckland Art Gallery Toi o Tāmaki
Jørn Utzon Award for International Architecture–
    Australian Institute of Architects –2012
Architecture Medal–NZIA (National)–2012
Architecture Award–Public–NZIA (National)–2012
International Architecture Award–Royal
    Institute of British Architects–2012
National Award in Public Service Architecture–
    Asia Pacific Property Awards–2013
Pinnacle Award for Design Effectiveness–
    Australian Design Biennale Awards–2012
Australian Designed International Project–
    Excellence in Timber Design–Australian
    Timber Design Awards–2012
International Architecture Award–Chicago Athenaeum:
    Museum of Architecture and Design and European
    Centre for Art Design and Urban Studies–2012
Best Design Award for Identity Development
    (Large scale)–Gold–Designers
    Institute of New Zealand–2012
Best Design Award for Environmental Graphics–Silver–
    Designers Institute of New Zealand–2012
Best Design Award for Visual Communication–Silver–
    Designers Institute of New Zealand–2012
Communication Design Award–IF Communication
    Design Award, Germany–2013
Project Achievement Award for Museum or
    Gallery Development–Museums Aotearoa:
    New Zealand Museums Awards–2012
Davis Langdon Excellence Award for projects over
    $50M–New Zealand Institute of Building–2012
Supreme Award 2012–New Zealand
    Institute of Building–2012
Hawkins Construction Heritage and Adaptive Reuses
    Property Award–NZ Property Council–2012
Supreme Award–NZ Property Council –2012
Education and Arts Property Industry Award–
    NZ Property Council–2012
Commercial Architectural Excellence–NZ
    Wood Timber Design Awards–2012
Indigenous Timber Showcase Award–NZ
    Wood Timber Design Awards–2012
Architecture Award–Heritage–NZIA Auckland–2011
Architecture Award–Public–NZIA Auckland–2011
Architecture Award–Heritage–NZIA National–2012
Communication Design Award–Type
    Directors Club, New York–2011

Australian School of Business
Architecture Award for Public Architecture–
    RAIA (NSW Chapter)–2008

Bayside Police Station
Public Buildings (New), Commendation—Australian
    Institute of Architects (Victoria)–2013
Public Design Award, Highly commended–
    Australian Interior Design Awards–2011
Best Ecologically Sustainable Design–Bayside
    Built Environment Awards–2010
Best New or Renovation to a Commercial Building–
    Bayside Built Environment Awards–2010
Most Creative Building Design–Bayside
    Built Environment Awards–2010
Interior Fitout Award–Commercial–
    Timber Design Awards–2011
Timber Panels–Timber Design Awards–2011
Civic and Community Shortlist–World
    Architecture Festival–2011

365 George Street, Sydney
Best Use of Glass–Master Builders
    Association Awards–2011

Blake Dawson Waldron, Canberra
National Interior Award–RAIA–1999
Canberra Medallion for Architectural Excellence–
    RAIA (ACT Chapter)–1999

Capella Apartments
Best New Commercial and Mixed Use Award–
    Randwick City Council–2006

Chancellery & Business School
Award of Excellence for Main Entry Colonnade–
    Illuminating Engineering Society of Australia & New
    Zealand (WA Division)–2004
Public Building over $20 Million–Master
    Builders Association (WA)–2005
Commendation (Civic Design)–RAIA (WA Chapter)–2005

Chemical Sciences Building
Highly Commended–Institute of
    Engineers Australia–2008
Chemical Sciences Building, UNSW–Award of
    Excellence (Education Building: $10m–$50m)–
    Master Builders Association (NSW)–2007
Chemical Sciences Building, UNSW–Urban Design Award
    (Public Building)–Randwick City Council–2008

The Concourse
Public Architecture Award–AIA (NSW Chapter)–2012
Philip Chun Award for Government Leadership–
    Property Council of Australia–2013
Best Public Building ($25m & over)–Master
    Builders Association Awards–2011
Best Use of Steel–Master Builders
    Association Awards–2011
Innovation Award for Construction Technique/Equipment–
    Master Builders Association Awards–2011
Outstanding Construction–Master Builders
    Association Awards–2011
National Public Buildings Award–over $50 million–
    Master Builders Association Awards–2011
Timber Veneers–Timber Design Awards–2011
Government Leadership for Urban Development–UDIA
    NSW Austral Bricks Awards for Excellence–2012

Creative Industries Precinct
Commendation Award–RAIA (Qld Chapter)–2005

Darling Quarter
Sir Arthur G. Stephenson Award for a Commercial
    Building–RAIA (NSW Chapter)–2013
Lloyd Rees Award for Outstanding Urban
    Design (with Aspect Studios and Lend
    Lease)–RAIA (NSW Chapter)–2013
Milo Dunphy Award for Sustainable Architecture–
    RAIA (NSW Chapter)–2013
City of Sydney Lord Mayor's Prize–RAIA
    (NSW Chapter)–2013
Best Office Development–World
    Architecture Festival–2012
International Architecture Award–Chicago Athenaeum
    Museum of Architecture and Design–2012
Winner–UN World Enviornment Day
    Award–Green Building–2013
Design Excellence Award–Australian Institute of
    Landscape Architects (AILA) NSW–2011
Presidents Award–International Federation
    of Landscape Architects–2012
Team Innovation Award–NSW National
    Association of Women in Construction
    (NAWIC) Awards for Excellence–2012
Australian Development of the Year—Property
    Council of Australia–2013
Best Office Development—Property
    Council of Australia–2013
Best Workplace Project—Property
    Council of Australia–2013
Best Sustainable Development–New Buildings—
    Property Council of Australia–2013
Master Builders Association and Clinton Recruitment
    Award for Team Innovation–National Association
    of Women in Construction–2011
Leisure Development–Asia Pacific–Asia Pacific

International Property Awards–2012
Mixed Use Development–Australia 5 Star–Asia
    Pacific International Property Awards–2012
Office Design Architecture–Highly Commended–Asia
    Pacific International Property Awards–2012
Office Development–Australia 5 Star–Asia Pacific
    International Property Awards–2012
Office Interior–Australia 5 Star–Asia Pacific
    International Property Awards–2012
Professional Excellence in Building High Commendation–
    Australian Institute of Building–2012
Dexus Property Group Environmental Award–
    Australian Property Institute–2011
Built Environment Awards–Banksia
    Environmental Awards–2012
Large Commercial Winner–BPN
    Sustainability Award–2012
Commissioning Project of the Year–Chartered
    Institution of Building Services Engineers–2012
Buildings and Structures Excellence Award–
    Engineers Australia Sydney Division–2012
Commercial Exterior Commendation–Intergrain
    Timber Vision Awards–2012
Landscape Commendation–Intergrain
    Timber Vision Awards–2012
Ovations Award Outstanding Client Service–
    Jones Lang LaSalle–2011
Public Playspaces–Over $1M–Kidsafe 2012
    National Playspace Design Awards–2012
Innovation–Playground–Lend Lease Awards–2011
Leadership in Safety–Construction–
    Lend Lease Awards–2011
Leadership in Safety–Excellence in Design–Lend Lease
    Awards Incident and Injury Free Global Awards–2011
Innovation–Façade Lighting–Lend Lease Awards
    Innovation and Excellence Award–2011
Construction–$400M and over–Master
    Builders Association (NSW)–2012
Construction–Energy Efficiency–Master
    Builders Association (NSW)–2012
Construction–Interior Fitouts–Master
    Builders Association (NSW)–2012
Development Excellence Awards Best Commercial
    Development–NSW Urban Taskforce–2012
Award for Parks–Parks and Leisure Australia–2012
Australia Award for Urban Design–Planning
    Institute of Australia–2012
NSW Development of the Year–Property
    Council of Australia / Rider Levett Bucknall
    Innovation and Excellence Awards–2013
Urban Design Award–Architecture–
    Sydney Design Awards–2012
Retail/ Commercial Development Award–Urban
    Development Institute of Australia–2012
Sustainable Development & Consultancy/
    Contracting High Commendation–Urban
    Development Institute of Australia–2012
Global Award for Excellence–Urban Land Institute–2012
Power and Energy Management Award–
    Zenith Awards–2012

Eastern Avenue Auditorium
Commendation (Public Building)–RAIA
    (NSW Chapter)–2003

**John Niland Scientia Building and
Red Centre**
Lloyd Rees Award for Excellence in
    Civic Design–RAIA–2000

John Niland Scientia Building
Sir Zelman Cowen Award–RAIA–2000
Sir John Sulman Award for Architectural
    Excellence–RAIA–2000
The Kevin Cavanagh Medal for Excellence in
    Concrete–Concrete Institute of Australia–2001
Award for Outstanding Concrete Structures–

Fédération Internationale du Béton (International
    Federation for Structural Concrete)–2002
Citation of Merit, Medium Structures–
    Lightweight Structures Association of
    Australia Design Awards–2000
National New Commercial Building Award
    for Construction Excellence–Master
    Builders Association (NSW)–2000
Outstanding Construction Award Educational
    Building $5M Plus category–Master
    Builders Association (NSW)–2000
Overall Winner for Construction Excellence–Master
    Builders Association (NSW)–2000
Randwick City Urban Design Award for Public
    Building–Randwick City Council–2004

Little Bay (Manta and Alaris) Apartments
Multiple Housing Commendation–RAIA
    (NSW Chapter)–2013
Residential Category–Multi Unit Housing –Randwick
    City Urban Design Awards –2013
Winner, Medium Density Development (Austral
    Bricks Award for Excellence)–Urban
    Development Institute of Australia–2011
Excellence in Housing Award for Integrated
    Housing (Open Price Category)–Master
    Builders Association Awards–2011

Macquarie University Library
Best Tertiary Building ($50M & Over)–Master
    Builders Association Awards–2011

Max Webber Library, Blacktown
Merit Award–Illuminating Engineering Society of
    Australia & New Zealand (NSW Division)–2006
Premier's Award–RAIA (NSW Chapter)–2007
Commendation (Public Building)–RAIA
    (NSW Chapter)–2006

Meta Apartments
Joint Winner (Adaptive Reuse Corporate/
    Government)–Energy Australia/National
    Trust Heritage Award–2005
Multiple Housing Commendation Award–
    RAIA (NSW Chapter)–2005

The Mint
Sir John Sulman Award for Outstanding
    Public Architecture–RAIA–2005
Greenway Award for Conservation (with Clive Lucas,
    Stapleton and Partners and the Historic Houses Trust
    of New South Wales)–RAIA (NSW Chapter)–2005
Lachlan Macquarie Award for Conservation (with Clive
    Lucas, Stapleton and Partners and the Historic
    Houses Trust of New South Wales)–RAIA–2005
Professional Excellence Award–Commercial Construction
    $10M–$50M–Australian Institute of Building–2005
Project of the Year–Commercial Construction
    $10M–$50M–Australian Institute of Building–2005
Professional Excellence Award–Heritage
    Construction $10M–$50M–Australian
    Institute of Building (NSW Chapter)–2005
Building Services Journal–Top 30 ground breaking
    buildings of the world–Chartered Institute of
    Building Services Engineers (UK)–2008
Interior Design Award (Public / Institutional)–
    Design Institute of Australia–2006
Joint Winner (Conservation–Energy Mangement)–Energy
    Australia/National Trust Heritage Awards–2005
Award of Excellence for The Mint–Illuminating
    Engineering Society of Australia & New
    Zealand (NSW Division)–2005
Award for Restoration ($10M–$25M)–Master
    Builders Association (NSW)–2005
Best Specialty Venue (National)–Meetings
    & Events Australia–2007
Best Specialty Venue–Meetings & Events

Australia (NSW)–2006
Stockland Award for Achievement in Design for Elizabeth
  Carpenter, Project Architect–National Association
  of Women in Construction (Australia)–2005
Commendation in the Category The Environment
  and Natural Resources for Conservation/
  Adaptation of The Mint Coining Factory, Sydney–
  NSW Premier's Public Sector Award–2005
Best Use of Western Red Cedar (Highly Commended)–
  Timber Development Association–2005

**Museum of Contemporary Art and
Sydney Harbour Moving Image Centre**
International Project Award Winner–AR/MIPIM–2003

Newcastle Museum
Public Architecture Commendation–
  AIA (NSW Chapter)–2012
Graph Building Heritage Award–Landcom 2012
  Lower Hunter Urban Design Awards–2012
Scooters & Mobility & Australasia Independent Living
  Aids Universal Access Award–Landcom 2012
  Lower Hunter Urban Design Awards–2012
Best Adaptive Reuse of a Historic Building ($9m &
  over)–Master Builders Association Awards–2011
Best NSW Regional & ACT Project–UDIA NSW
  Austral Bricks Awards for Excellence–2012
Urban Renewal Commendation–UDIA NSW
  Austral Bricks Awards for Excellence–2012

Red Centre
Sole Recipient, Honour Award for Design Excellence,
  Sustainable Design Awards Program,–AIA New York
  Chapter, Boston Society of Architects / AIA–2003
The Green Building Awards Bronze Medal–
  The Architecture Show Magazine & The
  Francis Greenway Society–2001

St Barnabas Church
Best Use of Steel–Master Builders
  Association Awards–2012
Construction–$10M–$25M–Master Builders
  Association Awards–2012

School of Information Technologies
Excellence in Construction Award, Educational
  Building $10m–$50m–Master Builders
  Association (NSW)–2006
Shortlist (Education)–Property Council Australia–2009

Sugar Dock, Jacksons Landing
Multi-Residential, Commendation–AIA
  (NSW Chapter)–2011

Surry Hills Library and Community Centre
Public Service Architecture, Highly Commended–2011
  Asia Pacific Property Awards–2011
National Architecture Award for Public Architecure–
  Australian Institute of Architects–2010
National Architecture Award for Sustainable Architecture–
  Australian Institute of Architects–2010
John Verge Award–Interior Architecture–Australian
  Institute of Architects (NSW Chapter)–2010
Milo Dunphy Award–Sustainable Architecture–Australian
  Institute of Architects (NSW Chapter)–2010
Public Architecture Award–Australian Institute
  of Architects (NSW Chapter)–2010
AIRAH award for excellence in sustainability–
  Australian Institute of Refrigeration,
  Airconditioning and Heating–2010
Best Use of Timber Panels–Highly Commended–
  Australian Timber Design Awards (NSW)–2009
Public or Commercial Buildings–Highly Commended–
  Australian Timber Design Awards (NSW)–2009
Finalist–Banksia Awards–2009
Public Building and Urban Design–BPN
  Sustainability Awards–2010

Emilio Ambasz Award for Green Architecture
  (runner-up), Architecture of Israel–2010
Highly Commended in Institutional Category–Interior
  Design of Excellence Awards–2010
Best New Global Design 2011–International
  Architecture Awards, Chicago–2011
Excellence in Construction Award–Public
  Buildings ($10-$25 million)–Master
  Builders Association (NSW)–2009
Finalist–National Interior Design Awards–2010
Sustainability Green Globe Award–NSW Government,
  Environment, Climate Change & Water–2010
Finalist–UN World Enviornment Day Award–2009
Winner, Environmental Excellence–Urban
  Development Institute Australia (NSW)–2009

Sydney Law School
General– High Commendation–Australian
  Institute of Building–2009
General– High Commendation–Australian
  Institute of Building (NSW)–2009
Best Use of Decorative Wood veneers–Australian
  Timber Design Awards (National)–2009
Interior Fit-out–Australian Timber Design
  Awards (National)–2009
Best Use of Decorative Wood veneers–Australian
  Timber Design Awards (NSW)–2009
Best Use of Timber Panels–Highly Commended–
  Australian Timber Design Awards (NSW)–2009
Interior Design–Australian Timber Design
  Awards (NSW)–2009
Public or Commercial Buildings–Highly Commended–
  Australian Timber Design Awards (NSW)–2009
Public Building– Highly Commmended–BPN
  Sustainability Awards–2009
Excellence in Construction Award–Tertiary
  Buildings (Over $25 million)–Master
  Builders Association (NSW)–2009
Public Architecture Commendation–RAIA–2009
Public Architecture Award–RAIA (NSW Chapter)–2009
Sustainable Architecture Award–RAIA
  (NSW Chapter)–2009
Urban Design Commendation–RAIA
  (NSW Chapter)–2009
Finalist, Educational Sector Awards–World
  Architecture News–2010

Tasmanian Museum & Art Gallery
MAGNA national winner–Museums Australia–2013

Tyree Energies Technology Building
Outstanding Construction Award–Master
  Builders Association (NSW)–2012
National Public Buildings Award–over $50 million–
  Master Builders Association Awards–2012
Tertiary Buildings–$50 million and over–Master
  Builders Association Awards–2012
Public Buildings Category–Randwick City
  Urban Design Awards–2013
Sustainability Category–Randwick City
  Urban Design Awards–2013
Finalist–UN World Enviornment Day Award–2013

Owen G. Glenn Business School
Innovate Gold Award of Excellence–Association of
  Consulting Engineers New Zealand–2009
Auckland Architecture Award (Public
  Architecture)–NZIA–2008
Merit award (Education & Arts)–Property
  Council New Zealand–2008
Shortlist (Education)–World Architecture Festival–2008

Atrium ceiling, Darling Quarter

383

Bibliography

Books

Asensio, P (ed.) 2003, 'Maroubra Apartment', *Sydney houses*, teNeues, Kempen, pp. 336–43

Barrett, M (ed.) 2011, 'Scientia, University of New South Wales', *The Phaidon atlas of contemporary world architecture*, Phaidon, London

Beaver, R (ed.) 2009, *In the realm of learning: the University of Sydney's new law school*, Images Publishing, Melbourne

Dokulil, H & Marreiros, S (eds.) 2007, 'Chancellery & Business School, Edith Cowan University', *Australia: architecture and design*, daab, Cologne

Frampton, K (ed.) (forthcoming), *Francis-Jones Morehen Thorp Monograph*, Oro Editions, Pt Reyes Station

Griffin, R (ed.) 2009, *The Mint project*, Historic Houses Trust of New South Wales, Sydney

Heritage Office & Royal Australian Institute of Architects NSW Chapter, 2008, 'The Mint: Coining factory to Historic Houses Trust head office and library, Macquarie Street, Sydney', *New uses for heritage places*, Heritage Council of NSW, Parramatta, pp. 36–7

Howells, T 2009, 'New Law School; Eastern Avenue Auditorium; School of Information Technologies', *University of Sydney architecture*, Watermark Press, Sydney pp. 78–80, 109, 197

Jackson, D 2005, 'Francis-Jones Morehen Thorp, Sydney' *10 x 10_2: 10 critics 100 architects*, Phaidon, London, pp. 120–3

Klaebe, H (ed.) 2006, 'Creative Industries Precinct, QUT', *Sharing stories: a social history of the Kelvin Grove Urban Village*, Focus Publishing, Sydney

Krauel, J & Broto, C (eds.) 2010, 'Business School, University of Auckland', *Today's educational facilities*, Links International, Spain, pp. 54–65

Krauel, J & Broto, C (eds.) 2010, 'Chancellery and Business School, Edith Cowan University', *Today's educational facilities*, Links International, Spain, pp. 222–39

Latham, P (ed.) 1994 'Allen Allen & Hemsley tenancy', *Architects & interior designers of Australia and New Zealand*, Images Publishing, Melbourne

McGillick, P & Bingham-Hall, P 2004, 'Scientia, University of NSW', *Sydney architecture*, Pesaro Publishing, Sydney, pp. 136, 169

McLeod, V (ed.) 2009, 'Chancellery & Business School, Edith Cowan University', *Detail in contemporary timber architecture*, Laurence King, London, pp. 18–21

Mostaedi, A (ed.). 2000, 'Woy Woy house', *New coastal houses*, Links International, Barcelona, pp. 180–91

Navone, N (ed.) 2008, 'Scientia, University of New South Wales; The Mint; Max Webber Library', *BSI Swiss architectural award*, Switzerland, Mendrisio Academy Press, Mendrisio, pp. 92–5

Orr, K (in press), 'Francis-Jones Morehen Thorp, Sydney', *The encyclopaedia of Australian architecture*, Cambridge University Press, Melbourne

Shaoqiang, W (ed.) 2010, 'Capella Apartments', *M3 modern architecture*, Sandu Publishing, China, pp. 206–9

Shaoqiang, W (ed.) 2010, 'Rose Bay Apartments', *M3 modern architecture*, Sandu Publishing, China, pp. 254–7

Stuebe, K & Parken, D (eds.) 2010, 'Surry Hills Library & Community Centre', *Inspire*, Australian Institute of Architects & Reveal Books, Melbourne, pp. 52–3, 137, 160–1

ThinkArchit, 2011, 'Capella Apartments', *The architecture design of apartment in the world*, China, pp. 308–13

ThinkArchit, 2011, 'Rose Bay Apartments', *The architecture design of apartment in the world*, China, pp. 314–9

Periodicals

Architecture Australia 2012, 'International Architecture - the Jorn Utzon Award', Vol 101 No 6 pp. 82-83

Architectural Review Australia, 2006, 'Museum of Contemporary Art', December, pp. 5

Architecture New Zealand, 2005, 'Auckland Art Gallery: Across the Board', October

Architecture of Israel, 2010, 'Surry Hills Library & Community Centre', no. 8, February, pp. 14–15

Barrett, M 2008, 'Crystal clear commercial', *Design Trends*, vol.24, no. 14, pp. 172–180

Barrett, M 2008, 'Degree of Excellence', *Commercial Design Trends*, vol. 24, no. 4, May, pp. 6–17

Belogolowsky, V 2012, 'Interview Richard Francis-Jones, *Tatlin News*, 3.69.2012 pp. 68-72

Bruhn, C 2006, 'The Mint', *Artichoke*, Interior Design Awards Special Edition, April, pp. 22–23

Cantrill, PJ 1997, 'Green Machine', *Architectural Review Australia*, December, vol.62, pp. 81–87

Chesterman, D 2010, '10x10 millenium projects: University of New South Wales', *Architecture Bulletin*, January–February, pp. 16–17

di Chiarabini, G, 2010, 'Re-interpreted dialects', *Inside Quality Design*, July–September, July–Spetember, pp. 28–35

Cook, M & Hopkinson, S 2011, 'Auckland Art Gallery Toi o Tāmaki, *ArchitectureNZ*, No 5 pp. 42-52

Crosling, J 1999, 'Revealing academia', *Architectural Review Australia*, Summer, pp. 84–91

Davey, P 2003, 'MIPIM future project preview', *Architectural Review* (London), May, no. 1275, pp. 4–5, 21

Davey, P 2003, 'MCA Moving Image Centre competition', *Architectural Review* (London), no. 1275, May, pp. 50–54

Drew, P 2009, 'The bridge that gathers', *Architectural Review Australia*, vol. 111, August–September, pp. 72–83

Drew, P 2009, 'Surry Hills Library & Community Centre', *Monument*, August–September, pp. 68–73

Drew, P 2005, 'A view to the city', *Architecture Australia*, May–June, pp. 34–38

Droege, P 2004, 'Compliance, conviction and the art of difference', *Architectural Review Australia*, January, pp. 33–35

Eichblatt, S 2006, 'Idea factories: art decisions', *Urbis*, vol.31, pp. 76

Fortmeyer, R 2010, 'Library down under', *GreenSource*, May–June, pp. 68–71

Green 2012, 'Surry Hills Library & Community Centre', Vol 16 pp. 64-69

Harding, L 2010, 'Surry Hills Library & Community Centre', *Architecture Australia*, vol. 99, no. 2, March, pp. 41–49

Hartoonian 2012, 'Building civitas', *Architecture Australia*, Vol 101 No 2 pp. 48-54

Hartoonian, G 2004, 'Landscape, the fabric of architecture', *Architecture Australia*, January–February, pp. 64–71

Hartoonian, G & Crosling, J 2001, 'Tertiary annex', *Architectural Review Australia*, June, pp. 58–66

Hawen, S 2009, 'The University of Sydney', *Landscape Architecture Australia*, no. 123, September, pp. 40–47

Hawkes, C 2011, 'Off the wall', *Trends*, v27 no5 pp. 6-33

Hawkes, C 2011, 'Open to view', *Commercial Design Trends*, Vol 27 No 15 pp. 42-47

Hawkes, C 2011, 'Embracing design: Commonwealth Bank Place, Sydney', *Commercial Design Trends*, Vol 27 No 15 pp. 16-25

Hawkes, C 2010, 'In the box seat', *Commercial Design Trends*, vol.26, no. 4, April, pp. 68–75

Heneghan, T 2006, 'Max Webber Library', *Architecture Australia*, May–June, pp. 86–95

Henrickson, G 2002, 'Scientia, University of New South Wales: exhibition and performance building', *Architectural Review* (London), no. 1263, May, pp. 44–47

Henrisken, J 2007, 'Is an art gallery Newcastle's ticket to urban renewal?', *Architecture Bulletin*, January–February, pp. 12

Hight, C 2009, 'The New somatic architecture', *Harvard Design Magazine*, no. 30, Spring–Summer, pp. 24–31

Hill, J 2007, 'Newcastle Regional Art Gallery Competition', *Architecture Bulletin*, January–February, pp. 10–11

Hyun, Y 2010, 'New Head Office for the Historic Houses Trust of New South Wales', *C3*, no. 311, July, pp. 98–107

Intelligente Architektur, 2004, 'Green machine', January, pp. 42–47

Jackson, D 2002, 'Today's arguments in Australian architecture', *World Architecture*, no. 145, pp. 17–18 and pp. 46–49

Jackson, S 2004, 'Sometimes landform, sometimes image', *Architecture Australia*, March–April, pp. 34–35

Kim, Y 2009, 'Business School, University of Auckland', *Concept*, no. 127, November, pp. 64–69

Kucharek, JC 2011, 'Personal touch', *RIBA Journal*, 11 pp. 69-72

Laboratory Design, 2009, 'University of New South Wales: New Projects, Chemical Sciences Building', June

Lester, M 2003, 'Booz Allen Hamilton', *Artichoke*, vol.3, no. 2, pp. 64–71

McGillick, P 2012, 'CBA Unplugged', *Indesign*, 49 pp. 70-91

McGregor, B 2005, 'Mint-making', *Architecture Bulletin*, January–February, pp. 16

McKay, B & Hunt, J 2008, 'Outreach program', *ArchitectureNZ*, vol.1, January, pp. 42–59

Mackenzie, D 2010, 'Surry Hills Library & Community Centre–so how does it work?', *Architecture Australia*, vol. 99, no. 2, March, pp. 101–104

Mackenzie, D 2007, 'Making current benchmarks the new entry–level', *Architecture Bulletin*, March–April, pp. 12

Mackenzie, D 2005, '"Total architecture" provides mint conditions', *Architecture Bulletin*, January–February, pp. 18–20

Mackenzie, D 2005, 'Historic buildings for the future', *Architecture Bulletin*, January–February, pp. 17

Mackenzie, D & Wright, S 2006, 'The Mint', *Architecture Bulletin*, March–April, pp. 10

de Manincor, J 2007, 'Capella Apartments', *Architectural Review Australia*, vol. 99, January, pp. 60–66

de Manincor, J 2005, 'The Mint', *Architecture Australia*, January–February, pp. 80–87

Meiqian, Q 2010, 'Faculty of Law, University of Sydney', *Interior Public Space*, no. 12, December, pp. 166–177

Meiqian, Q 2010, 'Surry Hills Library and Community Centre', *Interior Public Space*, no. 8, August, pp. 28–35

Moore, C 2006, 'Chancellery building and business school', *Architectural Record* (New York), no. 03, pp. 106–111

Mullazzani, M 2010, 'Beautiful and sustainable', *Casabella*, no. 786, February, pp. 24–34

Niski, D 2009, 'Australian School of Business: stairs', *Artichoke*, no. 27, May, pp. 60–63

Preston, M 2012, 'Darling Quarter', *Landscape Architecture Australia*, 135 pp. 48-53

Reboli, M 2006, 'The Mint', *Casabella*, no. 744, pp. 24–29

Ridgway, S 2003, 'Sam Ridgeway and Richard Francis-Jones, a conversation', *Architectural Theory Review*, vol.8, no. 1, pp. 1–13

Salhani, P 2009, 'Surry Hills Library and Community Centre, FJMT', *Architecture Bulletin*, September–October, pp. 17

Sang-worl, B 2010, 'Faculty of Law, University of Sydney', *Architecture & Culture*, no. 346, March, pp. 44–57

Sellars, S 2012, 'Crossing the Threshold', *Architecture Review*, 125 pp. 84-89

Sokol, D 2010, 'Turned inside-out', *GreenSource*, May, http://greensource.construction.com/features/Solutions/2010/may/1005_faculty_of_law_building.asp

Specifier 2011, 'Macquarie Library', 100 pp. 28-29

Specifier, 2010, 'Faculty of Law, University of Sydney', no. 90, August, pp. 100–103

Stead, N 2001, 'Formal geometries', *Architecture Australia*, vol.90 no. 04, July–August, pp. 57–61

Stevens, A 2012, 'Artful Weaving', *Indesign*, 51 pp. 156-168

Thalis, P 2005, 'The Mint', *Architectural Review Australia*, vol.91, May, pp. 60–67

TIME Pacific, 2005, 'Auckland Art Gallery: Finding Their Inner Spring', October

Watson, F & Hook, M 2010, 'Francis–Jones Morehen Thorp (fjmt)', *Architectural Design*, no. 204, March, pp. 118–125

Weirick, J 2001, 'Radar: competition', *Architecture Australia*, July–August, pp. 14–18

Wettbewerbe Aktuell, 2006, 'Erweiterung der Newcastle Region Art Gallery, Australien', October, pp. 41

Whittle, K 2011, 'Force for change', Architectural Review Australia, no. 119, April-May, pp. 70–77

Xu, Y 2010, 'Faculty of Law, University of Sydney', *World Architecture*, no. 243, September, pp. 72–77

Xu, Y 2006, 'The Mint, Sydney, Australia', *World Architecture*, no. 191, pp. 55–59

Yamane, K 2010, 'Faculty of Law, University of Sydney', *Detail* (Tokyo), no. 184, April, pp. 52

Yun, S 2010, 'Faculty of Law, University of Sydney', *Concept*, no. 138, October, pp. 58–69

Yun, S 2010, 'Mulitfunctional Community', *Concept*, no. 136, August, pp. 90–95

Published texts

Francis-Jones, R 2011, 'Architecture & material craft: FJMT', *Architectural Review Australia*, no. 119, April-May 2011, p. 45

Frampton, K & Francis-Jones, R 2009, 'The power of smallness: the Austrian Cultural Forum', *Skyplane*, vol. 5, pp. 55–7.

Francis-Jones, R 2009, 'Design' *The Mint project,* Historic Houses Trust of New South Wales, Sydney, pp. 46–53

Francis-Jones, R 2009, 'Last Words' *The Mint project,* Historic Houses Trust of New South Wales, Sydney, pp. 94–7

Francis-Jones, R 2009, 'Fragments of learning: movement and light', *In the realm of learning*, Images Publishing, Melbourne, pp. 14–7

Francis-Jones, R (ed.) 2008, *CV08: Critical visions*, Royal Australian Institute of Architects

Francis-Jones, R 2008, 'Critical Visions', *Architecture Australia,* March-April

Francis-Jones, R 2007, 'Crisis of the object: the architecture of theatricality', *Architecture Australia*. vol. 96, no. 4, July-August

Francis-Jones, R 2007, 'Time regained, *ArchitectureNZ*, 4 pp. 26-30

Francis-Jones, R 2005, 'The essence of Architectural Bulletin', *Architecture Bulletin*, pp. 6-7

Francis-Jones, R 2004, 'Introduction', *Tectonic form and critical culture*, Royal Australian Institute of Architects, pp. 10–1

Francis-Jones, R 2004, 'The intersection and dissection of theory and practice', *BE UNSW*, November, pp. 10–1

Francis-Jones, R 2003, 'Labour, work and architecture', *Architectural Review Australia*, March, p.

Francis-Jones, R 2002, 'Search for the universal', *On monumentality*, Royal Australian Institute of Architects, pp 8–9

Francis-Jones, R 2002, 'The (im)possibility of slowness: a note on globalisation, ideology and speed in contemporary architecture', *10x10: 10 critics 100 architects,*. Phaidon, London, pp. 433–4

Francis-Jones, R 2001, 'Groundplane', *Content*

Francis-Jones, R 2001, 'Culture and Place', *Architecture Bulletin*

Francis-Jones, R 2000, 'The challenge of livable housing', *Architecture Bulletin*, December, p. 16

Francis-Jones, R 2000, 'Sydney's search for the meaningful search of place', *Architecture Bulletin*, September, pp. 9–14

Francis-Jones, R 1999, 'Pavilions and platforms', *Architectural Review Australia*

Francis-Jones, R 1997, 'Architecture not language—a note on representation' *UME* vol. 3, pp. 50–1

Francis-Jones, R 1997, 'Between representation and commodification', Curtin University

Francis-Jones, R 1997, 'Passive design in architecture', *Architectural Review Australia*, vol. 62, December, pp. 90–2

Francis-Jones, R 1994, 'Architectural representation', *Proceedings from the RAIA debate*

Francis-Jones, R 1993, 'Labyrinth of Images', *Architecture Australia*, March

Francis-Jones, R 1992, 'A misguided view of Post-Modernism', *Architecture Bulletin*

Francis-Jones, R 1991, 'Yet another strand of Post-Modernism', *Architecture Bulletin*, June

Sydney Law School

Atrium, Darling Quarter

Contributors

Kenneth Frampton

Kenneth Frampton was born in the United Kingdom in 1930 and trained as an architect at the Architectural Association School of Architecture, London. After practicing for a number of years in the United Kingdom and in Israel, he served as the editor of the British magazine *Architectural Design*. He has taught at a number of leading institutions including the Royal College of Art, the ETH Zurich, EPFL Lausanne, the Accademia di Architettura in Mendrisio, and the Berlage Institute in The Netherlands. He is currently the Ware Professor of Architecture at the GSAPP, Columbia University, New York. He is the author of *Modern Architecture and the Critical Present* (1980), *Studies in Tectonic Culture* (1995), *American Masterworks* (1995), *Le Corbusier* (2001), *Labour, Work & Architecture* (2005), and an updated fourth edition of *Modern Architecture: A Critical History* (2007).

Jennifer Taylor

Jennifer Taylor (LFRAIA) is a Director of the International Committee of Architectural Critics (CICA), and is known primarily for her publications on contemporary Australian, Japanese and South Pacific architecture. She graduated from the University of Washington, Seattle, and has taught in many architectural schools throughout the world. Appointed University of Sydney 1970–1998, Queensland University of Technology since 1999.

She was awarded the Japan Foundation Fellowship in 1975 and 1994–5, the Inaugural RAIA Marion Mahony Griffin Award for writing and teaching in 1998 and the Inaugural RAIA National Education Prize in 2000. She received the UIA Jean Tschumi Prize honourable mention for architectural criticism in 1999 and 2002, and the Inaugural President's Medal of the AIA in 2010. Among her publications are *John Andrews: Architecture a Performing Art, Australian Architecture since 1960, Tall Buildings: 1945–70: Australian Business Going Up, The Architecture of Fumihiko Maki: Space, City, Order and Technology. Architecture in the South Pacific* is for publication 2013.

Richard Francis-Jones

Richard is the Design Director of fjmt and is Visiting Professor at the University of New South Wales. He is Fellow of the Australian Institute of Architects and in 2012 was made an honorary fellow of the American Institute of Architects.

He graduated from the University of Sydney with a Bachelor of Science (Architecture) in 1981 and a Bachelor of Architecture with First Class Honours and the University Medal in 1985. He attended Columbia University on an ITT Fellowship, where he studied under Kenneth Frampton, completing a Master of Science in Architecture and Building Design in 1987. He subsequently taught at Columbia University as an Adjunct Associate Professor of Architecture. He was the creative director of the Australian Institute of Architects' 2008 national conference, *Critical Visions: Form Representation and the Culture of Globalisation*, and is an editor of *Skyplane* and *Content: A Journal of Architecture*. Richard was President of the RAIA (NSW Chapter) from 2001–2 and was a member of the NSW Architects Registration Board from 2001–4.

Jeff Morehen

Jeff is the Managing Director of fjmt and has been responsible for the project delivery on many of fjmt's most significant and awarded commissions. He was Project Architect for the highly acclaimed John Niland Scientia Building at the University of New South Wales, Project Director for the multi-awarded Mint project, and was the Project Director for the University of Sydney's Sydney Law School and School of Information Technologies and integrated public domain projects.

Jeff has achieved considerable success in the delivery of high-profile public commissions and has particular expertise in the management of projects that involve demanding briefs, multiple stakeholders and constrained budgets. His expertise is diverse and extends to include specialisation in project management, contract administration and procurement, and environmental sustainability.

Forecourt façade detail, Owen G Glenn Business School, University of Auckland

Published by:
ORO Editions
Publishers of Architecture, Art, and Design
Gordon Goff: Publisher
www.oroeditions.com
info@oroeditions.com

Copyright © 2014 by ORO Editions
ISBN: 978-1-935935-14-8
10 09 08 07 06 5 4 3 2 1 First Edition

Graphic Design: Tim Harper
Edited by: Christine Kwong
Color Separations and Printing: ORO Group Ltd.
Printed in China.
Production Manager: Usana Shadday

Special thanks: Kenneth Frampton, Jennifer Taylor, Richard Thorp & Alicia McCarthy

This book was printed and bound using a variety of sustainable manufacturing processes
and materials including soy-based inks, aqueous-based varnish, VOC- and formaldehyde-
free glues, and phthalate-free laminations. The text is printed using offset sheetfed
lithographic printing process in 4 color on 157gsm premium matte art paper with an
off-line gloss aqueous spot varnish applied to all photographs.

ORO Editions makes a continuous effort to minimize the overall carbon footprint of
its publications. As part of this goal, ORO Editions, in association with Global ReLeaf,
arranges to plant trees to replace those used in the manufacturing of the paper produced
for its books. Global ReLeaf is an international campaign run by American Forests, one
of the world's oldest nonprofit conservation organizations. Global ReLeaf is American
Forests' education and action program that helps individuals, organizations, agencies, and
corporations improve the local and global environment by planting and caring for trees.

Library of Congress data: Available upon request

For information on our distribution, please visit our website
www.oroeditions.com

Francis-Jones Morehen Thorp
www.fjmt.com.au

Sydney studio
Level 5, 70 King Street, Sydney NSW 2000 Australia
t +61 2 9251 7077

Melbourne studio
Level 2, 56 Hardware Lane, Melbourne VIC 3000 Australia
t +61 3 9604 2500

UK studio
Belsyre Court, 57 Woodstock Road, Oxford OX2 6HJ United Kingdom
t +44 1865 29 2042